Can Abenor

Overcoming the Legacy of Japan's Lost Decades

Dennis Botman
Stephan Danninger
Jerald Schiff

INTERNATIONAL MONETARY FUND

© 2015 International Monetary Fund

Cover photo courtesy of Gregg Forte

Cataloging-in-Publication Data
Joint Bank-Fund Library

Can Abenomics succeed? : overcoming the legacy of Japan's lost decades / editors: Dennis Botman, Stephan Danninger, and Jerald Schiff. — Washington, D.C. : International Monetary Fund, 2015.
   pages ; cm

   Includes bibliographical references and index.
   ISBN: 978-1-49832-468-7 (paper)
   ISBN: 978-1-49830-233-3 (ePub)
   ISBN: 978-1-48434-124-7 (Mobipocket)
   ISBN: 978-1-48435-220-5 (Web PDF)

   1. Japan—Economic conditions—1989–   2. Stagnation (Economics) 3. Deflation (Finance)—Japan.   I. Botman, Dennis (Dennis Petrus Johannes).   II. Danninger, Stephan.   III. Schiff, Jerald Alan. IV. International Monetary Fund.

HC462.95.C35   2015

Disclaimer: The views expressed in this book are those of the authors and do not necessarily represent the views of the International Monetary Fund, its Executive Board, or management.

Please send orders to:
International Monetary Fund, Publication Services
P.O. Box 92780, Washington, DC 20090, U.S.A.
Tel.: (202) 623-7430   Fax: (202) 623-7201
E-mail: publications@imf.org
Internet: www.elibrary.imf.org
www.imfbookstore.org

Contents

Foreword   v
David Lipton

Acronyms and Abbreviations   vii

1. Abenomics: From the Lost Decade to the Three Arrows 1
   Jerald Schiff

2. Abenomics: Lessons Learned from Two Decades of Conventional and Unconventional Monetary Policies 11
   Dennis Botman

3. Can Abenomics Overcome the Headwinds from Population Aging? 29
   Dennis Botman

4. Japan's Fiscal Risks 51
   Ikuo Saito

5. Options for Fiscal Consolidation in an Aging Society 69
   Ikuo Saito

6. Japan's Growth Challenge: Needs and Potential 91
   Stephan Danninger and Chad Steinberg

7. Labor Market Reform: Vital to the Success of Abenomics 107
   Chie Aoyagi and Giovanni Ganelli

8. The Opportunities and Risks of Abenomics in the Financial Sector 125
   Serkan Arslanalp, Raphael Lam, and Malhar Nabar

9. Stimulating Private Investment and Innovation 147
   Joong Shik Kang

10. Japan's Role in the Global Economy and Spillover Effects of Abenomics 163
    Dennis Botman and Joong Shik Kang

Contributors   179

Index   183

Foreword

At the heart of Japan's economic challenge lie four, closely related, intertemporal problems: ending deflation, raising growth, securing fiscal sustainability, and maintaining financial stability. These objectives need to be achieved against the background of Japan's rapidly aging society, entrenched deflationary expectations, and a global economy that remains mired in subdued growth.

Most readers will be familiar with the following striking statistic: in 2013, Japan's level of nominal GDP was about 6 percent lower than it was in the mid-1990s. There can be little doubt that this in part is caused by persistent deflation. Nonetheless, it remains a challenge to quantify exactly how much of the slow growth was due to deflation rather than the typical post-bubble blues, population aging, and the waning effects of technological convergence. As a result, it is also difficult to measure how much living standards will improve from a successful reflationary effort and whether these potential gains are lower now than they would have been in the 1990s. Compared to other advanced countries, Japan has fared relatively well in terms of productivity growth, suggesting that the biggest bang for the buck will likely come from greater capital accumulation (domestic investment rather than outsourcing) and providing additional, high-quality, employment opportunities (rather than increasing part-time work with lower wages and less investment in human capital). The Bank of Japan's quantitative and qualitative easing measures should lead to greater portfolio rebalancing and financial risk taking, raise inflation expectations, and support aggregate demand, which, together with complementary fiscal and structural measures, should help greatly to revive Japan's economy and decisively end deflation.

Another striking statistic—unprecedented among advanced economies—is the debt-to-GDP ratio, which now tops 240 percent and has risen by 50 percentage points in the last five years. Restoring fiscal sustainability by putting the debt ratio on a firm downward path is a priority for Japan's future. Although bond yields in Japan have remained very low despite ever increasing government debt, this is partly due to special factors, including a marked home bias of Japanese investors. None of these special factors can be taken for granted in the future especially with the prospect of higher yields as the Bank of Japan exits from its quantitative easing policies after achieving its two percent inflation target. Indeed, managing the normalization of interest rates along all asset classes and maturities in a way that maintains economic and financial stability will depend, in no small part, on the credibility of the government's fiscal adjustment strategy.

Ambitious structural reforms are pivotal for lasting success of Abenomics. Ending deflation and eliminating the government debt overhang will be good for potential growth, but these efforts themselves depend a great deal on the economy's expected growth rate in the future. Specifically, ambitious labor market reforms would strengthen the monetary policy transmission channel and accelerate the attainment of the Bank of Japan's inflation target by enhancing the pass through of rising inflation expectations into higher wages. Ambitious structural reforms will support demand in the near term as expectations of permanent income rise. As we have seen recently in Europe, fiscal consolidation without faster growth is unlikely to succeed. A more dynamic Japan is also key from a multilateral perspective, by preventing excessive reliance on monetary and fiscal easing and an undue weakening of the exchange rate.

With much at stake and multiple goals, Japan clearly needs a comprehensive and coordinated set of reforms. This recognition lies at the heart of Abenomics and the chapters in this book offer detailed recommendations in the areas of monetary policy, fiscal adjustment, and structural and financial sector reforms to make Abenomics a success for Japan and the rest of the world.

The various recommendations in this book are presented as a package and, ideally, one would like to make progress on all three arrows of Abenomics equally and simultaneously, not least because they create mutual synergies. However, there is a clear recognition that the amount of emphasis on each policy area needs to be state-dependent. This was evident, for example, around the time of the consumption tax increase to 8 percent in April 2014. Faced with weak demand and a possible reversal of actual and expected inflation, the Bank of Japan significantly further scaled up its asset-purchase program in October 2014. The authorities also decided to delay the second consumption tax increase to 10 percent and adopt further fiscal stimulus while placing greater emphasis on formulating a medium-term consolidation plan to maintain fiscal credibility. The key take away from this experience is that most, if not all, of the agenda for Abenomics laid out in this book will likely have to be implemented for Japan's efforts to be successful, but the reader should remain mindful that priorities need to be recalibrated at times depending on how economic conditions unfold.

This is not just a book about Japan. The main message that policymakers should use all policy levers at their disposal in a coordinated manner when faced with persistently weak demand and high public and private balance sheet vulnerabilities extends to other important parts of today's global economic landscape. As such, policymakers around the world have much to learn from Japan's experience and from the analyses presented in this volume.

David Lipton
First Deputy Managing Director
International Monetary Fund

Acronyms and Abbreviations

BoJ	Bank of Japan
CPI	Consumer price index
DSA	Debt Sustainability Analysis (IMF)
ECG	Excess cost growth
FDI	Foreign direct investment
FLP	Female labor force participation
FTA	Free trade agreement
FY	Fiscal year (in Japan: April 1–March 31)
G7	Group of Seven
G20	Group of Twenty
GDP	Gross domestic product
GIMF	Global Integrated Monetary and Fiscal model (IMF)
IMF	International Monetary Fund
JGBs	Japanese government bonds
OECD	Organisation for Economic Co-operation and Development
QQE	Quantitative and qualitative monetary easing
R&D	Research and development
REIT	Real estate investment trust
SMEs	Small and medium-sized enterprises
TFP	Total factor productivity
TOPIX	Tokyo Stock Price Index
TPP	Trans-Pacific Partnership
VAR	Vector autoregression
VIX	Volatility index (Chicago Board Options Exchange Volatility Index)
ZIRP	Zero interest rate policy

CHAPTER 1

Abenomics: From the Lost Decade to the Three Arrows

JERALD SCHIFF

EMERGING FROM THE LOST DECADE

The last 20 years have not been easy for Japan. The "Lost Decade"—actually a decade and a half of low growth and deflation—was followed by the global financial crisis in 2008–09 and, in 2011, the tragic Great East Japan Earthquake. Policy responses over this period—including sizable fiscal stimulus and large, if piecemeal, monetary expansion—proved only marginally effective in the face of strong headwinds, most notably from a declining population and rapid aging. To provide some perspective, between 1997 and 2013, nominal GDP in Japan has *declined* more than 6 percent.

What Went Wrong?

Several factors were at play, but the collapse of the Japanese asset bubble in the early 1990s played a key role. In its wake, balance sheet repair in the banking system, corporate deleveraging, and household attempts to rebuild net worth all combined to suppress demand. The external shock from the Asian financial crisis in 1997–98 contributed to a deficiency of demand, creating the environment for an extended period of moderate deflation and stagnant growth.

Once deflation took hold, it worked its way through the economy in textbook fashion. Businesses began to hold off on investment and households stepped back from buying big-ticket items, delaying purchases on expectations that prices would decline. Financial strategies adjusted to the deflationary environment, with portfolio allocations across households and financial institutions shifting toward "safe assets" such as currency, deposits, and government securities which, despite low nominal yields, provided stable real returns. And firms grew reluctant to hire workers on the lifetime contracts that previously characterized the Japanese workplace, increasingly opting for "nonregular workers" with lower basic wages, less job security, fewer benefits, less training, and lower productivity.

Parts of the section on "What Went Wrong" are based on "From Deflation to Reflation: Japan's New Monetary Policy Framework, Effectiveness, and Broad Lessons," Speech by David Lipton, First Deputy Managing Director of the IMF, at the 2014 BoJ-IMES Conference on Monetary Policy in a Post-Financial Crisis Era, Tokyo, May 28.

As discussed in Chapter 2, demand management tools were deployed against this difficult backdrop in a variety of ways, but failed to decisively end deflation. In particular, the Bank of Japan (BoJ) provided monetary policy support through various means, cutting the policy rate to the zero lower bound and experimenting before other advanced economies did with quantitative easing and asset purchases. In hindsight, the experience points to the need for clear communication regarding the end objective and consistent implementation of policy easing toward that goal. But the failure of monetary policy also spotlights how difficult it is for a central bank to stimulate demand when confronted with powerful private sector imperatives to deleverage, repair balance sheets, and restore net worth.

As Chapter 3 highlights, a rapidly declining birthrate and high and rising life expectancies were aging and shrinking Japanese society at a nearly unprecedented rate throughout the Lost Decade, adding to the country's difficulties. This has contributed to falling potential growth, a tendency toward deflation, and sizable fiscal pressures (owing to large increases in social security spending).

Japan in Decline?

These developments left Japan, at the start of the second Abe administration at the end of 2012, mired in low growth, mild deflation, and nearly unprecedented public sector debt. More broadly, many had come to see Japan—at home and abroad—as a country in inevitable decline, with potential solutions difficult to imagine and even harder to pass through a fossilized political system.

But this view was always an exaggeration. Even as Japan's growth slowed and prices began their long gradual decline, its economy and society showed strengths.

- Per capita GDP and especially productivity continued to rise at rates that were broadly in line with other advanced economies.
- The rapid recovery from the earthquake and tsunami of March 2011 pointed to the admirable resilience of its people and the economy. Beyond the loss of life, the tragedy badly shook the economy: all nuclear power plants—accounting for a quarter of power—were shut down, and remain closed, while supply-chain disruptions brought production in parts of Japan to a virtual halt. Yet, growth had rebounded to above 4 percent by the first quarter of 2012.
- During the last 15 years, periods of reform were rewarded with renewed economic activity, most notably during the Koizumi period of 2001–06, suggesting that better results were possible.

Nevertheless, it was clear that Japan was facing enormous challenges. Persistent deflation had taken much of the air out of the economy. The combination of an aging population and decreasing work force, declining potential growth, and a rapidly rising public debt burden pointed clearly to the need for a new approach.

THE "THREE ARROWS": A BREAK WITH THE PAST

It was in this challenging context that Prime Minister Shinzō Abe, in late 2012 and early 2013, rolled out a comprehensive approach to reviving the Japanese economy, summarized by three policy arrows: aggressive monetary easing, flexible fiscal policy, and structural reforms to raise potential growth.

The idea was this: An escape from deflation triggered by monetary easing and fiscal stimulus would lower real interest rates and stimulate investment, consumption, and—with the yen at least temporarily weaker—exports. Structural reforms would boost confidence in the near term and ensure that higher growth was sustained over the longer term. Lower real funding costs and higher growth would improve debt dynamics. And a credible medium-term fiscal plan would curtail risks of a government bond rate spike and allow for a measured pace of adjustment. Complementarities among policies would be the key—all three arrows would be required for success. But if all went according to plan—a big and highly uncertain if—a more dynamic Japan would emerge, with higher growth and lower risk of a fiscal crisis in its future. This would be an important plus for the regional and global economy as well.

Abenomics: Changing Minds

But would it all work? That was less than obvious. What was being attempted under Abenomics was unprecedented, and nothing less than a leap from a low-growth deflationary equilibrium to a new equilibrium characterized by positive inflation and higher sustained growth. This requires a parallel shift toward more risk taking, requiring changes in expectations and behavior by businesses, consumers, and financial institutions. Confidence would be key, in both Japan's growth prospects as well as the government's ability to carry out needed reforms. These changes would not be easy to engineer and would require the firing of all three arrows. Failure could mean a slide back into deflation or, even worse, a loss in confidence in Japan's public finances with everything that might entail. But while risky, Abenomics is less so than the prior status quo, which seemed clearly headed for an unhappy ending.

Given the need to adjust long-held expectations, it is notable that the Abe administration had early and significant success in "changing the conversation" both in and about Japan. No student or observer of economics in 2012–13 could have missed the discussion of the "three arrows" of Abenomics. The prime minister himself appeared on the cover of *The Economist* as a super-hero in flight. Even J-pop groups recorded paeans to the economic policy named after the newly elected premier. It is clear that "Abenomics" was a remarkable branding success and, given the key role of expectations, this was not a trivial achievement. But high expectations are easily dashed and, in the end, just provide an opening for the right policies to do their job.

Monetary Policy: An End to Incrementalism

In April 2013, the Bank of Japan fired the first of the three arrows, announcing its new quantitative and qualitative monetary easing framework to achieve 2 percent inflation in a stable manner within about two years. The sheer size of the asset purchases marked a clear departure from the incremental approach of the past, as did forward guidance aimed squarely at sending the message that this framework would continue for as long as necessary to achieve its goals. Another difference is a clearer articulation of the idea—seen most evidently in the pact signed between the government and the BoJ in the early days of Abenomics—that the effectiveness of monetary policy depends on complementary fiscal and structural reforms to lift growth expectations and support price momentum.

As described in detail in Chapter 3, monetary policy was expected to be transmitted to prices and the real economy in four interrelated ways. First, quantitative and qualitative easing would hold down long-term real interest rates, raising domestic demand and reducing the output gap. Second, BoJ purchases of large amounts of Japanese government bonds from the books of financial institutions would lead to portfolio rebalancing, including higher domestic and overseas lending. Third, enhanced communication and increases in actual inflation would raise inflation expectations. Finally, the at least temporary depreciation of the yen would help raise inflation and close the output gap.

These important changes in monetary policy coincided with a significant decline in concerns over Europe, improving the global outlook and reversing sizable safe-haven flows into Japan. This had the fortunate near-term effect of adding to the depreciation of the yen, which declined about 24 percent in real effective terms from September 2012 until May 2013, and contributed to early gains in inflation and inflation expectations. However, this source of support for inflation eventually petered out, leaving the other transmission mechanisms to carry the load. Progress toward the 2 percent goal has been made, but the BoJ remains roughly only halfway there.

Fiscal Policy: Spend Now, Save Later?

The new government faced the delicate balancing act of addressing serious fiscal challenges without unduly compressing growth, in particular during the hoped-for "takeoff" period of Abenomics.

As Chapter 4 argues, a clear and convincing plan to reverse the long-term trend of rising government debt was needed urgently. Net public debt had increased from 13 percent in 1990 to 134 percent in 2012, while gross debt had surged to close to 240 percent, the highest among advanced economies on both measures. This rise in debt had so far been financed without problems, given domestic investors' large appetite for government bonds. But the contemporaneous experience in the European periphery had underlined that investor views can change quickly, and that confidence, once lost, was extremely costly to regain. Moreover, longer-term trends, including a shrinking population, declining household savings, and a shrinking current account surplus were not working in government's favor.

While adjustment was clearly necessary, the European experience playing out at the time also illustrated that adjustment without growth was unlikely to work. In this context, Abenomics proposed to use fiscal stimulus to help jump-start the economy in the near term while promising the needed adjustment over time. The bridge would be provided by a medium-term fiscal plan that was sufficiently concrete and credible to maintain the confidence of investors and avoid a sharp spike in government bond yields that would threaten the entire operation. However, given the long period of large deficits and growing debt and the inevitably gradual nature of any adjustment plan, maintaining this confidence would require, beyond promises, at least some upfront action.

Chapter 5 highlights that the adjustment plan itself would need to be as growth friendly as possible, relying on a package of measures that could deliver deficit reduction while improving incentives to work and invest. This adjustment would also need to include measures to both raise revenue and control spending—most notably rapidly growing social welfare spending—and ensure that the overall burden of this deep adjustment would be broadly shared.

The first year of Abenomics was, largely as expected, more about stimulus than adjustment, but that tide may be turning. Following a series of stimulus measures totaling about 1.5 percent of GDP over 2013–14, the government raised the consumption tax from 5 to 8 percent in April 2014, the first major step toward dealing with the sovereign debt burden. The government had planned a second increase, to 10 percent, in October 2015, but decided to delay this hike until 2017 given the weaker than expected economic growth following the April tax increase. Japan still finds itself only a very modest way toward the ultimate goal of reducing public debt as a share of GDP and, with the delay of the second tax increase, the formulation of a concrete medium-term plan has become particularly urgent. Such a plan is apparently in the works, to be articulated in 2015, and much will be riding on it.

The Third Arrow: Raising Potential Growth

As Chapter 6 makes clear, Abenomics will not ultimately succeed if it relies solely on fiscal and monetary policy stimulus. Rather, a hand-off to sustainable and private sector-led growth, together with a substantial rise in potential growth from its current low level of about ½ percent per year—to something like 1½ or even 2 percent—is urgently needed. The necessary transformation will be difficult but, as discussed in the chapter, not unprecedented. A permanent exit from moderate deflation would get Japan part of the way there—reversing the costs of deflation outlined above—but much of the heavy lifting will need to come from a comprehensive series of structural reforms, summarized in a new growth strategy.

Japan has not suffered from a lack of growth strategies over the past decade and a half, although one would be hard pressed to find any impact on economic performance. These strategies have tended to avoid the most fundamental roadblocks to growth, which have also typically been the most politically difficult to address. However, early on in the Abe administration there was real hope that "this time will be different." First, by boldly launching the first two arrows, the prime minister emphasized his focus on growth. In addition, the political environment for reform had improved considerably, with the ruling Liberal Democratic Party capturing sizable majorities in both houses of parliament and with the prime minister's popularity at impressive levels.

The government's growth strategy has proceeded more tentatively than many had hoped, but the broad contours can now be seen, notably in the revised growth strategy of June 2014. To offset the demographic decline in the workforce, the strategy aims to increase labor force participation among women, older workers, and—in a closely proscribed manner—foreign workers. Participation in the Trans-Pacific Partnership and other trade agreements would help further integrate Japan with rapidly growing Asian markets, raise inward and outward foreign direct investment, and incentivize much-needed deregulation in agriculture and the services sector. Special economic zones could serve as "laboratories" for a variety of forms of deregulation. A lower corporate tax rate and improved corporate governance would help bring down high corporate savings. And a range of policies would transform the stable financial sector into a growth engine. Still, a more ambitious and better-defined program of structural reforms will likely be needed to ensure a significant, sustained rise in growth.

Chapter 7 looks in particular at the need for aggressive labor market reforms, which could enhance many aspects of economic performance. As noted above, efforts to bring more workers into the labor force are critical, but measures thus far go only a short way toward achieving this. But the dual nature of the Japanese labor market—with a sizable and growing segment of the labor force in "nonregular" positions alongside the traditional heavily protected and better-compensated regular workers—also raises important challenges. Notably, this duality appears to limit labor productivity by dulling incentives for training and contributes to a low female labor force participation rate, as women face challenges of reentering the regular track after childbirth. A reduction in this duality—for example, through the use of a new labor contract that bridges the gap between regular and nonregular workers—would seem promising, but the government has not yet taken it up.

Financing Growth

While not officially an "arrow" of its own, the financial sector plays a crucial role in the new policy framework. Abenomics is all about encouraging risk taking, which will require a different sort of financial sector, more proactive in searching out lending opportunities and nurturing new enterprises. At the same time, increased risk taking will require a somewhat different focus for financial oversight.

As highlighted in Chapter 8, the Japanese financial system, while sound, could do more to support growth. Venture capital and other financing for start-ups lag badly behind those in other advanced economies, while less dynamic small and medium-sized enterprises (SMEs) are kept alive via loan guarantees.

The new monetary policy framework already provides a window for financial institutions to support growth. The BoJ's purchases already amounted to some 70 percent of newly issued Japanese government bonds when it launched its quantitative and qualitative easing in April 2013 and this has risen further with the expansion of the program in October 2014. With government bond exposures declining, banks can more assertively seek opportunities at home or abroad. In fact, domestic lending is picking up, rising some 3 percent on an annual basis, including to SMEs, after many years of decline. Some larger banks are increasingly focusing on expansion to foreign markets, in particular in rapidly growing emerging Asia, with foreign profits accounting for as much as one-third of total profits. Nonetheless, some financial institutions—notably regional banks, insurance companies, and pension funds—have maintained strong demand for government bonds, continuing a wait-and-see approach, while banks hold large excess reserves with the BoJ.

Structural reforms can help eliminate bottlenecks to financial intermediation. In particular, the existing credit support system for SMEs tends to weaken both credit risk assessment by banks and incentives for restructuring or exit of nonviable SMEs. At the same time, risk capital is limited for start-ups. This significantly dampens the natural process of entry and exit critical to economic dynamism. It will be important to gradually phase out credit guarantees to restore credit discipline and replace them with more targeted support for businesses. More diverse sources of funding also need to be encouraged, including asset-based lending. And the reform of the governance and investment rules of the government pension fund has the potential to provide funding to venture capital funds and other innovative sources of financing.

The transition to a higher-risk/growth equilibrium could pose challenges, although these appear manageable. For example, with the flattening of the yield curve, banks—particularly regional banks—may be pressured to take excessive risks to raise profitability. As more and more financial institutions move abroad, they also face making risk assessments in new economic settings and bear some increase in funding risks in overseas activity. Financial regulators will need to be alert to such risks.

Investing for the Future

Of course, for productive lending to take off, strong demand from credit-worthy borrowers is needed. Indeed, amid ample liquidity, in the aggregate, the low growth of credit until now has been primarily caused by weak demand rather than an unwillingness of banks to lend.

As discussed in Chapter 9, investment in Japan has been on a declining trajectory since the onset of the Lost Decade, and the nation's capital stock has aged dramatically, even while corporate savings have continued to rise. Reversing these trends would go a long way toward ensuring the success of Abenomics. The chapter finds that investment responds most strongly to expectations about future economic performance and certainty about economic policies. This suggests that an ambitious reform program can have a positive economic impact even in the near term. Financing constraints are also an important limiting factor for SMEs, especially for new entrants and the services sector, pointing again to the need for financial sector reforms.

IS IT WORKING?

So, the Abe administration, together with the Bank of Japan, has put some very significant policy changes in place, and a number of others are in the pipeline. What has this all meant to actual economic performance? Is Abenomics working?

The monetary policy "big bang" has raised actual and expected inflation far more effectively than many imagined possible. This has lowered real interest rates and raised asset prices, contributing to stronger consumption, credit demand, and, more recently, investment. The government took the politically difficult decision to go ahead with raising the consumption tax in April 2014. Although this had a larger than expected adverse impact on growth and confidence, the economy now appears to be slowly getting back on its feet and the outlook still features above potential growth in the coming quarters. Compensation is rising at the strongest pace in many years, albeit with only modest increases in base wages. There are initial signs that export volumes will finally start to rise, which should bode well for investment growth going forward. Taken together, this would support the hand-off from stimulus to more sustainable sources of aggregate demand, which so far has been elusive.

Yet, it is clear that Japan is not fully back. While wages and exports have begun to pick up, the sustainability of those trends remains in doubt, with much resting on the government's policies continuing to engender confidence.

Specifically, all considered, exports and, by extension, investment growth, have remained surprisingly flat and net exports a drain on GDP, despite the large yen depreciation. In part, this likely reflects the so-called "J-curve," that is, the observation that trade balances typically improve following depreciation, but only with a delay. But there also appear to be important underlying trends holding back exports, including the acceleration of Japanese firms' production moving abroad and the loss of competitiveness in former bellwether industries, such as electronics. These trends highlight the continued headwinds facing the economy and point to the need for serious thinking about how to maintain high value-added and skill-intensive production within Japan.

And, while much progress has been made, much can still go wrong. A new bout of global financial volatility or a slowdown in global growth could act as a brake on domestic activity and cause the yen to appreciate just as the economy is taking off.

But the bigger risk is domestic: that through complacency or political obstacles, Japan gets only a partial version of Abenomics, missing important elements of fiscal or structural reform, and leading the country back to deflation or to a more generalized loss in confidence, including in its ability to address its public debt problem.

WHAT DOES ABENOMICS MEAN FOR THE WORLD?

The success or failure of Abenomics, and of Japan more generally, is of great significance to the rest of the world. Despite 15 years of low growth, Japan remains the third largest economy and among the largest net creditors and trading nations. It is also wrestling with an unprecedented public debt burden, for which failure could have major negative implications for the global economy.

As Chapter 10 explains, Abenomics can impact other countries in a variety of ways, with the net impact on any single country difficult to determine. The weakening of the yen would tend to impose costs on countries that are direct competitors, such as Korea. At the same time, the important upstream role that Japan plays in the Asia supply chain means that lower prices for its inputs would benefit regional economies. Portfolio rebalancing by Japanese financial institutions and households would generate capital outflows, including to emerging Asia, the desirability of which would depend on the macroeconomic situation in each recipient country. Thus far, such spillovers have been subdued, with net outflows limited and Japanese exports yet to rise in a decisive manner. But if Abenomics is to succeed, it will likely generate larger spillovers along the lines laid out above.

While these individual channels are important, the overriding point is that a dynamic and growing Japan would undoubtedly be a boon for its neighbors, its region, and the global economy.

WHAT'S NEXT?

To deliver on this vision, Japan must overcome a series of daunting challenges. Fiscal adjustment on a large scale and over a decade or more will be needed. The population will continue to grow older and smaller. And the global economy will undoubtedly suffer from further episodes of volatility or even crisis. Even success will bring new challenges, such as an eventual Bank of Japan exit from large-scale asset purchases. Against these potential difficulties, the country will need to demonstrate steadfastness in implementing its reform agenda. This book offers suggestions in each policy area to complete this economic transformation.

CHAPTER 2

Abenomics: Lessons Learned from Two Decades of Conventional and Unconventional Monetary Policies

DENNIS BOTMAN

Japan's experience with a liquidity trap in the mid-1990s and its subsequent Lost Decade experience with slow growth, deflation, and below-potential output have stimulated a lively debate about what went wrong (Leigh 2010). A number of authors attributed much of the economy's disappointing performance to "exceptionally poor monetary policymaking" (Bernanke 2000, 150). Kuttner and Posen (2002, 536) find that "Japanese fiscal policy was contractionary over much of the 1990s," and attribute part of the protracted downturn to insufficient fiscal stimulus. Moreover, each time the economy appeared to get back on its feet, adverse shocks such as the Asian financial crisis, the bursting of the dot-com bubble, and the global financial crisis beset the country (Figure 2.1).

Ito and Mishkin (2006) discuss various channels through which deflation harms an economy. First, with downward rigidity in nominal wages, very low inflation may prevent real wages from declining during times of weak labor demand, raising the natural rate of unemployment. However, in Japan, annual compensation is relatively flexible—especially for hourly paid, part-time female employees—as part comes in the form of bonuses tied to company and individual performance. Second, (unexpected) deflation redistributes wealth from borrowers to lenders, reducing the collateral of, and creating incentives for excessive risk taking by, borrowers. Third, it reduces fiscal space, not only through higher real interest payments, but also because of less tax revenues (reverse bracket creep). Fourth, it reduces the effectiveness of conventional monetary policy. For these reasons, unless it is the result of a favorable productivity shock, persistent deflation thus has costs as it undermines the effective functioning of financial markets and the ability of macroeconomic policies to stabilize the economy. Negative effects on consumer and business confidence likely amplify these channels.

In this chapter we review the emergence of deflation and conduct of monetary policy during the last two decades. We draw lessons in four broad areas. First, the experience during the Lost Decade suggests that a policy rule with a higher inflation target and more aggressive monetary easing in response to economic slack would have substantially improved the economy's performance and would have avoided the zero bound on nominal interest rates.

Figure 2.1 Inflation and Deflation in Japan, 1990–2010 *(Percent)*

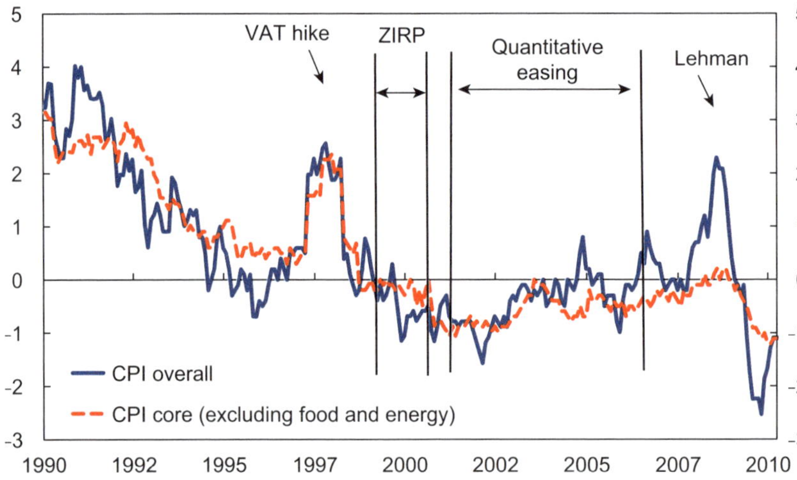

Source: CEIC database.
Note: CPI = consumer price inflation, VAT = value-added tax, ZIRP = zero interest rate policy.

Second, the subsequent period of unconventional monetary and credit easing policies had a statistically significant impact on bond yields and equity prices. Once the health of the banking sector improved and the corporate sector had made progress on deleveraging, these measures also started to show some effectiveness in supporting real activity, contributing to higher growth and lower unemployment. Furthermore, the composition of asset purchases matters, with private assets being particularly effective by reducing corporate risk premiums. The evidence suggests, however, that the impact of quantitative and other monetary easing was weaker on inflation, inflation expectations, and the exchange rate. All combined, this evidence suggests that the size and composition of asset purchases matters and that more aggressive monetary easing was needed to shift Japan's stable inflation expectations and relatively flat Phillips curve.

Third, since the global financial crisis, an intensive global debate has emerged about the importance of forward guidance and central bank communications, and transparency more generally, for the monetary policy transmission channel. In Japan, the nature of forward guidance has changed substantially during the past two decades, with increased clarity about price stability objectives following greater recognition of the need to move inflation expectations in a sustainable manner.

Fourth, during the Lost Decade, efforts to end deflation and revive growth have been criticized for lacking sufficient monetary and fiscal policy coordination. More recently, amid the onset of falling labor force participation rates owing to population aging and dwindling fiscal space, calls for greater policy coordination have included the need for ambitious structural reforms.

The Bank of Japan (BoJ) has taken these four lessons to heart when, as part of Abenomics, it embarked on a radical change in monetary policy when it adopted the quantitative and qualitative monetary easing (QQE) framework in April 2013. QQE included the adoption of a higher inflation target, more aggressive monetary easing including through the purchase of risk assets and longer-duration government securities, as well as improved communication and forward guidance. With the other two arrows of Abenomics—flexible fiscal policy and bold structural reforms—policy coordination has been strengthened substantially, promising the creation of a virtuous cycle that will not only end deflation and raise growth, but also restore fiscal sustainability.

In this chapter we discuss these four lessons in detail as well as the broad characteristics of QQE. In Chapter 3, we will discuss the effects of QQE so far and the potential medium-term implications and risks, taking into account the other elements of Abenomics in the context of a rapidly aging society.

MONETARY POLICY FOLLOWING THE BURSTING OF THE BUBBLE

Ito and Mishkin (2006) provide a detailed assessment of Japanese monetary policy and deflation from the mid-1990s onward. As they noted, it was remarkable that, during the bubble period, the consumer price index (CPI) inflation rate remained relatively low even though asset prices were rising rapidly. This presented difficult choices for monetary policymakers, with tightening starting in 1989 in combination with more direct measures to limit increases in land prices, such as containing bank lending to real-estate-related projects and companies, and higher taxes on realized capital gains on land sales.

As such, Japan was a front-runner in the debate about the role of monetary policy in the face of an emerging bubble. Important questions in this regard relate to (1) the difficulty in identifying bubbles ex ante; (2) to what extent risks to financial stability should be part of the central bank's objective function; and (3) whether these risks are best addressed through traditional monetary policy instruments or whether they require more targeted measures. A significant body of work in this area has emerged since the global financial crisis (2008–09), with an emerging consensus view that risks to financial stability should be addressed mainly using macroprudential tools, on the grounds that financial and price stability are distinct and imperfectly aligned objectives and thus need to be addressed separately (see IMF 2010). Such tools include capital requirements and buffers, forward-looking loss provisioning, liquidity ratios, and prudent collateral valuation. Furthermore, all potentially systemic institutions and markets should be within the macroprudential regulatory perimeter, and central banks should play a key role whether or not they serve as the main regulator.

In early 1990, as the bubble burst, stock prices started to decline, losing more than 60 percent of their peak value by summer 1992. At that time, quarter-on-quarter GDP had contracted. Land prices started to decline in 1991. As Ito and Mishkin (2006) note, lending to the real estate sector from banks slowed after 1991, but nonbank financial intermediaries picked up the slack. During 1992–95, nonperforming loans started to rise rapidly, possibly impairing the effectiveness of successive rounds of monetary easing that started in April 1992 and saw the policy rate reach 0.5 percent by September 1995.

During this time, the inflation rate declined from just about 2 percent in early 1992 to 0 percent by mid-1995. Surprisingly, the Japanese yen appreciated during this period, complicating efforts to jump-start the economy and contributing to disinflation first and subsequently to deflation. Some began to question whether the BoJ had fallen behind the curve given the stagnant economy and falling inflation (Ito and Mishkin 2006).

As Figure 2.1 illustrates, recovery began in mid-1995, with growth exceeding 3 percent in 1996, and headline and core inflation picking up, aided by yen depreciation. The recovery strengthened in the first half of 1997, partly as a result of front-loading of (durable) consumption in anticipation of a consumption tax increase from 3 percent to 5 percent in April of that year. Economic growth slowed significantly in the second half of 1997 and deteriorated in 1998 following the Asian financial crisis.

Ito and Mishkin (2006) describe Japanese financial market stress during 1997–98, noting that banks were losing capital as a result of high ratios of nonperforming loans and falling asset prices. Three large banks failed and, amid financial sector deleveraging, a severe credit crunch occurred. From this point onward, mild deflation emerged and the newly independent BoJ reduced the overnight call rate to 0.15 percent in February 1999, the beginning of the zero interest rate policy (ZIRP), which was temporarily ended—with hindsight prematurely—in August 2000 when interest rates were hiked despite the forward guidance that ZIRP would continue "until deflationary concerns subside."

LESSONS FROM MONETARY POLICY DURING THE LOST DECADE

Leigh (2010) investigates how the BoJ conducted interest rate policy as economic conditions deteriorated in the 1990s and, through counterfactual simulations, assesses to what extent alternative policy rules could have yielded superior economic outcomes. The results provide evidence of a downward drift in the implicit inflation target from about 2.5 percent in the early 1980s to about 1 percent in 1995. The finding of a declining path for the implicit inflation target during this period is consistent with findings for other central banks. Overall, the results suggest that there was nothing "exceptional" about Japanese interest-rate policy during the early 1990s.

The task of easing monetary policy was complicated by a simultaneous decline in the natural interest rate. Estimates displayed in Figure 2.2 suggest that the natural rate declined from about 4 percent in the early 1980s to about 1 percent in the mid-1990s. The decline was particularly sharp after 1991, and the estimate is not significantly different from zero by 1995:Q4. This sharp decline in the natural interest rate coincides with the bursting of the asset-price bubble and could, following Cúrdia and Woodford (2009) and Gertler (2003), be interpreted as an increase in financial sector stress. As a result, on average, despite substantial interest rate cuts, the actual real policy rate remained above the natural rate during 1991–95.

Figure 2.2 Japan's Natural Rate of Interest, 1982–1996 *(Percent)*

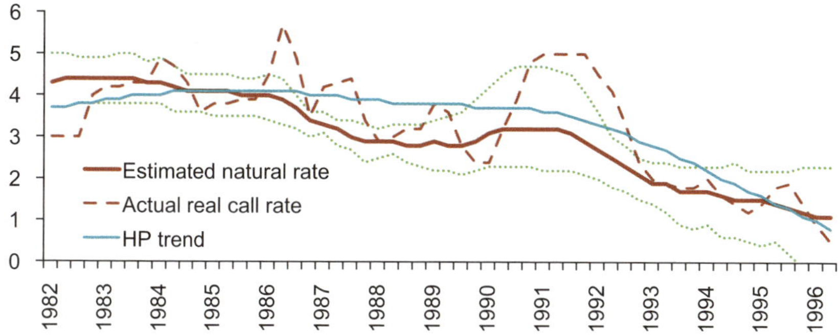

```
—— Estimated natural rate
- - Actual real call rate
—— HP trend
```

Source: Leigh (2010).
Note: Solid line indicates the median of the estimated posterior distribution. Fine dashes indicate 95 percent confidence bands. HP trend = trend calculated using the Hodrick-Prescott filter.

As noted in the previous section, substantial "bad luck" characterized the post-bubble period. The negative shocks in the early 1990s can be interpreted as reflecting the decline in investment spending that followed the bursting of the stock- and land-price bubbles in 1991–92. The shocks during 1997–99 appear to be associated with the domestic banking crisis, the consumption tax hike, and the effects of the Asian financial crisis. The contractionary shocks starting in 2001 could reflect the recession that started after the collapse of the dot-com bubble in the United States.

In addition, a number of observers attributed part of the deflation during the 1990s to supply-side shifts, as documented in Posen (2000). Indeed, Leigh (2010) finds a number of deflationary disturbances starting in the late 1990s. Such supply shocks are interpreted as benign under normal circumstances, reflecting declining markups and firm monopoly power. But when nominal interest rates are at the zero lower bound, they raise real interest rates and thus depress output.

Leigh (2010) conducts counterfactual exercises to investigate whether alternative interest-rate policy approaches could have helped Japan improve its macroeconomic performance. First, the author examines how the economy would have evolved if the implicit inflation target had risen in 1993:Q1, with everything else remaining unchanged. Krugman (1998) suggested a higher inflation target for Japan to anchor inflation expectations well above zero and avoid deflation. Other things being equal, a higher inflation target implies a higher steady-state nominal interest rate, with more room for interest-rate cuts before reaching the zero bound. The estimated decline in the natural rate of interest in the 1990s underlines the need for such a higher inflation buffer.

The results indicate that a higher inflation target would have warded off deflation and prevented zero interest rates during 1993–95. A key channel for this is that the higher inflation target anchors inflation expectations at the higher rate, and this increase in expected inflation translates into higher inflation in line with the forward-looking component of the aggregated supply equation. In addition, the increase in inflation expectations reduces real interest rates because the nominal interest rate rises only gradually toward its new long-run level. This short-run decline in real interest rates stimulates output, which in turn raises inflation further relative to the actual path. Nonetheless, inflation would not have reached the targeted level as the unexpected shocks to inflation were deflationary over almost the entire period of analysis. Also, under an otherwise unchanged monetary policy rule, the associated improvement in output performance is short-lived and small.

Next Leigh (2010) examines whether economic performance would have been better under a Taylor rule that responds more vigorously to deviations of output from potential. In this counterfactual scenario, the policy rate would have been reduced to zero much sooner. Although inflation rises slightly, the economy would still have experienced several quarters of deflation. However, output would have fallen by less as a result of the additional monetary stimulus provided.

These results suggest that a combination of a higher inflation target with an aggressive policy response to the output gap could potentially have made a substantial difference. Indeed, Leigh (2010) finds that such a rule would have achieved greater stabilization than any one of the components alone. The intuition for this finding is that the higher inflation target provides the policy space to cut interest rates in response to the deflationary shocks, while the stronger output-gap coefficient provides the "will" to use that additional space vigorously.

Another alternative that has been proposed for Japan is a policy rule that targets the price level rather than the inflation rate. The rationale for price-level targeting is that any spell of deflation must be followed by an economic expansion with higher inflation that returns the price level to its target. The anticipation of this intensified future inflation reduces real interest rates during the deflationary period, moderating the associated output contraction. The results suggest that economic performance would have benefited substantially from price-level targeting. Specifically, following the onset of the contractionary shocks, counterfactual output still falls below potential, but the downturn is relatively shallow, and output returns to potential by 1995. During each of the subsequent contractionary shocks, output rebounds more quickly than under the estimated policy rule.

This final counterfactual simulation therefore yields an interesting result: price-targeting would have delivered a more stable macroeconomic performance than the combination of a higher inflation target with a more vigorous output-gap response. At the same time, however, while price targeting appears to perform well in the face of the deflationary shocks considered here, it is worth recognizing a possible concern in times of high inflation. In particular, as Friedman (2003) emphasizes, price-level targeting implies the need for potentially costly monetary policy contractions following one-time increases in the price level.

THE EMERGENCE AND EFFECTIVENESS OF QUANTITATIVE EASING

High public debt and large fiscal deficits limited the fiscal space to close the wide output gap, whereas close-to-zero interest rates limited the scope for further reducing the policy rate. As a result, unconventional monetary easing that included large-scale asset purchases emerged as a policy instrument to support the recovery. The BoJ introduced quantitative easing in March 2001, together with a change in the operating target from the short-term interest rate to the current account balance.

The BoJ expanded purchases of long-term Japanese government bonds and increased the current account balance targets stepwise from March 2001 through October 2002. It targeted further increases in the current account balance through January 2004. The central bank exited quantitative easing in March 2006, amid signs that the economy was emerging from deflation.

Following the global financial crisis, the BoJ increased the pace of its government bond purchases and adopted a number of unconventional measures to promote financial stability. The measures included a fixed-rate funds-supplying operation, increased purchases of government securities, and a clearer policy commitment to the zero interest rate policy. The overall objective of the various measures was to achieve sustainable growth and price stability.

At the time, a key innovation in the BoJ's series of monetary easing steps was the October 2010 introduction of a new asset purchase program under its Comprehensive Monetary Easing policy. The purchases in this program comprised private sector financial assets—corporate bonds, commercial paper, exchange-traded funds and real estate investment trusts (REITs)—in addition to government securities.

Against this background, Lam (2011) assesses whether the BoJ's easing measures, particularly the asset-purchase program, were comprehensive and effective in affecting financial markets. For this, he uses an event study to analyze (1) how financial markets responded following the announcement of the BoJ's easing measures; (2) whether the impact came mostly from the announcement of the program or the actual asset purchases; and (3) to what extent buying private risky assets or government securities was more effective in reducing risk premiums.

In Lam's (2011) event study, the impact of monetary easing is measured as the change in asset returns and volatility. Financial indicators include equity prices, sovereign and corporate bond yields, exchange rates, inflation expectations, and the term premium. To assess the significance of events, he compares the percentage change of financial indicators around the event window against that in a typical trading day: (1) two trading days, defined to be $t + 1$ versus $t - 1$ where t refers to the event day; and (2) five trading days—allowing an assessment of whether the initial two-day effect persists or wanes after a week. Overall, five events are related to announcements of new programs and over 30 events to subsequent expansion of purchases or exits of earlier programs.

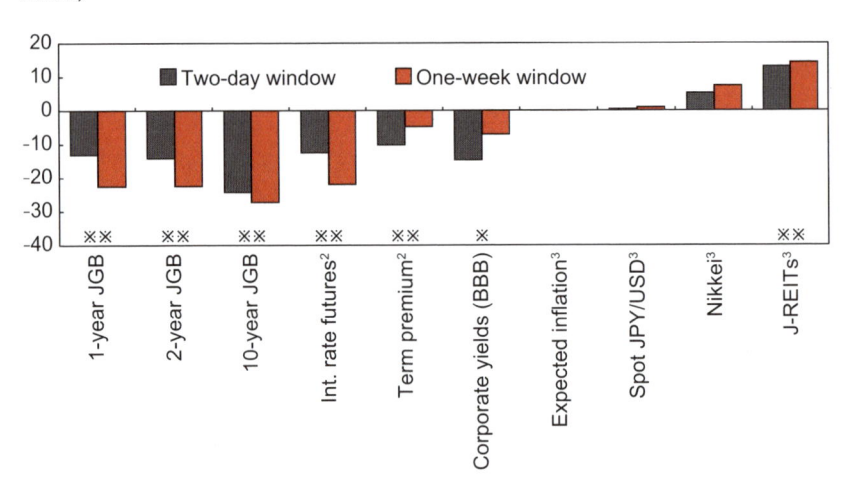

Figure 2.3 Impact of Monetary Easing on Financial Markets *(Basis points, unless otherwise stated[1])*

[Bar chart comparing Two-day window and One-week window impacts across: 1-year JGB (✕✕), 2-year JGB (✕✕), 10-year JGB (✕✕), Int. rate futures[2] (✕✕), Term premium[2] (✕✕), Corporate yields (BBB) (✕), Expected inflation[3], Spot JPY/USD[3], Nikkei[3], J-REITs[3] (✕✕)]

Sources: Bloomberg, L.P.; and IMF staff estimates.
Note: JGB = Japanese government bonds, J-REITs = Japanese real estate investment trusts.
[1] Events defined as the announcement dates of monetary easing by the Bank of Japan. Symbol ✕ denotes statistically significant at the 5 percent level.
[2] Refers to three-month interest rate futures and the term premium defined as 10-year net of 2-year sovereign yields.
[3] In percent.

Overall, the BoJ's monetary easing measures had a positive impact on financial markets (Figure 2.3). The impact is broad based and extends beyond the assets the central bank purchases.

- *Government securities.* Sovereign yields across all maturities declined in three out of the five events at the 5 percent significance level. The 10-year government bond yield fell a cumulative 24 basis points while the two-year Japanese government bond yield fell 14 basis points compared to a 0.1 basis point change in a typical trading day. The initial fall in sovereign yields appeared to persist, reinforcing the decline in the following week. Declines of shorter maturity yields were not significant when Comprehensive Monetary Easing was introduced, in part because those yields were already very low.

- *Corporate bonds.* Corporate yields across investment grades decreased a cumulative 15–22 basis points in the two-day window (with a *p*-value of around 0.05), though the impact stayed broadly the same throughout the week. Bond issuance also improved following the announcement of the asset-purchase program (Bank of Japan 2011).

- *Equity markets.* Stock and futures markets strengthened in four out of the five easing events, cumulatively increasing 5–7 percent in the week after. The impact was statistically significant (*p*-value below 0.05). The implied volatility in the equity market generally declined following the monetary easing measures.

- *REITs*. Prices of REITs in particular surged 14 percent cumulatively following the monetary easing events, reflecting large BoJ purchases in a relatively small market. The initial impact was also reinforced during the rest of the week.

But the easing measures had no appreciable impact on the yen exchange rate and inflation expectations. Spot and forward yen rates against the U.S. dollar changed little and were not significantly different from movements during typical trading days. Inflation expectations derived from breakeven rates based on inflation-linked bonds remained unchanged within the event windows. Ueda (2011) also finds no evidence that the BoJ's policy actions had an impact on the exchange rate, which may instead have been driven by external factors, particularly interest-rate differentials, risk appetite, and safe-haven flows.

Most of the impact on financial markets came from the announcement of new easing measures, rather than from subsequent purchases (Figure 2.4). The BoJ's measures had the largest impact on the financial and real estate sectors. Financial sector stock prices, notably the major banks and insurance companies, rose strongly relative to the market index. A comparison of the BoJ's easing measures and those of the U.S. Federal Reserve shows similar effects, with two notable exceptions. First, the Federal Reserve's large-scale asset purchases had a stronger impact on global financial markets, including in Japan and the euro area, compared with the limited global spillovers of the BoJ's measures. Second, the Federal Reserve's easing measures were found to have influenced the U.S. dollar exchange rate and domestic inflation expectations (D'Amico and King 2010, Yellen 2011), while the BoJ's measures appeared to have had no such effects.

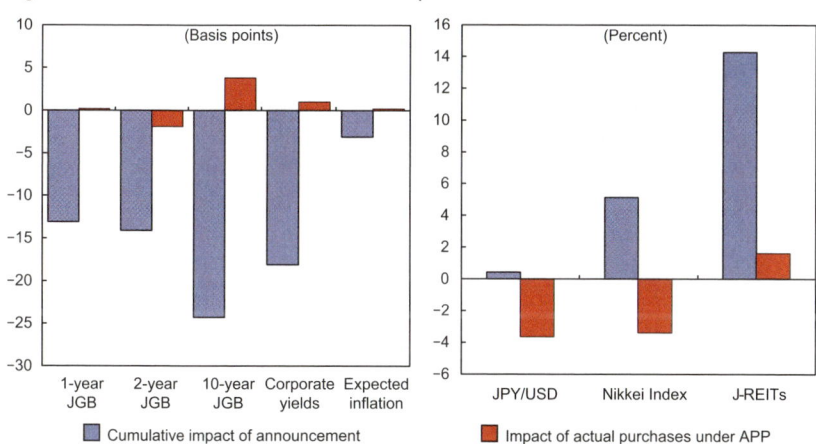

Figure 2.4 Announcement and Purchases: Impact on Financial Markets

Sources: Bloomberg, L.P.; and IMF staff estimates.
Note: APP = assest-purchase program, JGB = Japanese government bonds, J-REITs = Japanese real estate investment trusts.

Besides raising asset prices, the asset-purchase program contributed to lowering the probability that tail risks would materialize in financial markets. Implied volatility based on options prices in the equity market fell nearly a cumulative 10 percent after the BoJ's easing, suggesting an improvement of investor risk appetite—one of the objectives under the Comprehensive Monetary Easing—for the subsequent months, lasting until the March 2011 earthquake and tsunami. Markets' perceived risk of a double-dip recession also receded, as indicated by the decline in the implied volatility of out-of-the-money call and put options—a measure of the cost of insuring against extreme tail risk events. And business and consumer confidence generally improved following an easing event.

In sum, the key findings are that unconventional monetary policies had a statistically significant impact on bond yields, risk sentiment, and equity prices, but no notable effect on the exchange rate or inflation expectations. In terms of the impact on economic activity, as noted in Berkmen (2012), research on the effectiveness of the earlier episodes of quantitative easing yielded mixed results, with most pointing to limited effect. The reasons cited included a dysfunctional banking sector, which impaired the credit channel, and weak demand for loans during a period when firms were deleveraging. The situation, however, improved following the strengthening of banks' balance sheets and the restructuring of the corporate sector after the banking crisis of the late 1990s.

For example, nonperforming loans declined from 8.4 percent in 2002 to 2.5 percent in 2007 and have remained low since then. In addition, the corporate sector reduced its debt-to-equity ratio from about 200 percent to less than 100 percent over the same period. Both of these factors may have helped restore the credit channel and demand for funds during the 2000s. Indeed, Berkmen's work, using a structural vector autoregression (VAR) model, suggests that unconventional monetary policies were more effective in stimulating growth, reducing unemployment, and, to some degree, raising inflation after financial stability had been strengthened.

Does the composition of asset purchases matter? Lam (2011) assesses the potential impact of a further expansion of the asset-purchase program, using a portfolio rebalancing framework as in Neely (2010) to analyze a hypothetical scenario of the potential impact on financial markets if Comprehensive Monetary Easing had not included private asset purchases. Lam's (2011) calculations show that including private risky assets in the program was a key factor supporting asset prices. Specifically, the rise of equity prices would have been 2–3 percent less if the BoJ had not directly purchased the exchange-trade funds and Japanese real estate investment trusts.

The model also suggests that, if the target purchase level had been expanded, it would have further supported asset prices (Figure 2.5). Specifically, an additional purchase of ¥1 trillion of government securities beyond the targeted level would have a limited impact on sovereign yields and equity markets, especially given the already-low level of interest rates. However, the same amount of additional purchases of corporate bonds and commercial paper would have a larger impact by lowering the risk premium in the corporate sector. In addition, purchasing an additional ¥500 billion in equities-related assets would have reduced long-term sovereign yields by about 30 basis points and raised equity prices 3 percent.

Figure 2.5 Impact of a Hypothetical Expansion of the Asset-Purchases Program

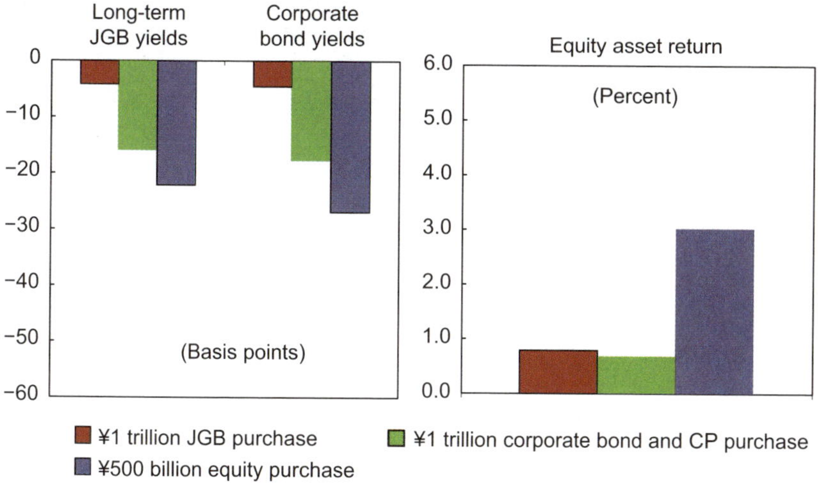

■ ¥1 trillion JGB purchase   ■ ¥1 trillion corporate bond and CP purchase
■ ¥500 billion equity purchase

Sources: Neely (2010); and IMF staff estimates.
Note: JGB = Japanese government bonds; CP = commercial paper.

THE IMPORTANCE OF COMMUNICATION AND FORWARD GUIDANCE

The importance of central bank communication and transparency for shaping the public's expectations has been well recognized. Such expectations in turn affect current financial conditions and thereby output, employment, and inflation over time. As Bernanke (2013, 5) notes, "the Federal Reserve, like many central banks around the world, has made significant progress in recent years in clarifying its goals and policy approach, and in providing regular information about the future path of policy that it views as most likely to attain its objectives. This increased transparency about the framework of policy has aided the public in forming policy expectations, reduced uncertainty, and made policy more effective."

The role of central bank communication becomes particularly important when the transmission of monetary policy is impaired by a weak financial system, when interest rates are near the zero lower bound, and when fiscal space is more limited. Specifically, under these conditions, monetary policy can remain powerful as the degree of accommodation provided by monetary policy depends not just on the current value of the policy rate, but on public expectations of future settings of that rate (see Bernanke 2013).

Indeed, recent research suggests that the communication channel, or more specifically the nature of forward guidance, has important implications for asset prices. Such forward guidance is provided implicitly, through speeches and, in the United States, testimony by monetary board members, and explicitly through regular central bank statements. Campbell and others (2012) find evidence that the Federal Reserve's Federal Open Market Committee communications were successful in affecting expectations of macroeconomic forecasters and market participants during the past decade. Femia, Friedman, and Sack (2013) and Raskin (2013) also show that the committee's more explicit forward guidance has conveyed important information about the Federal Reserve's policy reaction function, which has led to a more accommodative policy.

Recent research finds that guidance about the future course of monetary policy is a more effective tool for providing monetary accommodation at the zero bound compared to quantitative easing. Although key announcements of U.S. asset-purchase programs have been found to lower 10-year government bond yields, increasingly this effect is attributed to the signaling of the future monetary policy stance rather than to the direct effects of the purchases themselves. Kiley (2012) finds that declines in long-term interest rates brought about by a decline in the term premium has about one-half of the effect of a similar decline in long-term interest rates brought about through a reduction in short-term interest rates (also see IMF 2013).

The fact that several major central banks are now grappling with the zero lower bound has further stimulated this interest in the role of central bank communication and transparency. The BoJ has been at the forefront of experimenting with forward guidance since 1999, with various modifications to strengthen its effectiveness.

Shirai (2013) discusses the evolution of forward guidance in Japan. Under the ZIRP (1999–2000), the BoJ "will maintain a zero-interest rate policy until deflationary pressures are dispelled" (Shirai 2013, 12). Although this was an open-ended commitment, it was generally criticized for being vague. In addition, the ZIRP was lifted on August 11, 2000 even though the recovery was still fragile, overseas risks were elevated following the bursting of the dot-com bubble, and the inflation rate was still negative.

As Ito and Mishkin (2006) note, communications were weak when quantitative easing was introduced in March 2001, with no indication why the policy change would be effective, particularly in light of previous statements by BoJ officials that such policies might not be helpful and could result in balance sheet risks. Also, the BoJ clarified that its aim for CPI, excluding fresh food, was to show an inflation rate of stably zero percent or an increase year-on-year, but this change too was not explained, which led to a decline in the credibility of the bank according to some observers.

As Shirai (2013) notes, in March 2003, the expression "stably zero percent or an increase" was clarified along two dimensions. First, not only should the most recent core CPI register zero percent or above, but also that such tendency should be confirmed over a few months; and second, that the prospective core CPI would not be expected to register below zero percent. This type of forward guidance was contingent on the state as it was linked to the continuation of the quantitative easing policy. One challenge during this time was that CPI figures were retroactively revised downward and all the positive numbers became negative.

Under the Comprehensive Monetary Easing policy that started in 2010, forward guidance was strengthened by the statement that the BoJ will maintain the virtually zero interest rate policy until price stability is in sight on the basis of the understanding of medium- to long-term price stability, on the condition of no significant risk. "Understanding" refers to a positive range of 2 percent or lower, with the midpoint at 1 percent. This type of guidance is also state contingent, linking it to the zero interest rate policy. It also introduced a conditional commitment for the first time by providing a clear description of the economic conditions under which the monetary easing policy would be maintained, in this case by linking it to a threshold on the inflation outlook.

In February 2012 the forward guidance was strengthened further. The BoJ stated that it would "continue its zero interest rate policy and asset purchases until it judges that the 1% goal is in sight." The price stability goal in the medium to long term is a positive range of 2 percent or lower. The state-contingent nature of the guidance linked it to both the zero interest rate policy and asset purchases. The phrase "understanding" was replaced with "goal" (the consensus of all policy board members).

Overall, the BoJ's forward guidance was clarified and incrementally strengthened during these successive revisions. Compared with other central banks trying to formulate monetary policy at or near the zero lower bound for interest rates, Japan's experience remains, to some extent, unique and more challenging. This is because its guidance, together with other monetary measures, aims to raise and anchor inflation expectations to end deflation amid a relatively flat Phillips curve. This recognition prompted still further refinements to forward guidance when the central bank adopted QQE, with a greater emphasis on medium- to long-term market and public expectations of the future monetary policy stance.

POLICY COORDINATION

Bernanke (2003) suggested that monetary and fiscal policy coordination may be required during a period of protracted deflation. As noted in Eggertsson (2006), many economists believe it was wartime spending that finally pulled the United States out of the Great Depression when short-term nominal interest rates had been close to zero for several years. Similarly, in Japan during the early 1930s, Finance Minister Korekiyo Takahashi abolished the gold standard and implemented large fiscal stimulus. In addition, the central bank directly underwrote government bonds. This policy has been credited with ending deflation at the time and has to some extent been referenced as a historical precedent for the current Abenomics policy.

Fiscal coordination does not necessarily imply fiscal stimulus, but could take the form of other measures as well, depending on the situation. For example, Ito and Mishkin (2006) noted that, after the domestic bubble burst, many economists called for fiscal injections to either close or rehabilitate financial institutions that had become unviable. Although the government at the time guaranteed all deposits and suspended the deposit insurance ceiling, capital injections only started in

1998–99, which were effective in restoring market confidence as evidenced by declining risk premiums.

As noted in Eggertsson (2006), on the surface it might appear that there has been monetary-fiscal coordination in Japan that nonetheless was ineffective in ending deflation: the BoJ maintained interest rates near zero, while the budget deficit ballooned and the gross public debt started to exceed 150 percent of GDP by the mid-2000s. Furthermore, recent research has pointed out that fiscal multipliers tend to be larger when interest rates are near zero, which would also suggest that stimulus must have had some positive effects.

Eggertsson's (2006) analysis, however, suggests that deficit spending is only effective if fiscal and monetary policies are coordinated. If there is no coordination, deficit spending has no effect. This may help explain the weak response of the Japanese economy to the rise in deficits. This occurs when deficit spending has not been accumulated in the context of a coordinated reflation program by the Ministry of Finance and the BoJ, where each actor takes the other parties' actions into consideration. Second, the effects of real government spending do not only work through current spending as the conventional wisdom maintains, but also through expectations about future spending.

Indeed, under optimal fiscal policy, expectations about future spending are even more important than current spending and in this regard the stop-go fiscal stimuli that were introduced, as described in Kuttner and Posen (2001), may have weakened the overall effectiveness. Interestingly, Eggertsson's (2006) analysis suggests that even in the absence of coordination, spending (in contrast to deficit) multipliers remain high, but Kuttner and Posen (2001) show that a substantial part of the increase in the deficit in Japan was the result of weaker revenue collection following the bursting of the bubble as well as temporary tax cuts.

More recently, a third leg of policy coordination has been advocated. Owing to population aging, the labor force participation rate has been declining, reducing potential growth and adding to already high fiscal consolidation needs through rising health care and social security expenses. Aging can also exert downward pressure on the natural rate of interest (see Chapter 3) which, other things being equal, tightens monetary conditions, complicating the exit from deflation. As such, it has been suggested that important synergies exist among monetary, fiscal, and structural reforms to end deflation, revive growth, and restore fiscal sustainability.

THE NEW MONETARY POLICY FRAMEWORK

The lessons learned in these four areas were taken onboard when Abenomics was launched in 2013. For the first lesson, the BoJ adopted a higher inflation target of 2 percent supported by the QQE framework to achieve it in a stable manner with a time horizon of about two years. For the second, the central bank embarked on an unprecedented asset-purchase program, targeting a doubling of the monetary base—its new operational target—by 2014 to around 54 percent of GDP. It also changed the composition of asset purchases, with greater emphasis on longer-dated government securities and expanding purchases of risk assets

Figure 2.6 Monetary Base Target and Balance Sheet Projections *(Trillion yen [on the left side] and percent of GDP [on the right side])*

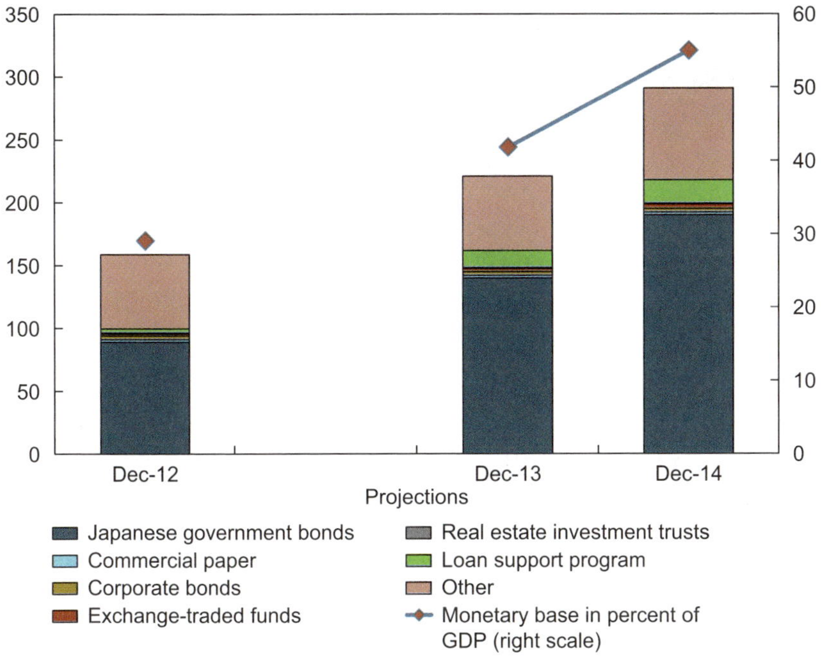

- Japanese government bonds
- Commercial paper
- Corporate bonds
- Exchange-traded funds
- Real estate investment trusts
- Loan support program
- Other
- Monetary base in percent of GDP (right scale)

Source: Bank of Japan.

such as commercial paper, corporate bonds, exchange-traded funds, and Japanese REITs (Figure 2.6).

The QQE transmission channel has four interconnected components:

- Reducing long-term real interest rates and risk premiums. QQE has the potential to lower the term premium through purchases of longer-dated government securities. Additional purchases of risk assets would contribute to higher business investment, durable goods consumption and residential investment by reducing the funding cost of firms and households, improving firms' balance sheets, and through the wealth effect.

- Portfolio rebalancing. BoJ purchases exceed the net issuance of government securities over the next two years, particularly in the 5- to 10-year segment, which would lead to portfolio rebalancing among investors and financial institutions, including toward riskier assets and credit extension at home or abroad.

- Raising inflation expectations, including through stronger communication, would lower long-term real interest rates, thereby stimulating near-term activity.

- Exchange rate depreciation, which is a product of these channels, is a crucial mechanism for QQE to work as it would raise import prices as well as support higher inflation by helping to close the output gap through positive wealth effects and higher exports.

On October 31 2014, the BoJ further expanded its QQE program. The BoJ decided to accelerate its purchases of Japanese government bonds to an annual pace of 80 trillion yen (compared to around 50 trillion yen before), extend the average remaining maturity of JGBs purchases to around 7–10 years (an extension of about three years at most), and triple its purchases of exchange-traded funds and Japanese real estate investment trusts. The BoJ's move was aimed at maintaining momentum in formulating inflation expectations. Specifically, long-term expectations stopped increasing during 2014 and were hovering around 1 percent. The inflation outlook remained largely unchanged and, taking into account these additional measures, the BoJ forecast is to meet its inflation target of 2 percent by the end of fiscal year 2015.

In terms of the third lesson, the BoJ further strengthened forward guidance and communication by clarifying the price stability objective and its relation to monetary policy: it stated that it is committed to continue with easing until 2 percent inflation is achieved in a stable manner.

Finally, in terms of policy coordination, monetary and fiscal policies were more explicitly linked in January 2013 with the issuance of the joint statement of the government and the BoJ on overcoming deflation and achieving sustainable economic growth. Aside from the aforementioned monetary measures, the statement emphasized the need for flexible fiscal policy and ambitious growth reforms. Institutional arrangements were also strengthened to monitor progress with these reforms through the Council on Economic and Fiscal Policy.

The new framework thus addresses the four key issues that have hampered a sustained exit from deflation in the past. What have been the effects so far and will it be successful? We discuss this next in Chapter 3.

CONCLUSION

Criticism of Japan's monetary policy during the past two decades includes the slow pace and insufficiency of easing, stop-go approaches, asset purchases that were concentrated on relatively short-term government bonds, ineffective communication and forward guidance, and insufficient policy coordination. These factors contributed to the emergence of a deflationary mindset and raised questions about the BoJ's credibility and therefore its ability to shift inflation expectations in a sustained manner.

In this chapter we reviewed monetary policy in Japan during the past two decades, which offered four key lessons. First, the experience during the Lost Decade suggests that a rule with a higher inflation target and more aggressive monetary easing in response to economic slack would have substantially improved the economy's performance and would have avoided the zero bound on nominal interest rates. Second, the experience with the BoJ's easing measures suggests they had a statistically significant impact on bond yields, risk sentiment, and equity prices, but no notable effect on the exchange rate or inflation expectations. The impact stemmed mainly from the announcement effect rather than from the actual operations or purchases. The composition of asset purchases matters, with private assets being particularly effective by reducing corporate risk premiums. Third, recent research suggests that forward guidance and clear central bank communications more generally have important ramifications on expectations and economic activity, potentially surpassing the effects of asset purchases. Fourth, coordination between monetary and fiscal policy may be needed to overcome deflation and, with a rapidly aging population, structural reforms may be instrumental as well.

The Bank of Japan has taken these lessons to heart when, as part of "Abenomics," it adopted the QQE framework in April 2013 and, consistent with its commitment, expanded it further in October 2014. Quantitative and qualitative monetary easing included the adoption of a higher inflation target, more aggressive monetary easing including through the purchase of risk assets and longer-duration government securities, as well as improved communication and forward guidance. The next chapter discusses the potential effects of QQE while taking into account the country's rapid demographic change.

REFERENCES

Bank of Japan. 2011. *Financial Markets Report*, February, Tokyo: Bank of Japan.

Berkmen, P.S. 2012. "Bank of Japan's Quantitative and Credit Easing: Are They Now More Effective?" IMF Working Paper No. 12/2. International Monetary Fund, Washington, DC.

Bernanke, B.S. 2000. "Japanese Monetary Policy: A Case of Self-Induced Paralysis?" In *Japan's Financial Crisis and Its Parallelsto U.S. Experience*, edited by Ryoichi Mikitani and Adam S. Posen. Special Report 13, September 2000. Institute for International Economics, Washington, DC, 149–66.

———. 2003. "Some Thoughts on Monetary Policy in Japan." Speech before the Japan Society of Monetary Economics, Tokyo, Japan, May 31, 2003.

———. 2013. "Communication and Monetary Policy." Speech at the National Economists Club Annual Dinner, Herbert Stein Memorial Lecture, November 19, Washington, DC.

Campbell, J.R., C.L. Evans, J.D.M. Fisher, and A. Justiniano. 2012. "Macroeconomic Effects of Federal Reserve Forward Guidance." *Brookings Papers on Economic Activity*, Spring. Brookings Institution, Washington, DC.

Cúrdia, V., and M. Woodford. 2009. "Credit Frictions and Optimal Monetary Policy." BIS Working Papers No. 278. Bank for International Settlements, Basel.

D'Amico, S., and T.B. King. 2010. "Flow and Stock Effects of Large-Scale Treasury Purchases." Federal Reserve Board, Staff Working Papers in the Finance and Economics Discussion Series (FEDS), No. 2010-52. Federal Reserve Board, Washington, DC.

Eggertsson, G.B. 2006. "Fiscal Multipliers and Policy Coordination." Federal Reserve Bank of New York Staff Reports No. 241.

Femia, K., S. Friedman, and B. Sack. 2013. "The Effects of Policy Guidance on Perceptions of the Fed's Reaction Function." Federal Reserve Bank of New York Staff Reports No. 652.

Friedman, B.M. 2003. "Comments and Discussion." *Brookings Papers on Economic Activity* 1. Brookings Institution, Washington, DC.

Gertler, M. 2003. "Comments and Discussion." *Brookings Papers on Economic Activity* 1. Brookings Institution, Washington, DC.

International Monetary Fund. 2010. "Central Banking Lessons from the Crisis." IMF Policy Paper. Washington, DC.

———. 2013. "Unconventional Monetary Policies—Recent Experience and Prospects." Background Paper, April. Washington, DC.

Ito, T., and F.S. Mishkin. 2006. "Two Decades of Japanese Monetary Policy and the Deflation Problem." In *Monetary Policy under Very Low Inflation in the Pacific Rim*, edited by T. Ito and

A. Rose, NBER East Asia Seminar on Economics, Vol. 15. Chicago: University of Chicago Press, 131–202.

Kiley, M.T. 2012. "The Aggregate Demand Effects of Short- and Long-Term Interest Rates." Finance and Economics Discussion Series, Working Paper No. 2012-54, Federal Reserve Board, Washington, DC.

Krugman, P. 1998. "It's Baaack! Japan's Slump and the Return of the Liquidity Trap." *Brookings Papers on Economic Activity* 2: 137–205. Brookings Institution, Washington, DC.

Kuttner, K.N., and A.S. Posen. 2001. "The Great Recession: Lessons for Macroeconomic Policy from Japan." *Brookings Papers on Economic Activity* 2: 93–185. Brookings Institution, Washington, DC.

———. 2002. "Fiscal Policy Effectiveness in Japan." *Journal of the Japanese and International Economies*, 16 (4): 536–58.

Lam, R.W. 2011. "Bank of Japan's Monetary Easing Measures: Are They Powerful and Comprehensive?" IMF Working Paper No. 11/264. International Monetary Fund, Washington, DC.

Leigh, D. 2010. "Monetary Policy and the Lost Decade: Lessons from Japan." *Journal of Money, Credit and Banking*, 42 (5): 833–57.

Neely, C. 2010. "The Large-Scale Asset Purchases Had Large International Effects." Federal Reserve Bank of St. Louis, Working Paper.

Posen, A.S. 2000. "The Political Economy of Deflationary Monetary Policy." in *Japan's Financial Crisis and Its Parallels to U.S. Experience*, edited by Ryoichi Mikitani and Adam S. Posen, Special Report 13, 194–208, Institute for International Economics, Washington, DC.

Raskin, M.D. 2013. "The Effects of the Federal Reserve's Date-Based Forward Guidance." Finance and Economics Discussion Series, Federal Reserve Board, Washington, DC.

Shirai, S. 2013. "Monetary Policy and Forward Guidance in Japan." Presentation at the International Monetary Fund, Washington DC.

Ueda, K. 2011. "The Effectiveness of Non-Traditional Monetary Policy Measures: The Case of the Bank of Japan." CARF Working Paper, CARF-F-252. Center for Advanced Research in Finance, Tokyo.

Yellen, J. 2011. "Unconventional Monetary Policy and Central Bank Communications," Speech at the U.S. Monetary Policy Forum, New York, on February 25.

CHAPTER 3

Can Abenomics Overcome the Headwinds from Population Aging?

DENNIS BOTMAN

The adoption of the quantitative and qualitative monetary easing (QQE) framework, together with the higher inflation target and stronger coordination with fiscal and structural policies marked a clean break from previous, more incremental attempts to end deflation and revive growth. What have been the effects of the new policies so far? What can we expect amid underlying headwinds from population aging? And what are the potential risks, including for the Bank of Japan (BoJ) balance sheet and financial stability? We discuss these issues in this chapter.

QQE and successive rounds of fiscal stimulus had an immediate impact on asset markets. The depreciation of the yen and the stock market rally boosted business and consumer confidence and growth well above potential during 2013, while inflation and inflation expectations posted multiyear highs. For the near term, the key issue is whether the recovery can gradually transition to a self-sustained, rather than stimulus-driven, recovery. This requires higher basic wages, an increase in investment, and a more substantial pickup in exports as well as progress with portfolio rebalancing among financial institutions.

We use the IMF's Global Integrated Monetary and Fiscal (GIMF) model to assess the potential medium-term implications of Abenomics.[1] We place particular emphasis on the rapid aging of Japan's population. This demographic shift not only has implications for potential growth and fiscal sustainability, but possibly also for the ability to escape deflation in a sustained manner. Specifically, we address the following questions, based on Anderson, Botman, and Hunt (2014):

- Under an unchanged monetary policy reaction function, what are the key channels and quantitative effects through which population aging affects inflation and the neutral real interest rate?
- To what extent do life-cycle saving considerations neutralize the impact of aging on growth and inflation?
- How does fiscal consolidation interact with the effects of aging on inflation?
- To what extent can Abenomics counter the effects of aging on the economy?

---
[1]See Kumhof and others (2010) for a detailed description of GIMF.

We conclude the chapter by discussing the potential risks of Abenomics. In the near term, this includes the possibility that the handover from stimulus- to private-sector-led growth remains incomplete, for example because of a lack of basic wage growth or continued weakness in investment and exports. In addition, there is a risk that monetary policy will become overburdened, including from insufficient progress on medium-term fiscal consolidation and structural reforms. We also discuss the exit strategy, risks to the BoJ balance sheet, and financial stability risks from unconventional monetary policy as a prelude to a fuller discussion in Chapter 9.

INITIAL EFFECTS OF ABENOMICS

The announcement of the new policy regime in December 2012 was followed by a quick set of actions. In February 2013, the Diet approved new debt-financed spending amounting to 1.4 percent of GDP for 2013–14. In April 2013, the BoJ introduced QQE to achieve its new inflation target with a time horizon of about two years and committed to continue easing until inflation is stabilized at 2 percent. In June 2013, the government affirmed its fiscal consolidation goals of halving the primary deficit by fiscal year (FY) 2015—from the FY2010 level— and achieving a primary surplus by FY2020. The announcement also included a broad outline of a comprehensive growth strategy, which targets to raise investment, employment, and productivity. In October 2013, the first stage of the consumption tax hike in April 2014 was confirmed and, at end-2013, a fiscal stimulus package of 1.2 percent of GDP to be disbursed over two years was adopted to mitigate its effects on the economy. At the same time, the contours of potentially important reforms emerged, including framework legislation for special economic zones, the adoption of a bill to encourage farmland consolidation, and the commencement of Trans-Pacific Partnership negotiations.

Financial and exchange markets were buoyant in early 2013 and the immediate aftermath of QQE. From September 2012 to mid-April 2013, the Nikkei rose about 80 percent, with large gains for export-oriented firms and financial institutions (Figure 3.1). The rise in the stock market occurred in tandem with the strong depreciation of the yen (down 17 percent in real effective terms between end-December 2012 and end-June 2013). Upon adoption of the BoJ's new QQE framework in April, bond yields declined briefly to historic lows, with the 10-year rate reaching 45 basis points.

In line with these developments, growth started to accelerate sharply in early 2013. First-quarter GDP growth jumped to 4.1 percent (seasonally adjusted annual rate) after two quarters of stagnation in mid-2012. Wealth effects from rising equity values stimulated consumption, particularly on luxury goods. One way to illustrate the initial success of the new policies is to compare the components of real GDP growth during 2013 relative to what was predicted to happen prior to the launch of Abenomics. For the latter we use the IMF's quarterly forecasts made in the October 2012 *World Economic Outlook* (Figure 3.2). As can be observed, fiscal stimulus played an important role in boosting growth, whereas investment and exports did not immediately react. Regarding trade, the forecasts made

Botman | 31

Figure 3.1 Equity Market Performance *(Index, July 2012 = 100)*

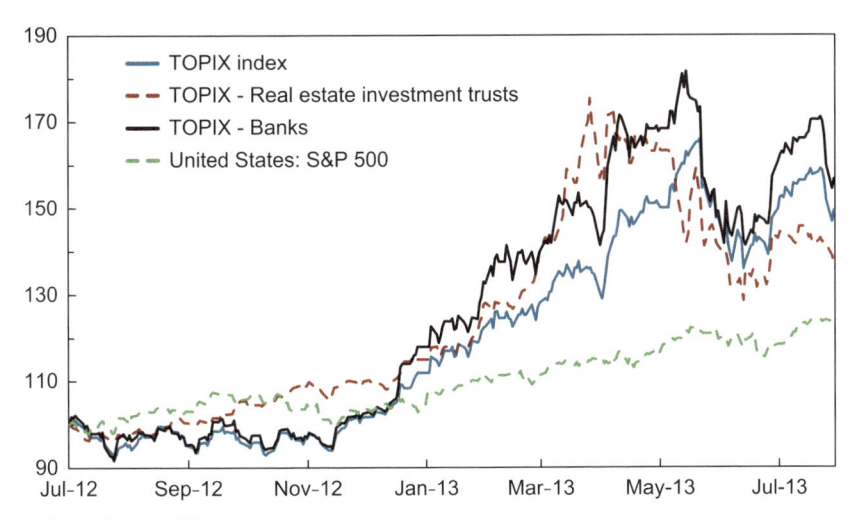

Source: Bloomberg, L.P.
Note: TOPIX = Tokyo Stock Price Index.

Figure 3.2 Components of Real GDP in Abenomics' First Year *(Index, 2012:Q4 = 100)*

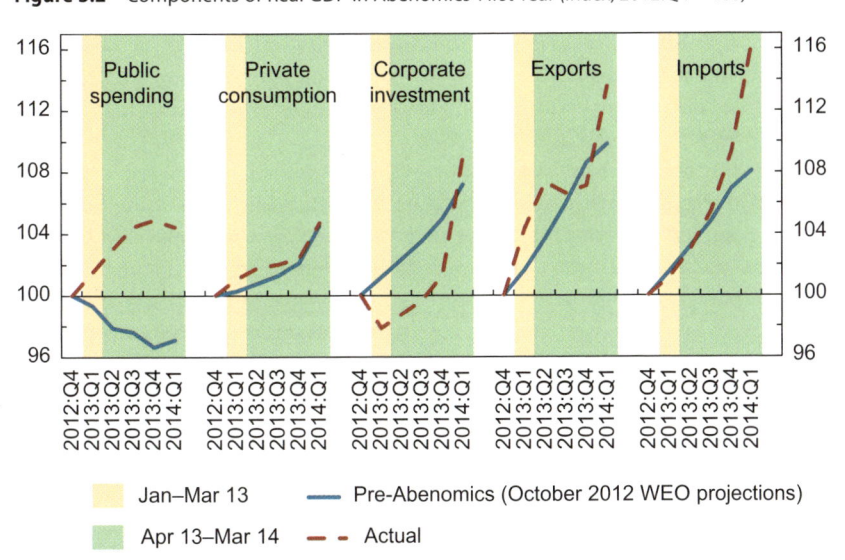

Source: IMF, *World Economic Outlook* (WEO); and IMF staff estimates.
Note: Compares IMF forecasts made prior to Abenomics and actual outturns.

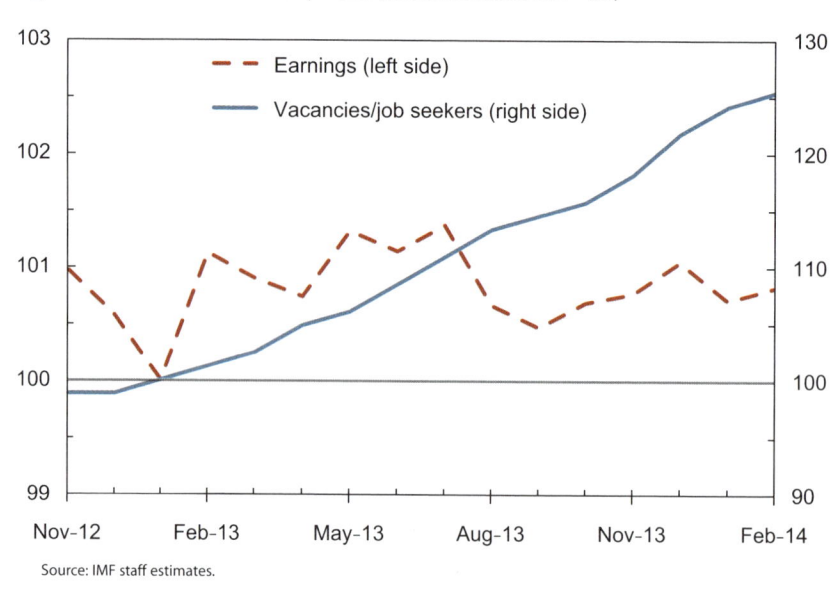

Figure 3.3 Labor Market Developments *(Index, December 2012 = 100)*

Source: IMF staff estimates.

pre-Abenomics were done under constant exchange rates. Thus, the rise in exports was driven by the expectation of higher partner country growth and the rise in imports by stronger domestic demand. The actual outcomes were very close to these predictions suggesting that the weakening of the yen itself had a very modest impact on export volumes and did not dampen real imports. Although the unemployment rate declined further and the vacancy-to-applicant ratio continued to rise, this tightness in the labor market did not translate into higher basic nominal wages (Figure 3.3).[2]

The four transmission channels of QQE mentioned in Chapter 2 worked broadly as expected, with yields remaining stable and low amid rising inflation, pushing real lending rates into negative territory. As the yen weakened, inflation expectations among a broad range of indicators started to rise (Figure 3.4). Although market-based indicators, including from swaps, can be distorted because of relatively low liquidity, while the near-term measures of inflation expectations are affected by the consumption tax increases, longer-term measures suggest that expectations are slowly converging on the BoJ's inflation target. Surveys of professional forecasters also confirm this. As the Phillips curve has been relatively flat, rising inflation expectations that shift the curve upward are essential to achieve the BoJ's inflation objectives.

Headline inflation increased to multiyear highs, and although this initially reflected higher food and energy prices, over the course of 2013 price increases became broader based. The gradual increase in core inflation, particularly for components such as reading and recreation and transportation and communication,

---

[2]See Chapter 7 for a detailed discussion on labor market developments.

Figure 3.4 Long-Term Inflation Expectations *(Annual percentage points)*

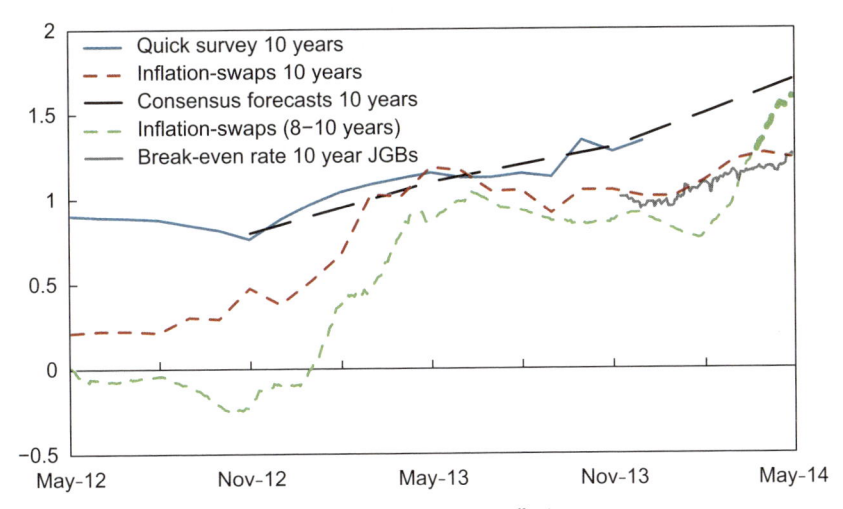

Sources: Bloomberg, L.P.; Consensus Forecasts; Quick Survey; and IMF staff estimates.
Note: JGBs = Japanese government bonds.

Figure 3.5 Inflation in Abenomics' First Year *(Year-over-year percent change)*

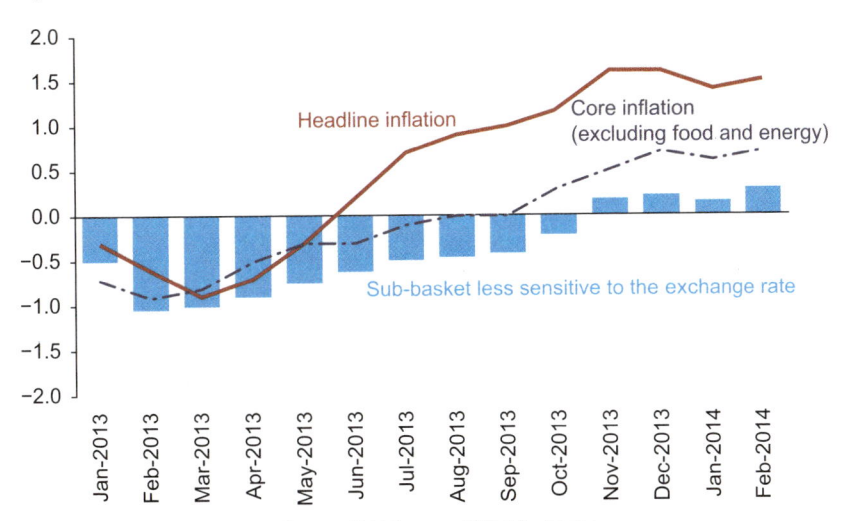

Sources: Bloomberg, L.P.; Consensus Forecasts; Quick Survey; and IMF staff estimates.

was evidence for this. Together these comprise close to 40 percent of the index. Nonetheless, the exchange rate depreciation played an important role in pushing up both headline and core inflation (Figure 3.5) with prices of certain capital goods remaining in deflationary territory.

For portfolio rebalancing, the initial effects of Abenomics were more mixed. Lending increased to small and medium-sized enterprises and large corporations, but was mainly flat to households (Figure 3.6, panel 1). Banks, particularly the large ones, have reduced their holdings of Japanese government bonds, but like insurance companies and corporate pension funds, did not significantly reduce their holdings of relatively risk-free assets. This is in contrast to households, public pension funds, and other financial intermediaries such as securities investment trust companies (Figure 3.6, panel 2; see also Chapter 9).

Figure 3.6 Portfolio Rebalancing During Abenomics' First Year

1. Japan Domestic Bank Lending *(Year-over-year percent change)*

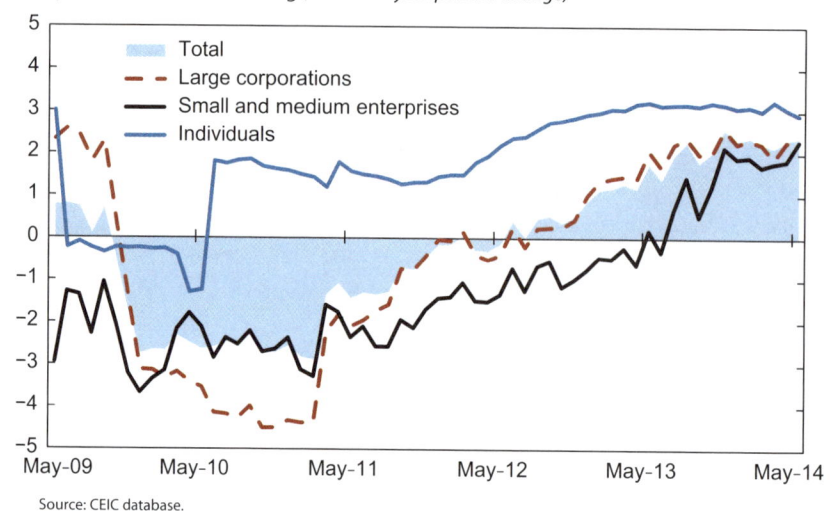

Source: CEIC database.

2. Currency, Deposits, and Government Bond Holdings, December 2013 *(Percent of total portfolios)*

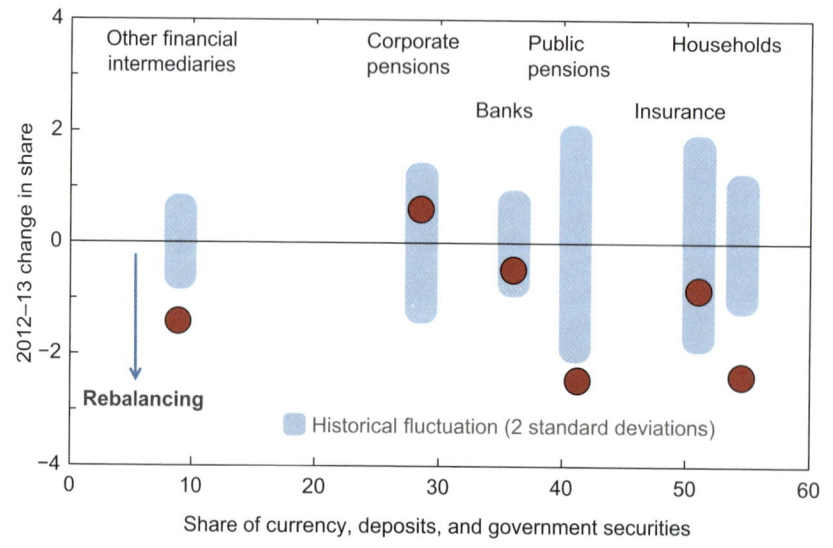

Sources: Bank of Japan Flow of Funds data; Haver Analytics; and IMF staff estimates.

3. Banks' Lending and Reserves *(Index, December 2012 = 100)*

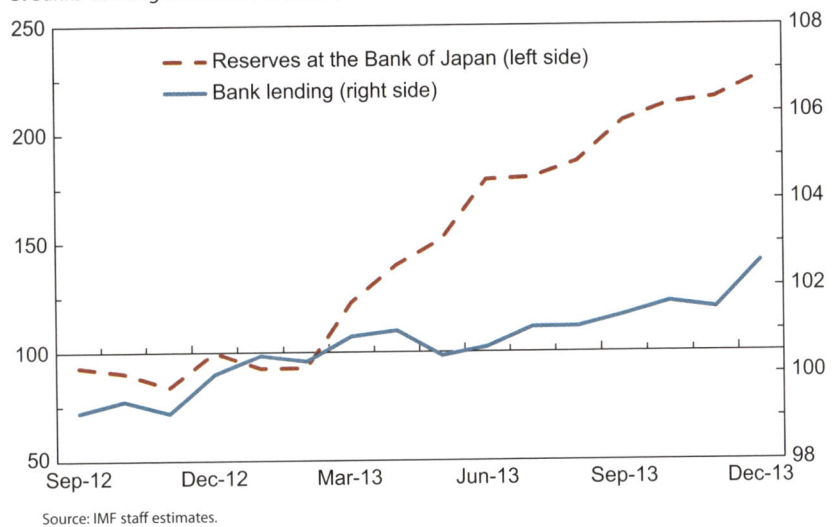

- - - Reserves at the Bank of Japan (left side)
—— Bank lending (right side)

Source: IMF staff estimates.

4. International Transaction in Securities[1] *(Trillion yen)*

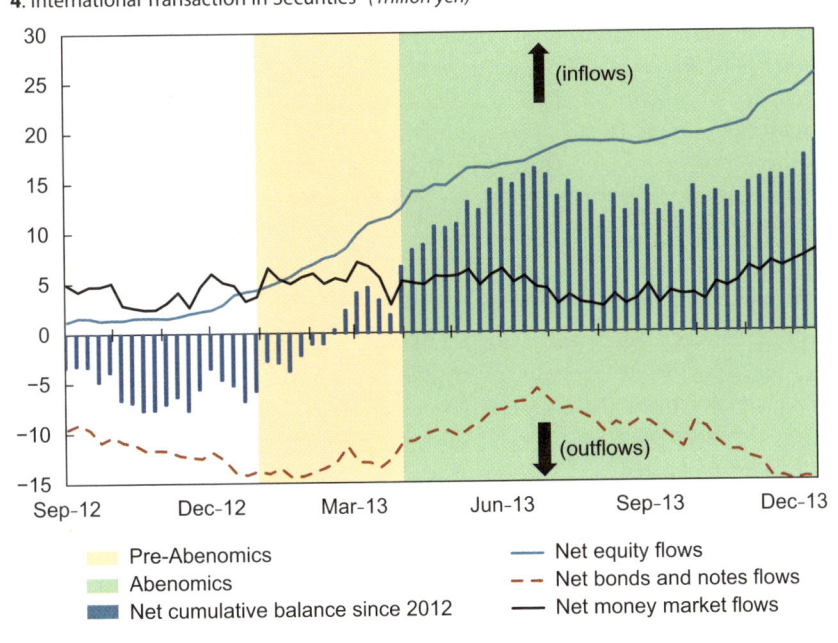

(inflows)

(outflows)

Pre-Abenomics
Abenomics
Net cumulative balance since 2012
—— Net equity flows
- - - Net bonds and notes flows
—— Net money market flows

Source: Japan Ministry of Finance.
[1] Cumulative positions since January 2012.

Instead, banks have mainly used the newfound financial room to accumulate excess reserves at the BoJ (Figure 3.6, panel 3). In terms of international transactions, the first year of Abenomics showed some increase in gross outflows—mainly to advanced economies—but at the same time even larger inflows, particularly into the equity market (Figure 3.6, panel 4).

Although the initial phase of Abenomics was successful, progress increasingly became uneven toward the end of 2013 and into 2014. Consumer confidence started to decline, albeit from high levels, around the summer of 2013 all the way through the April 2014 consumption tax increase. As basic wages were rising only moderately, real purchasing power started to decline, which, together with subdued export and investment growth and mixed progress on the structural reform front, implied that the transition from a stimulus-driven to private-demand-led recovery increasingly became elusive. Furthermore, the effects of the April consumption tax increase to 8 percent were stronger and longer lasting than anticipated, halting the recovery in its tracks by 2014:Q3. Progress on actual and expected inflation also stalled with the waning effects of the initial exchange rate depreciation. These developments led the BoJ to significantly scale up its monetary easing in October 2014, followed by the government's decision to delay the second increase in the consumption tax rate to 10 percent.

AGING AND POTENTIAL IMPLICATIONS FOR EXITING DEFLATION

With the initial phase of Abenomics behind us, what can be expected going forward? To address this question, we need to take into account Japan's rapidly aging population, with implications for growth, inflation, and debt dynamics, the three areas that Abenomics attempts to tackle. Large gains in longevity and virtually no immigration imply Japan is "aging in fast forward." Life expectancy is the highest in the world, the working-age population started to decline around the early 1990s, and the baby-boom generation (born in 1947–49) started retiring in 2007 (Figure 3.7).

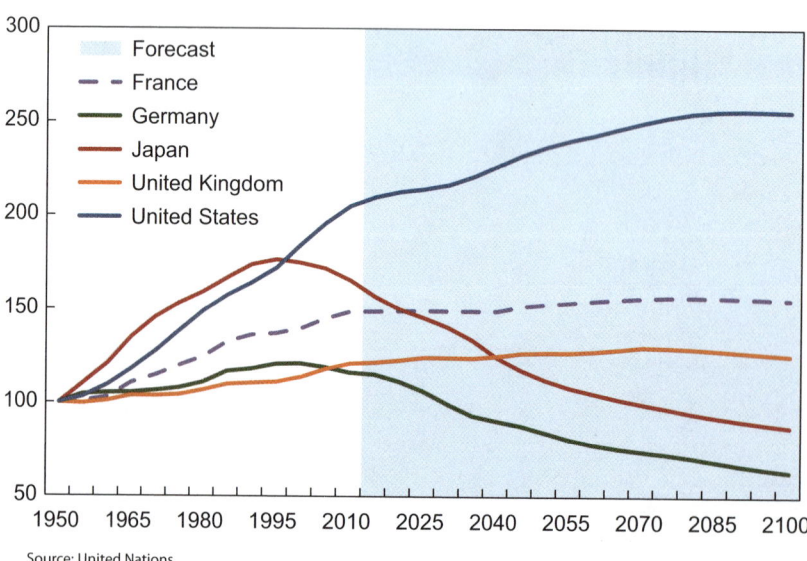

Figure 3.7 Working-Age Population in Selected Countries, 1950–2100 *(Index, 1950 = 100)*

Source: United Nations.

The old-age population will continue to increase disproportionately in coming years, while the fertility rate declined markedly during the past decades.

Population aging could impact inflation dynamics by affecting relative prices, the output gap, and potential growth, among other channels. In particular, deflationary pressures could arise from:

- *Changes in relative prices, including from land.* A shrinking or aging population would lower the price of land (for example, because the elderly live in smaller houses). Land is not only a fixed factor of production, but also affects wealth and thereby consumer behavior. In addition, a decline in labor force participation affects real wages. The extent to which relative price changes occur between land, labor, and capital will depend partly on labor market characteristics—in Japan, wage growth has lagged productivity growth despite declining labor force participation and the absence of immigration. In addition, aging leads to secular shifts in consumption patterns as the elderly's preferences differ from those of the young, with less spending on housing, transportation, communication, and education, and more spending on medical, utilities, and other consumption expenditures (Figure 3.8). To what extent this shift affects inflation dynamics depends on the flexibility of supply to adapt to these changes in demand. In turn, this may be affected by the extent to which there may be substitution from market to regulated prices and from traded to nontraded goods, although this will be difficult to capture empirically.

Figure 3.8 Average Expenditure Share by Household Age, *1995–2010 (Percent)*

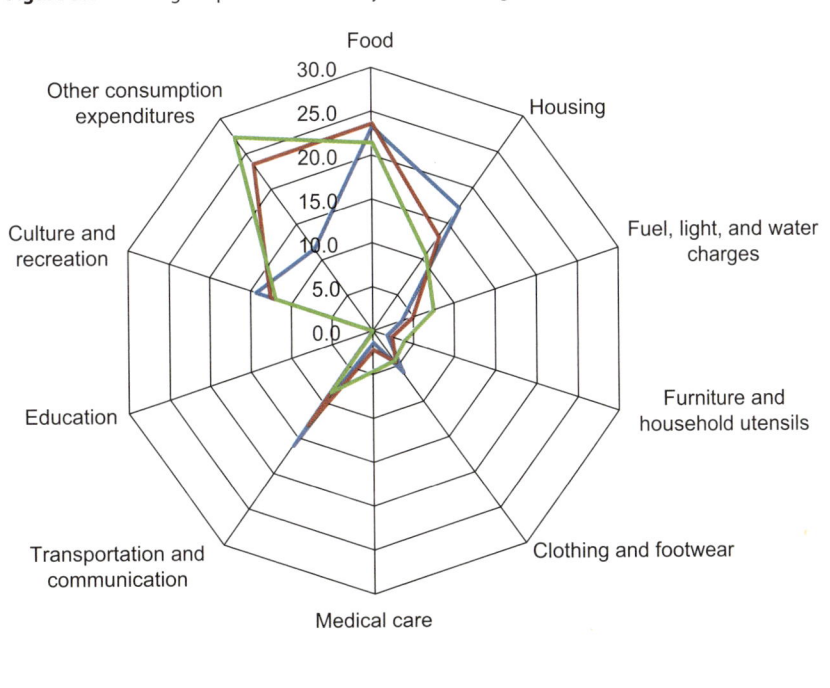

Sources: Ministry of Internal Affairs and Communications; Statistical Survey Department, Statistics Bureau; and IMF (2013b).

- *Life-cycle saving considerations* could have wealth implications by affecting asset prices, including the exchange rate following repatriation of foreign assets. As the population ages, aggregate portfolio rebalancing toward safe assets is likely to occur, potentially pushing government bond yields down (see IMF 2013a).

- *Greater excess supply as a result of fiscal consolidation.* In many countries, advanced and emerging market alike, aging will lead to higher government outlays on pensions and health care and a shrinking tax base. Coupled with the elevated initial deficit and debt levels, the expectation of a rising risk premium and fiscal consolidation would lead to a sustained period of output growth below potential and deflationary pressures. In contrast, unsustainable government debt dynamics could increase fears of debt monetization and, therefore, expectations of high inflation in the absence of a credible medium-term fiscal consolidation plan. It should be noted, however, that projections for aging-related fiscal expenditures are relatively modest in Japan—although new work suggests that health care spending could rise faster than previously expected (Kashiwase, Nozaki, and Saito 2014). As a result, the fiscal channel will be driven mainly by the high initial debt and deficit levels. In addition, the composition of government spending could change, with fewer outlays on human (education) and physical (public investment) capital accumulation, although the resulting effects on the output gap are not clear a priori.

- *Changes in policy objectives affected by political economy considerations.* Young cohorts do not initially have any assets, and wages are their main source of income. Hence, they prefer relatively low real interest rates and high real-wage growth. Older generations work less and prefer higher rates of return on their saving and relatively low inflation (Bullard, Garriga, and Waller, 2012). The latter will depend on institutional factors, for example, the extent of pension indexation. As such, aging could affect a central bank's perception of what its objective function should look like and thus the level of its inflation target and the speed with which it pursues it. Whether or not this is relevant for Japan is unclear, as the BoJ has recently adopted a higher inflation target to be achieved through aggressive monetary easing, to some extent defying the political economy hypothesis, or at least suggesting that this can be trumped by other economic considerations if a country has been stuck in deflation.

Some of these channels have been studied in the literature. For example, in the United States, it has been observed that the elderly population spends a relatively higher share of income on health care, for which prices have risen faster than the overall consumer price index. This has led to the development of an experimental price index to track inflation for the population aged 62 and older (Cashell 2010).

Konishi and Ueda (2013) suggest that negative correlations between inflation and demographic aging have been observed across developed nations recently.

They analyze this phenomenon from a political economy perspective by embedding the fiscal theory of the price level into an overlapping-generations model. They assume that short-lived governments successively make decisions about income tax rates and bond issues, taking into account political influence from existing generations and the expected policy responses of future governments. Their analysis reveals that the effects of aging depend on its causes; aging is deflationary when caused by an unexpected increase in longevity, but is inflationary when caused by a decline in the birth rate. Ikeda and Saito (2012) study the effects of demographic changes on the real interest rate in Japan. Using a dynamic general equilibrium model, they find that a decline in the labor-force participation rate reduced the real interest rate, which is amplified by falling land prices in the presence of collateral constraints. Nonetheless, they suggest that total factor productivity growth is a more important source of variations in the real interest rate.

In their paper, aging affects the real interest rate by changing the demand and supply of loanable funds.[3] First, household saving rises as the number of wage earners relative to the number of consumers in the household declines. This puts downward pressure on the real interest rate. This is consistent with Lindh and Malmberg (1998 and 2000) who, for a sample of Organisation for Economic Co-operation and Development countries, find that increases in the population of net savers dampen inflation, whereas the younger retirees fan inflation as they start consuming out of accumulated pension claims. Second, as firms' demand for capital and land declines, downward pressure on the real interest rate emerges from reduced demand for loanable funds. Third, firms' collateral falls as land prices decline, leading to a further decline in the demand for loanable funds.

A key distinction of our approach is that the GIMF is an open-economy model and therefore effects on the real interest rate occur only to the extent that developments in Japan affect the global supply and demand for saving. As a result, in the GIMF, the majority of the action occurs through changes in relative factor prices, including from fiscal consolidation. Furthermore, as in Hoshi and Ito (2012), we postulate that Japan has now entered the state in which we should start to see a decline in the saving rate as the population ages. In addition, consumption by retirees will in part be funded by running down Japan's sizable net foreign asset position. The effect on the neutral real interest rate will then also depend on the response of the real exchange rate following repatriation of savings.

Katagiri (2012) studies the effects of aging on growth, unemployment, and inflation using a multisector new Keynesian model with job creation and destruction. Aging leads to a shift in aggregate demand from durable goods to services which, owing to various labor market frictions, increases the structural unemployment rate. In addition, productivity in the nonmanufacturing sector has been lower than in

---

[3]Other studies that use computable general equilibrium models to study the effects of aging on the aggregate saving rate include Miles (1999) for the United Kingdom and western Europe, and Chen, İmrohoroğlu, and İmrohoroğlu (2007) and Braun, Ikeda, and Joines (2009) for Japan.

the manufacturing sector, implying that these demand shifts reduce aggregate productivity growth. Since estimates of aging have increased annually, the repeated upward revisions are treated as unexpected shocks to the economy. All considered, the author finds deflationary effects of aging in Japan through these channels.

THE EFFECTS OF AGING ON INFLATION AND GROWTH

Indeed, in popular debate a view appears to have emerged that exiting deflation has become more challenging because of aging. However, there is scant theoretical or empirical work on the potential relationship between these factors, with most research on aging focusing on the effects on growth and fiscal sustainability. To some extent this may be due to the monetarist doctrine: whether or not aging exerts downward pressure on prices is irrelevant as a central bank committed to do whatever it takes should remain capable of anchoring inflation expectations to the target.

Nonetheless, the extent to which aging affects the neutral rate and requires adapting macroeconomic policies to anchor inflation expectations remains a relevant and, to a large extent, unaddressed question. In this chapter we use the GIMF model to quantify the overall impact of aging on growth and to determine if the corrective macroeconomic and structural policies envisaged under Abenomics can stem the tide. The model, however, imposes limitations on the analysis. For example, in principle, monetary policy will react endogenously to any effects of aging on inflation consistent with the central bank's objective function, although there remains the open issue of to what extent this will be effective under the zero lower bound. Therefore, to isolate the effect of aging on inflation we would need to keep monetary policy constant. However, this can only be imposed in the GIMF for a few periods, as the model would otherwise become unstable. As such, any deflationary effects from aging will be observed in the simulations through its effects on both the "shadow" policy rate and the inflation rate.[4]

The effects of aging on the neutral real interest rate operate through changes in inflation pressures and rising risk premiums. First, as a large proportion of the population moves into retirement, the labor force will decline, with implications for both supply and demand. Second, without labor income, retirees will draw down their savings to finance consumption expenditures. Finally, as private domestic saving declines, it has been argued that Japan will need to increasingly tap foreign investors to meet its high public financing requirement, which would likely require higher interest rates, modeled here as a rising sovereign risk premium over time. We have layered these various channels to illustrate their relative contribution to the overall deflationary effects from population aging.

In the first layer of the simulation exercise (blue line in Figure 3.9), the labor force in Japan declines by 1 percent a year for 30 years. This magnitude is calibrated to match the decline in the United Nations median forecast for Japan's

---

[4]The "shadow" policy rate is defined as the rate that would be observed in the absence of the zero lower bound.

Figure 3.9 Effects of Aging on Growth and Inflation

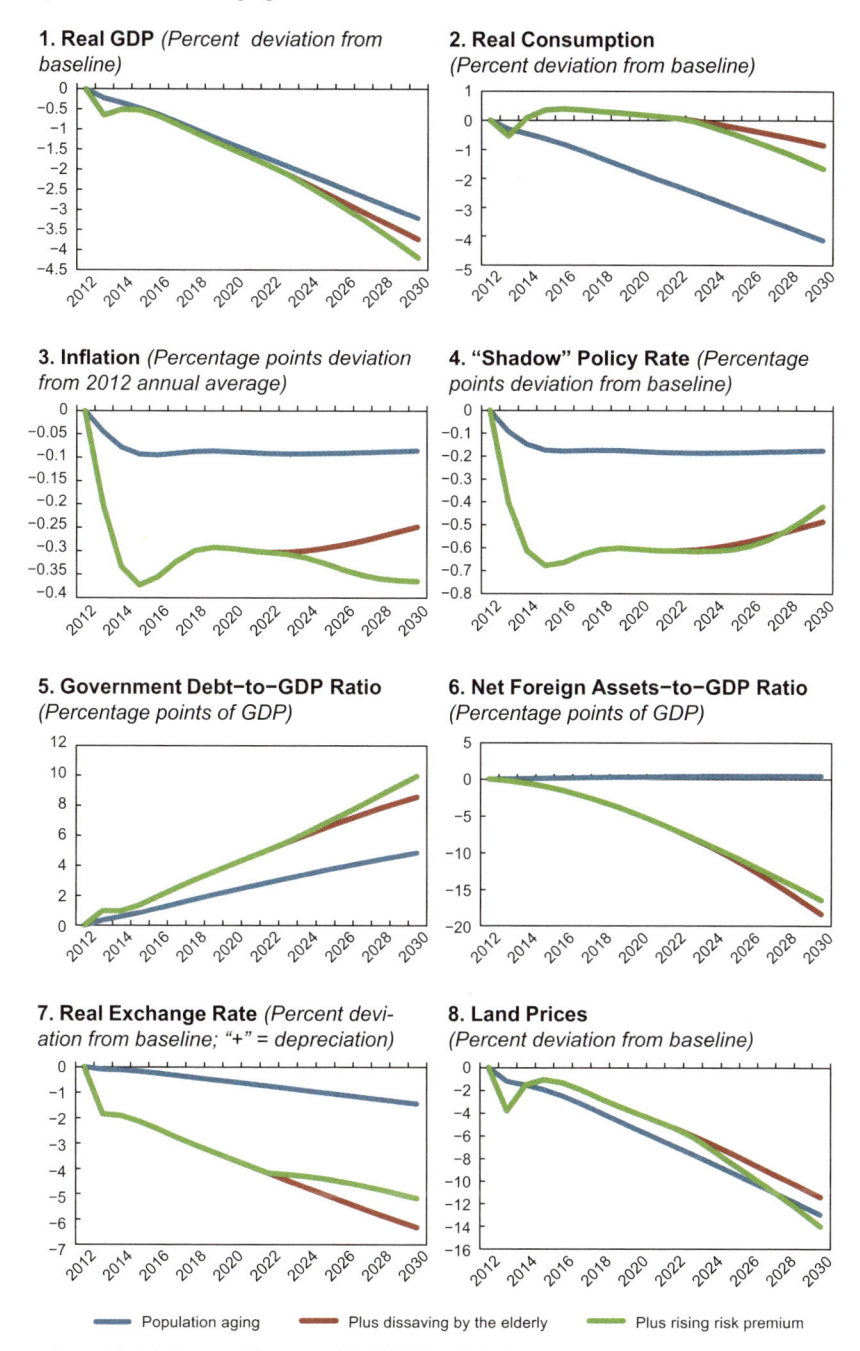

1. Real GDP *(Percent deviation from baseline)*

2. Real Consumption *(Percent deviation from baseline)*

3. Inflation *(Percentage points deviation from 2012 annual average)*

4. "Shadow" Policy Rate *(Percentage points deviation from baseline)*

5. Government Debt-to-GDP Ratio *(Percentage points of GDP)*

6. Net Foreign Assets-to-GDP Ratio *(Percentage points of GDP)*

7. Real Exchange Rate *(Percent deviation from baseline; "+" = depreciation)*

8. Land Prices *(Percent deviation from baseline)*

— Population aging   — Plus dissaving by the elderly   — Plus rising risk premium

Source: IMF, Global Integrated Monetary and Fiscal (GIMF) model simulations.

working age population. As the labor force declines, consumption and investment both fall. Both demand- and supply-side factors serve to decrease the overall demand for factors of production. A falling labor supply results in a higher real wage, which induces firms to move back along their supply curves, reducing demand for both capital and land. At the same time, falling demand implies that the return to all factors of production is declining, also reducing demand for capital, labor, and land. Lower demand for land causes its price to fall as well. The decline in the labor supply is similar in nature to a negative, economy-wide productivity shock, and, with less output to sell to the rest of the world, the Japanese currency appreciates. The appreciated real effective exchange rate results in increased demand for imports, as foreign goods become relatively cheaper compared to domestic goods. Declining demand for domestic output, falling land prices, and cheaper imports all exert continuous downward pressure on inflation. The calibrated aggressiveness of the monetary policy rule results in a reduction in the shadow policy rate of about 20 basis points, but this still results in inflation falling by about 10 basis points. The public debt-to-GDP ratio rises gradually over the simulation horizon owing to the trend decline in nominal GDP.

In the second layer (red line in Figure 3.9), it is assumed that the Japanese saving rate declines by just over 0.1 percent of GDP a year for 30 years. Specifically, the Japanese household saving rate has been gradually decreasing since the early 1990s, from about 15 percent of disposable income at that time to about zero percent in 2011. This decline in the saving rate partially occurred because of demographic changes (aging). The importance of demographic changes was outlined by Hoshi and Ito (2012). One can use the Annual Family Income and Expenditure Survey to determine the autonomous effect of aging on this decline in the saving rate. Older households have a lower (or negative) saving rate and their share has considerably increased throughout the last 20 years.

For the decomposition exercise, we used the savings rate reported by Iwaisako and Okada (2010) (Table 3.1). Notably, the saving rate changed significantly after the financial crisis of 1997–98. The role of demographic factors assumes the same saving rate throughout the whole sample. Demographic factors accounted for about 4 percentage points (one-third) of the decline in the aggregate saving rate (Table 3.2). The role of aging has gained importance since 1998, and about 3 percentage points out of the 5-percentage-point decline was due to this factor (the change in propensity to consume added another 2 percentage points). As

TABLE 3.1

Saving Rate for Different Age Groups								
	20–29	30–44	45–49	50–54	55–59	60+	60+ Non-employed	60+ Employed
1991–1997	0.278	28.8	23.6	26.1	32.3	1.7	−11.0	21.7
1998–2010	0.265	31.8	26.2	25.4	27.8	−9.4	−23.9	14.4

Source: Iwaisako and Okada (2010).

TABLE 3.2

Demographic Factors in Declining Household Saving			
	1991–2011	1991–1997	1998–2011
Change in net saving rate (%)	−13.5	−8.2	−5.3
Demographics	−3.8	−1.0	−2.8
C/Y	−2.3	...	...
Other	−7.4	−7.2	−2.5

Source: IMF staff calculations.
Note: C/Y = consumption quote; ... = not available.

such, aging subtracts about 0.1 to 0.2 percentage point from the saving rate each year, and for the simulations we use the lower bound of this estimate.

Dissaving by the elderly exerts further deflationary pressures through real exchange rate appreciation. Interestingly, one might expect that dissaving by retirees would be inflationary: while aggregate supply declines owing to a falling labor supply, aggregate demand remains supported by retirees' spending from their saving, as can be observed in Figure 3.9, panel 2. However, for Japan, dissaving by the elderly results in a repatriation of foreign saving, which in turn leads to real exchange rate appreciation. The deflationary impact from currency appreciation more than offsets the inflationary effects from higher demand for consumption goods.

As domestic saving declines while the government financing requirement remains large, Japan will need to increasingly rely on foreign investors. This is likely to exert upward pressure on long-term interest rates. This scenario is simulated through a rising risk premium, which adds further deflationary pressures (green line in Figure 3.9). The simulation assumes that the risk premium rises by five basis points per year, leading to a further contraction in output and accumulation of government debt. The combined impact of all three aging channels is to raise the public debt by 10 percentage points of GDP by 2030, relative to the baseline, and to lower inflation by about 0.3 percentage points on average during 2013–30, despite a decline in the shadow policy rate by about 60 basis points on average during the same period.

CAN ABENOMICS STEM THE TIDE?

As aging exerts downward pressure on growth and exacerbates deflationary pressures, what are the policy options available to counter these effects? Regarding fiscal policy, space for stimulus is limited; it is an inadequate instrument given that aging affects growth persistently; and we need to consider the necessity for significant medium-term fiscal consolidation in Japan to restore debt sustainability. The latter arises not only because an aging population exerts fiscal pressures (see Chapter 4), but especially because the starting fiscal position is characterized by high deficits and debt.

To put debt on a downward trajectory, an adjustment of 1 percent of GDP is assumed to occur each year during 2016–25, over and above the adjustment that is already in the baseline, which includes the increase in the consumption tax rate to 10 percent and the waning of stimulus and earthquake-reconstruction spending in the near term (IMF 2013a). This adjustment is assumed to be divided between revenue (consumption tax increases account for 66 percent of the needed adjustment) and expenditure measures (lower public consumption accounts for 34 percent of the needed consolidation) (purple line in Figure 3.10). Even though this would avoid the rise in the risk premium, consumption and land prices decline markedly, exerting more downward pressure on the shadow policy rate and inflation. Fiscal consolidation more than offsets the decline in private saving resulting from aging, leading to a further accumulation of net foreign assets.

As illustrated in Figure 3.10, the effects of fiscal consolidation to maintain debt sustainability on the neutral real interest rate far exceed the autonomous effects of population aging, including through the real exchange rate. This may provide a cautionary tale for other aging economies that will likely experience increasing debt sustainability pressures owing to rising health care and pension spending, albeit from a better starting position than Japan.

As additional medium-term fiscal consolidation is unavoidable, the focus shifts next to whether structural reforms and the more aggressive monetary policy reaction function under QQE can overcome the deflationary pressures and maintain growth prospects. This is precisely at the heart of Abenomics. Our results indicate that combining fiscal consolidation with structural reforms and aggressive monetary easing to achieve the new inflation target can offset the effects of aging (orange line in Figure 3.10). In the simulation it is assumed that structural reforms raise potential growth by 0.25 percentage point by 2015 and 0.50 percentage point by 2018.

Provided that inflation expectations converge quickly toward the 2 percent inflation target—through aggressive monetary easing and effective forward guidance—such a policy package has substantial benefits by overcoming the deflationary effects of aging, while supporting growth and fiscal sustainability. The positive effects on growth and fiscal sustainability are mainly due to the rise in inflation expectations, which lowers the real interest rate and stimulates investment. Together with modestly higher potential growth following structural reforms, this substantially reduces the net debt-to-GDP ratio—albeit relative to a sharply rising debt-to-GDP ratio in the baseline.

POTENTIAL MACROECONOMIC AND EXIT RISKS

The analysis above suggests that all three arrows of Abenomics are needed to achieve the BoJ's inflation target in a stable manner amid headwinds from population aging. As Chapter 9 discusses, such a complete package of reforms also improves financial stability by reducing interest rate risks as financial institutions reduce holdings of Japanese government bonds and expand higher-yielding domestic and international lending portfolios instead. Not surprisingly, therefore, the key macroeconomic risks stem from incomplete Abenomics as well as the eventual exit from unconventional policies.

Botman | 45

Figure 3.10 Effects of Abenomics' Three Arrows

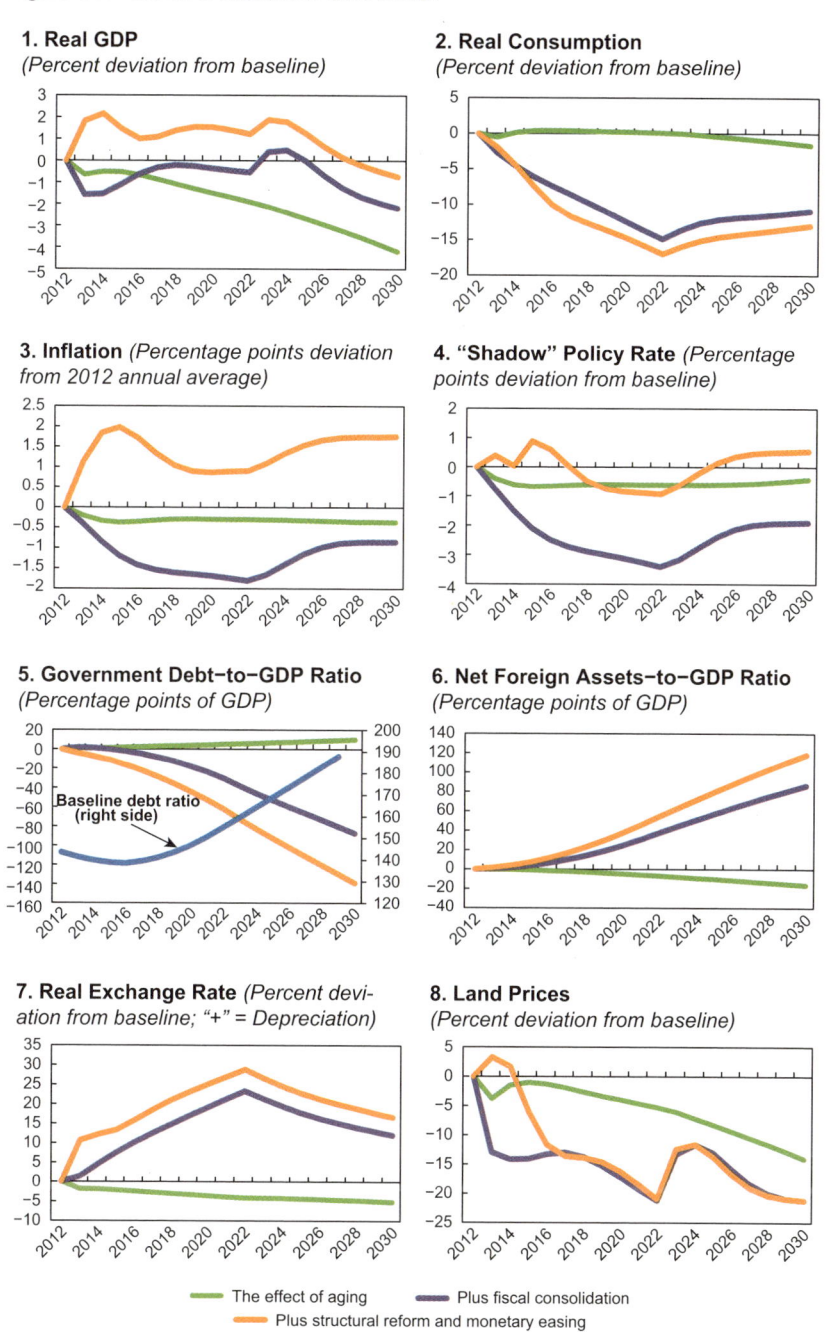

1. Real GDP
(Percent deviation from baseline)

2. Real Consumption
(Percent deviation from baseline)

3. Inflation *(Percentage points deviation from 2012 annual average)*

4. "Shadow" Policy Rate *(Percentage points deviation from baseline)*

5. Government Debt-to-GDP Ratio
(Percentage points of GDP)

6. Net Foreign Assets-to-GDP Ratio
(Percentage points of GDP)

7. Real Exchange Rate *(Percent deviation from baseline; "+" = Depreciation)*

8. Land Prices
(Percent deviation from baseline)

— The effect of aging
— Plus fiscal consolidation
— Plus structural reform and monetary easing

Source: IMF, Global Integrated Monetary and Fiscal (GIMF) model simulations.

Specifically, much uncertainty remains concerning to what extent inflation expectations will adjust over the medium term in response to QQE. Furthermore, the effects of structural reforms on potential growth are difficult to gauge. One could thus consider a scenario in which (1) fiscal stimulus boosts activity in the short term; (2) long-term inflation expectations adjust to QQE, but in a sluggish manner; and (3) potential growth remains stuck owing to the absence of ambitious structural reforms or because such reforms have smaller effects than assumed in the simulation above. In this case, there may be an overreliance on fiscal stimulus in an attempt to close the output gap and boost inflation in the near term. However, medium-term fiscal adjustment and a rising risk premium causes output and public debt to eventually fall below the pre-Abenomics baseline (IMF 2013a).

Alternatively, monetary policy could become overburdened in such a scenario to support activity and prevent yields from rising. With greater uncertainty about fiscal and financial stability, this may trigger capital outflows and exchange rate depreciation, undermining not only Japan's recovery, but also adversely affecting trading partners—especially in the region.

Additionally, tail risks could be triggered under an incomplete Abenomics scenario. Given high debt, a self-fulfilling sell-off of Japanese government bonds remains a possibility, in the event that a convincing medium-term debt reduction strategy is lacking, and markets could shift their perception of BoJ bond purchases toward debt monetization. Yields could spike, undermining domestic and global financial stability, increasing the risk of a reversal in emerging market capital flows and putting pressure on the BoJ to maintain an accommodative stance for longer, possibly at the cost of its credibility and ability to efficiently manage inflation.

Finally, even if Abenomics is successful in ending deflation and raising potential growth, important risks could stem from the eventual exit from QQE amid elevated BoJ balance-sheet exposure. As noted in Yamaoka and Syed (2010), in theory, exit from unconventional easing involves a number of seemingly straightforward central bank operations to maintain activity close to potential and ensure price stability: (1) halting extraordinary interventions; (2) downsizing and normalizing the central bank balance sheet; (3) selling purchased assets, if necessary; and (4) raising short-term interest rates.

However, in practice, the exit is more complicated. Yamaoka and Syed (2010) argue that uncertainties about the outlook for economic activity and inflation and the precise transmission mechanism of unconventional policies complicate the timing, pace, and sequencing of an exit strategy. In addition, to return to a positive policy rate, central banks usually need to eliminate the excess bank reserves accumulated through their unconventional operations, or at least neutralize the potential undesirable effects on credit growth and inflation as activity picks up. Some portion will contract automatically, as exceptional liquidity facilities are terminated and short-lived assets mature. However, the rest necessitate selling assets acquired by the central bank or other ways of sterilizing excess reserves to facilitate the necessary rate hike, such as by paying interest or issuing central bank bills.

The BoJ has experience with exiting from quantitative easing: it signaled the start of its exit strategy in March 2006 by announcing that it would gradually drain liquidity while keeping the overnight rate at virtually zero. By July 2006, it had smoothly transitioned to a more normal monetary framework, having downsized its balance sheet before raising the policy rate. Clear communication, transparent conditions governing future actions, flexibility, and market confidence about the adequacy of tools and underlying strategy for absorbing excess liquidity helped the BoJ manage an orderly exit. A revival of risk appetite through a restructuring of financial sector and debtor balance sheets, together with prudence and safeguards introduced during the entry stage of its unconventional operations, was also important (Yamaoka and Syed 2010).

Japan's experience during 2006, albeit premature in hindsight, as noted in Chapter 2, was successful and smooth in its technical aspects, practicalities, and associated communication strategies. After the BoJ officially announced the termination of quantitative easing, it reduced its balance sheet and excess bank reserves within a few months, although not all the way back to their late-1990 levels. Moreover, the exit did not result in any obvious disruption to financial markets. There was also no evidence of abrupt portfolio shifts or heightened volatility in both safe and risky assets (Yamaoka and Syed 2010).

As the BoJ's purchases are now skewed more toward longer-dated Japanese government bonds and private sector assets compared with the past, balance sheet risks may be commensurately higher, which may make the exit more complicated this time around. As noted in IMF (2013a), balance sheet risks could stem from implicit or explicit valuation losses as a result of a rise in interest rates, declines in operating income when central banks increase their holdings of long-dated securities with low coupon interest rates, and possible impairment losses on assets with credit risk.

CONCLUSION

Abenomics had a strong start, but, along a number of indicators, progress stalled toward the end of 2013 and, following the consumption tax increase to 8 percent in April 2014, uncertainty has increased about whether a successful handover from a stimulus-driven to a more self-sustained recovery is in the cards. This transition needs to occur against various structural headwinds, with population aging being a common thread that could hamper higher investment, rising wages, greater domestic rather than overseas production, and portfolio rebalancing away from safe assets.

Indeed, aging is expected to reduce the labor force participation rate and thereby impact potential growth. At the same time, it affects other factors of production, such as the rate of return to capital accumulation and land prices. Through these factors, aging affects potential growth, permanent income, and inflation, with implications for the neutral rate. Furthermore, aging tends to be associated with higher government outlays for health care and pensions, exacerbating already high fiscal consolidation needs in Japan. The prospect for sustained fiscal consolidation may dampen inflation dynamics by widening the output gap. In addition, while dissaving by the elderly during retirement could possibly support aggregate demand at the time when aggregate supply is declining, this needs to be weighed against possible exchange rate effects from repatriation of foreign assets, both with possible implications for underlying inflationary pressures.

Our findings suggest that aging tends to exert deflationary pressures through changes in relative prices. These include changes in nominal wages as labor force participation declines, triggering adjustment in the price of capital and land as well. Furthermore, dissaving by the elderly affects the neutral rate and also the real exchange rate through repatriation of foreign saving. Finally, as Japan's financing requirement remains large under baseline policies, while aggregate saving declines owing to life-cycle dynamics, the risk premium starts to rise gradually. In combination and under an unchanged monetary policy reaction function, this reduces inflation persistently, despite a decline in the shadow policy rate.

In addition, fiscal consolidation needs are large in Japan, mainly because of the high initial deficit and debt levels and, to a more limited extent, as a result of further increases in aging-related government expenditure (such as health care). We found that medium-term fiscal consolidation that puts the debt-to-GDP ratio on a downward trajectory through a combination of revenue and expenditure measures exerts substantial downward pressure on the neutral rate. In fact, the effect is larger than the combined direct effects of aging. This is a channel that is not only relevant for Japan, but likely also for other countries that experience fiscal pressure from population aging.

We also showed that these pressures can be overcome with a full package of reforms that includes, besides medium-term fiscal consolidation, bold structural reforms, and a sufficiently aggressive monetary policy reaction function, which at the zero lower bound should include unconventional monetary easing and strong forward guidance. Such a package of reforms generates powerful economic synergies, particularly as rising inflation expectations push down the real interest rate, stimulating capital formation, whereas bold structural reforms raise permanent-income expectations, thereby stimulating aggregate demand and helping to close the output gap.

Structural headwinds from aging justify the aggressive approach the BoJ has taken to strengthen the credibility of its policy rule. On the structural front, measures that directly address the effects of population aging are likely to be most effective. These include stimulating female and elderly labor force participation as well as greater opportunities for immigration, particularly in areas with labor shortages (see Chapters 6 and 7 for further discussion). Prior to the launch of Abenomics, a comprehensive and coordinated approach to exit deflation and revive growth was lacking and it is likely that the declining working-age population since the mid-1990s contributed to the mild deflation, on average, observed during the last two decades.

Although Japan is ahead of the curve in the pace of population aging, it is not unique. Many other advanced economies will experience rapid population aging in coming years (although not necessarily declining working-age populations) amid elevated debt-sustainability concerns in light of rising health care and pension outlays and high initial debt levels. Disinflation risks are also rising in a number of advanced economies (Moghadam, Teja, and Berkmen 2014) and are generally above the pre–global financial crisis average (IMF 2014). In this regard, while some of the findings in this chapter are Japan specific (such as the starting point of two decades of entrenched deflationary expectations and high net foreign assets), broader lessons for aging economies with low inflation and rising fiscal outlays owing to health care and pension spending are that ambitious structural reforms and an aggressive monetary policy reaction function are needed to reduce the risk of falling into a deflationary trap.

An incomplete package of policies will put financial stability at risk (Chapter 9), including by potentially overburdening monetary and fiscal policy. These risks are not just relevant for Japan, but also for the broader global economy through implications for the exchange rate, global financing conditions, and trade flows (see Chapter 10 for more on Japan's role in the global economy). An additional risk stems from the eventual exit from unconventional easing. Although past experience provides a useful marker, both the size and composition of asset purchases will present new challenges for the BoJ when the time comes to exit.

REFERENCES

Anderson, D., D. Botman, and B. Hunt. 2014. "Is Japan's Population Aging Deflationary?" IMF Working Paper No. 14/139. International Monetary Fund, Washington, DC.

Braun, R.A., Ikeda, D., and D.H. Joines. 2009. "The Saving Rate in Japan: Why It Has Fallen and Why It Will Remain Low." *International Economic Review* 50 (1): 291–321.

Bullard, J., C. Garriga, and C.J. Waller. 2012. "Demographics, Redistribution, and Optimal Inflation." Presented at the 2012 BoJ-IMES Conference, Demographic Changes and Macroeconomic Performance, Tokyo.

Cashell, B.W. 2010. "A Separate Consumer Price Index for the Elderly?" U.S. Congressional Research Service.

Chen, K., A. İmrohoroğlu, and S. İmrohoroğlu. 2007. "The Japanese Saving Rate between 1960 and 2000: Productivity, Policy Changes, and Demographics." *Economic Theory* 32 (1): 87–104.

Hoshi, T., and T. Ito. 2012. "Defying Gravity: How Long Will Japanese Government Bond Prices Remain High?" NBER Working Paper No. 18287. National Bureau of Economic Research, Cambridge, Massachusetts.

Ikeda, D., and M. Saito. 2012. "The Effects of Demographic Changes on the Real Interest Rate in Japan." Bank of Japan Working Paper No. 12-E-3, Tokyo.

International Monetary Fund. 2013a. "Japan: 2013 Article IV Consultation." IMF Country Report No. 13/253, International Monetary Fund, Washington, DC. www.imf.org/external/pubs/ft/scr/2013/cr13253.pdf.

———. 2013b. "Japan: Selected Issues." IMF Country Report No. 13/254, August 2013, International Monetary Fund, Washington, DC. http://www.imf.org/external/pubs/ft/scr/2013/cr13254.pdf.

———. 2014 (April). *World Economic Outlook: Recovery Strengthens, Remains Uneven.* World Economic and Financial Surveys. Washington, DC: International Monetary Fund. http://www.imf.org/external/pubs/ft/weo/2014/01/.

Iwaisako, T., and K. Okada. 2010. "Understanding the Decline in Japan's Saving Rate in the New Millennium." PRI Discussion Paper Series No 10A-06, Ministry of Finance, Tokyo.

Kashiwase, K., M. Nozaki, and I. Saito. 2014. "Health Spending in Japan: Macro-Fiscal Implications and Reform Options." IMF Working Paper No. 14/142. International Monetary Fund, Washington, DC.

Katagiri, M. 2012. "Economic Consequences of Population Aging in Japan: Effects through Changes in Demand Structure." Institute for Monetary and Economic Studies (IMES) Discussion Paper No. 2012-E-3, Bank of Japan, Tokyo.

Konishi, H., and K. Ueda. 2013. "Aging and Deflation from a Fiscal Perspective." IMES Discussion Paper Series 2013-E-13, Bank of Japan, Tokyo.

Kumhof, M., D. Laxton, D. Muir, and S. Mursula. 2010. "The Global Integrated Monetary Fiscal Model (GIMF) Theoretical Structure." IMF Working Paper No. 10/34. International Monetary Fund, Washington, DC. http://www.imf.org/external/pubs/cat/longres.cfm?sk=23615.0.

Lindh, T., and B. Malmberg. 1998. "Age Structure and Inflation—A Wicksellian Interpretation of the OECD Data." *Journal of Economic Behavior and Organization* 36 (1): 19–37.

———. 2000. "Can Age Structure Forecast Inflation Trends?" *Journal of Economics and Business* 52 (1–2): 31–49.

Miles, D. 1999. "Modelling the Impact of Demographic Change upon the Economy." *The Economic Journal* 109 (452): 1–36.

Moghadam, R., R. Teja, P. Berkmen. 2014. "Euro Area—'Deflation' Versus 'Lowflation.'" IMF Direct blog. http://blog-imfdirect.imf.org/2014/03/04/euro-area-deflation-versus-lowflation/.

Yamaoka, H., and M. Syed. 2010. "Managing the Exit: Lessons from Japan's Reversal of Unconventional Monetary Policy." IMF Working Paper No. 10/114. International Monetary Fund, Washington, DC.

CHAPTER 4

Japan's Fiscal Risks

Ikuo Saito

Japan has the highest debt-to-GDP ratio among the advanced economies, most of this debt held domestically, exposing the country to important risks from a negative feedback loop between the sovereign and financial sectors. Indeed, although interest rates remain low, a spike in yields is one of the key tail risks the country faces, with potentially important implications for the rest of the world. It is therefore not surprising that restoring fiscal sustainability is a cornerstone of Abenomics. Reducing deficits and debt is also critical for rebalancing portfolios toward riskier and more productive investments, another key pillar of Abenomics, and for an eventual return to a conventional monetary policy framework. This chapter describes Japan's current fiscal situation, its outlook, and key risks, and Chapter 5 discusses reform options to achieve sustainability in a growth-friendly and equitable manner.

We first review what has driven the rapid rise in debt, which can be boiled down to large domestic shocks (the bursting of the bubble and the 2011 earthquake and tsunami) and external shocks (the Asian financial crisis in 1997–98 and the global financial crisis) as well as structural factors such as aging. Specifically, the Lost Decade, which reduced the efficacy of monetary policy, as shown in the previous chapters, is one of the culprits. A sharp economic slowdown after the bubble burst and subsequent extended sluggish growth reduced revenue and prompted the government to embark on unprecedented fiscal expansion. In the interim, the government at times tried fiscal consolidation, but the need to support economic growth quickly overtook these attempts.

Aging has been a second factor contributing to the buildup of debt, and may have contributed more to the deteriorating fiscal picture than cyclical and structural economic slowdowns.[1] According to the Japanese Ministry of Finance, the increase in the central government's debt between fiscal year (FY)1990 and FY2012 was attributable more to the increase in social security spending than to higher public works spending. Aging will remain a burden on the fiscal outlook. For example, Kashiwase, Nozaki, and Saito (2014) estimate that public health spending can increase a further 3.5 percentage points of GDP in the next two decades, with more than half of the increase a result of the aging population.

---

[1] See Chapter 3 for a discussion of the impact of aging on growth and inflation.

Despite the rise in debt, yields have remained low, which begs the question: who funds Japan's debt? More than 90 percent of Japanese government bonds (JGBs) are held domestically (Figure 4.1). This share is considerably higher than that of other advanced economies (Figure 4.2). Tokuoka (2010) estimates that the household sector finances about 50 percent of JGBs either directly, or indirectly through banks and pension funds. Lam and Tokuoka (2011) point out that, especially over the last decade, a gradual increase in deposits and a trend decline in corporate loans have provided additional space for investments in JGBs. More

Figure 4.1 Holders of Japanese Government Bonds, 2014:Q2 *(Percent; figures in parentheses represent percentage point changes since 2013:Q1)*

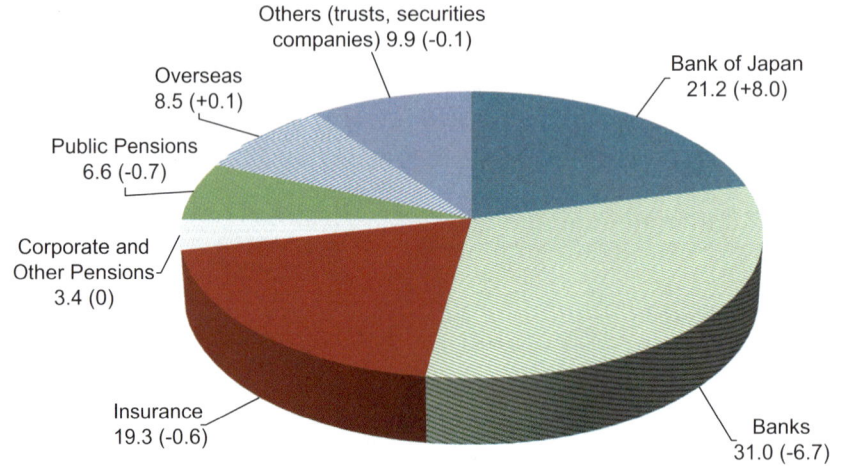

- Bank of Japan 21.2 (+8.0)
- Banks 31.0 (−6.7)
- Insurance 19.3 (−0.6)
- Corporate and Other Pensions 3.4 (0)
- Public Pensions 6.6 (−0.7)
- Overseas 8.5 (+0.1)
- Others (trusts, securities companies) 9.9 (−0.1)

Source: Bank of Japan Flow of Funds data.

Figure 4.2 Share of Public Securities Held Domestically *(Percent of total public securities)*

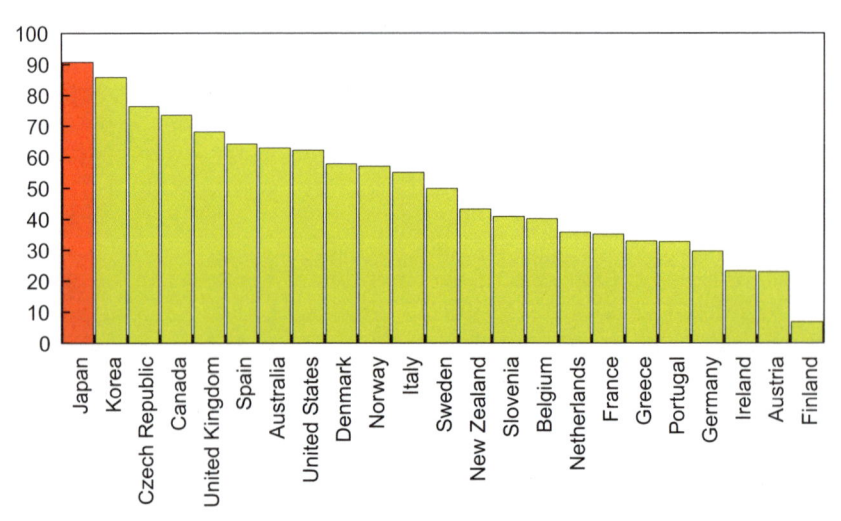

Countries (in order): Japan, Korea, Czech Republic, Canada, United Kingdom, Spain, Australia, United States, Denmark, Norway, Italy, Sweden, New Zealand, Slovenia, Belgium, Netherlands, France, Greece, Portugal, Germany, Ireland, Austria, Finland.

Source: Arslanalp and Tsuda (2014).

recently, under its quantitative and qualitative monetary easing (QQE) framework, the Bank of Japan (BoJ) has emerged as a key buyer in the JGB market. Although financing and refinancing needs are high, this domestic investor base has provided a stable financial resource and has kept yields low, including because of high demand for safe assets by the aging population.

What is the outlook for debt? We use the debt sustainability analysis framework (in IMF 2014a), which suggests that under current plans gross debt-to-GDP ratio will remain high, albeit relatively stable, at 240 percent of GDP for the next five years. This is due to the planned consumption tax rate increase to 10 percent,[2] waning stimulus and earthquake reconstruction spending, and a favorable differential between growth and interest rates. However, the gross debt ratio is projected to start rising again around 2020 and reach over 280 percent of GDP in 2030. This means that, even with successive increases in the consumption tax rate to 10 percent and the initial success of Abenomics in boosting growth, the debt path remains unsustainable under current policy settings, a view that is in line with the Japanese government's own projections.

Given this, the international community, including the IMF and the Group of Twenty (G20), has urged Japan to take action.[3] At a G20 meeting in 2010, Japan made a commitment to halve the primary deficit in FY2015 from the FY2010 level and achieve primary balance in FY2020. These are important objectives, although the FY2020 goal is beyond reach under currently announced policies and, more importantly, merely to achieve the primary balance is not sufficient to put debt on a downward path. Hence the need for further adjustment.[4]

The outlook for Japan's debt is subject to important downside risks. First, risks to the funding structure of JGBs are not explicitly considered in the debt sustainability analysis. Specifically, Japan currently relies on foreign creditors only marginally, with ample and stable domestic funding, including from the BoJ's purchases in the context of QQE. However, this favorable condition is not expected to continue forever putting downward pressure on yields. Tokuoka (2010) finds that Japan-specific factors, such as the large net financial wealth of the household and corporate sectors and the low share of foreign holdings, have contributed to lowering JGB yields, but domestic financial resources are not infinite and indeed domestic saving is expected to decline with population aging, as noted in Chapter 2.

Hoshi and Ito (2012) and Arslanalp and Lam (2013) also argue that Japan will need to rely more on external financing in about 10 years as its domestic financial assets will be exceeded by the amount of outstanding JGBs. In addition, QQE will eventually unwind. Arslanalp and Lam (2013) conclude that, without fiscal consolidation measures, long-term JGB yields are estimated to reach 4½ percent in 2020, a 3 percentage point increase from 2012. Further pressure on yields could come from reduced demand for safe assets (Lam and Tokuoka 2011).

---

[2]The government announced the delay of the tax hike in November 2014.
[3]Concerns are understandable as for example, IMF (2012) shows that a spike in JGB yields would reduce output in other countries by 1–4 percent if accompanied by contagion to global risk premiums.
[4]Potential options are laid out in Chapter 5.

Combined with a second downside risk of lower growth in the event of incomplete Abenomics, a higher interest growth differential would further worsen debt dynamics. On the other hand, Abenomics, if more successful than expected in boosting growth over the medium term, could pose an upside risk (IMF 2013). Furthermore, debt projections are vulnerable to macroeconomic shocks, in addition to shifts in financing conditions. For example, the stochastic debt sustainability analysis simulations in IMF (2013) show that even with substantial further fiscal consolidation (10 percent of GDP), the debt ratio may not decline, with a 25 percent probability.

A third downside risk stems from the impact of demographic changes on the fiscal accounts. For example, the above-mentioned increase in health spending (of 3.5 percentage points of GDP) suggested by Kashiwase, Nozaki, and Saito (2014) is only partially reflected in the IMF's debt sustainability analysis. In addition, the pension system may need additional public financial support.

In the rest of the chapter, we discuss the key determinants of the debt dynamics, both in the past and going forward, and the main reasons yields have remained low so far. We next detail the key risks around the debt outlook, including from a less favorable interest–growth differential and from population aging, and draw conclusions.

WHAT HAS DRIVEN THE RAPID RISE IN DEBT?

The gross debt-to-GDP ratio skyrocketed from less than 70 percent in 1990 to 240 percent in 2012. The net debt ratio increased from about 10 percent to 130 percent during the same period. The global financial crisis and the March 2011 earthquake accelerated the increase, but the gross and net debt-to-GDP ratios were already 180 and 80 percent of GDP in 2007, respectively. These debt levels are in stark contrast to the average gross debt-to-GDP ratios of the G20 advanced economies, which was about 80 percent in 2007 and 115 percent in 2012 (IMF 2014b). Japan only once previously experienced such a high debt ratio—during World War II. This section discusses how Japan has accumulated such high debt in such a relatively short time frame.

Disappointing economic performance is one usual suspect. The starting point of the rapid rise in debt coincides with the end of the bubble economy. The recession triggered by the bursting of an inflated asset market and the following lost (two) decade(s) not only reduced revenue through automatic stabilizers, but also led the government to embark on discretionary fiscal expansion of unprecedented magnitude. The tax revenue-to-GDP ratio peaked at 21 percent in 1990 and declined to 16 percent in 2004, reflecting the economic slowdown and various tax reduction measures. The ratio recovered somewhat to 17 percent in 2012 after a slide owing to the global crisis, but remains considerably lower than 20 years ago. On the other hand, total expenditure increased by 10 percentage points to 41 percent of GDP during the same period.

The various stimulus packages contributed to the rapid rise in spending. In Japan, such stimulus is provided through supplementary budgets, and there has been at least one supplementary budget each year since 1990, with 40 in total, including the most recent one submitted to the Diet in January 2015.[5] It is difficult to evaluate the effectiveness of past stimuli, but some measures were not well designed to support the economy. For example, the Cabinet Office (2012) estimates that only 25 percent of cash benefits introduced in 2009 raised consumption. Likewise, Hori and others (2002) find that merely 10 percent of cash benefits to children and the elderly in 1998 (the Shopping Coupon Program) did so. The impact of subsidies designed to promote the consumption of specific goods, such as eco-friendly automobiles and appliances is inconclusive. Such subsidies seem to have had smoothing effects by supporting consumption right after the crisis, but whether they succeeded in producing additional demand is uncertain and they may have created distortions between subsidized and other goods.

Another factor stems from population aging, which affects the fiscal situation directly and indirectly: directly by putting pressure on social security spending, especially on pension and health and long-term care, and indirectly by reducing economic growth potential. In this regard, aging may contribute more to the deteriorating fiscal picture than economic slowdowns. According to the Ministry of Finance, 37 percent of the increase in the central government's debt between FY1990 and FY2012 was attributable to an increase in social security spending, compared to 12 percent of public works spending. During FY1990–2010, pension spending more than doubled from 5.2 percent to 10.9 percent of GDP, as did public health and long-term care spending, from 4.1 percent to 8.3 percent, on a general government basis. On the other hand, public investment contributed more in the 1990s, but less so since then.

Against headwinds from aging and sluggish economic growth, the government did try to maintain fiscal discipline. It achieved a fiscal surplus from 1988 through 1992, not only because of favorable economic conditions and an asset-price boom, but also because of fiscal reforms including the introduction of the consumption tax, with a 3 percent rate in April 1989. Since then, however, the fiscal balance has never returned to positive territory, for the reasons mentioned above. In the mid-1990s, Japan embarked on comprehensive tax reform, designed to be roughly revenue neutral, to support the economy by increasing the rate of the broad-based, less distortionary consumption tax, while reducing the personal income tax rate.[6] However, in hindsight, the consumption tax hike from 3 to 5 percent in April 1997 was ill timed. The summer that year saw the Asian financial crisis, which had a negative spillover on the Japanese economy through trade and financial linkages with the region. Although the majority of studies, including Keen and others (2011) and Ihori (2010), argue that the recession following the

---

[5]Including supplementary budgets for reconstruction after the Great Hanshin-Awaji Earthquake (January 1995) and the Great East Japan Earthquake (March 2011).
[6]Reduction of the personal income tax started in 1995.

crisis was not due to the consumption tax hike,[7] the fiscal contraction it implied certainly did not help. The government formulated stimulus packages of an unprecedented size—12 trillion yen (2.3 percent of GDP) in April 1998 and 16 trillion yen (3.1 percent of GDP) in October 1998, even larger than the stimulus after the Lehman crisis in 2008. In parallel, the Fiscal Structure Reform Act enacted in November 1997, which included a comprehensive policy package to restore fiscal health from a medium-term perspective, was suspended after only one year given economic contraction for three consecutive quarters from 1997:Q4 to 1998:Q2.

The Koizumi administration (April 2001–September 2006) restarted fiscal consolidation efforts amid high approval ratings and a favorable economic situation. It used the newly created Council on Economic and Fiscal Policy to formulate a growth and fiscal reform plan (the so-called *Honebuto no Hoshin* or large-boned principles) every summer from 2001. The goal of achieving the primary balance of the central and local governments in FY2011 was adopted in the 2006 plan. As a result, the fiscal deficit declined from 8 percent of GDP in 2000 to 2 percent of GDP in 2007.

However, again, external shocks and the subsequent economic slowdown pushed Japan back into large deficits, and the FY2011 goal had to be discarded. Although direct exposure to the Great Recession, or to subprime mortgages, was relatively modest, the country experienced one of the world's largest drops in growth in 2008–09 (see also Chapter 10). Responding to the shock, the government and the Diet were quick to formulate a series of fiscal packages in October 2008 and January and May 2009, which were followed by other stimuli in January and November 2010. The fiscal deficit increased 8.3 percentage points in two years to 10.4 percent of GDP in 2009, of which 6.7 percent was due to a rise in expenditure.

Another shock beyond the government's control happened on March 11, 2011: the Great East Japan Earthquake. The government initially estimated reconstruction expenditure at around 19 trillion yen (4.0 percent of GDP) for the first five years, formulated three reconstruction-related supplementary budgets in 2011, and created a reconstruction special account from FY2012. The total amount of reconstruction spending is currently estimated to amount to 25 trillion yen. The fiscal deficit bounced back to 9.8 percent of GDP in 2011 as a result, after a small reduction in 2010, and remained elevated at 8.5 percent in 2013.

Fiscal consolidation has been a key issue in the G20 since the initial response to the global financial crisis. At the G20 Toronto Summit in June 2010, Japan committed to halving the primary deficit of central and local governments combined in FY2015, from the FY2010 level (6.6 percent of GDP), achieving primary balance in FY2020, and steadily reducing the debt ratio thereafter.[8] To achieve these goals the government adopted a multiyear spending cap framework and formulated a comprehensive reform plan of the tax and social security

---

[7]Growth in the second quarter of 1997 was negative, led by a contraction in private consumption, but total and private consumption growth returned to positive territory in the third quarter.

[8]Other advanced economies "committed to fiscal plans that will at least halve deficits by 2013 and stabilize or reduce government debt-to-GDP ratios by 2016" (the G20 Toronto Summit Declaration, June 27, 2010).

systems, including a two-stage consumption tax rate hike from 5 to 8 percent in April 2014 and to 10 percent in October 2015.

After the Liberal Democratic Party regained control of the Lower House in December 2012, Prime Minister Shinzo Abe embarked on fiscal expansion while maintaining the internationally committed fiscal goals. He obtained Diet approval for a fiscal package of 1.4 percent of GDP to kick-start the economy in early 2013, and another of 1.2 percent of GDP in February 2014 to soften the negative impact of the first stage of the consumption tax hike, which took effect in April 2014. In December 2014 Prime Minister Abe announced his intention to delay the second-stage tax hike to April 2017 and formulate another stimulus to secure economic recovery. Following this announcement he won a landslide victory in snap elections.

In sum, the rapid deterioration of Japan's debt is due to cyclical as well as structural factors (declining growth potential and aging). Various fiscal packages amid domestic and external shocks were formulated to stimulate the economy and, more recently, help end deflation. Notwithstanding the new fiscal stimuli under Abenomics, consolidation efforts are slowly progressing, but will such efforts be sufficient?

WHAT IS THE DEBT OUTLOOK?

What is the outlook for Japan's debt? The IMF's debt sustainability analysis framework is designed to answer this question.[9] Both concepts of gross and net debt are important in Japan's case, as the government has substantial financial assets.[10] Generally speaking, gross debt is a more relevant concept to capture liquidity risks, while net debt is a better proxy for solvency risks. That said, gross debt is typically the primary indicator as it is easier to compare internationally and because it is not always crystal clear if financial assets are readily available for debt repayment.

Aside from the IMF, the Japanese government regularly conducts long-term economic and fiscal projections. The Cabinet Office published its latest projections in July 2014.[11] It estimates the government will achieve the FY2015 deficit goal by a small margin, while it will not meet the FY2020 primary balance goal under current policies. The gross debt-to-GDP ratio will stabilize at about 185 percent of GDP under the baseline scenario until the last projection year, FY2023. Four points are worth noting. First, the analysis is based on current policies and thus assumes that the consumption tax rate will be raised to 10 percent at a uniform rate, without further fiscal stimulus. If multiple rates were to be

---

[9]Other than the government's projections and the IMF's debt sustainability analysis mentioned in this chapter, the Fiscal System Council released long-term fiscal projections in April 2014. It shows that the gross debt ratio will reach more than 600 percent of GDP in FY2060 under current policies. The Daiwa Institute of Research (2013) estimates that the debt-to-GDP ratio of the central and local governments will rise to 280 percent in 2040 after a temporary stabilization at about 245 percent.
[10]Including pension assets for future payments and foreign reserves accumulated through interventions.
[11]The numbers cited are on a central and local government basis and include reconstruction-related spending and revenue measures.

Figure 4.3 Japan: Gross Public Debt in the Baseline *(Percent of GDP)*

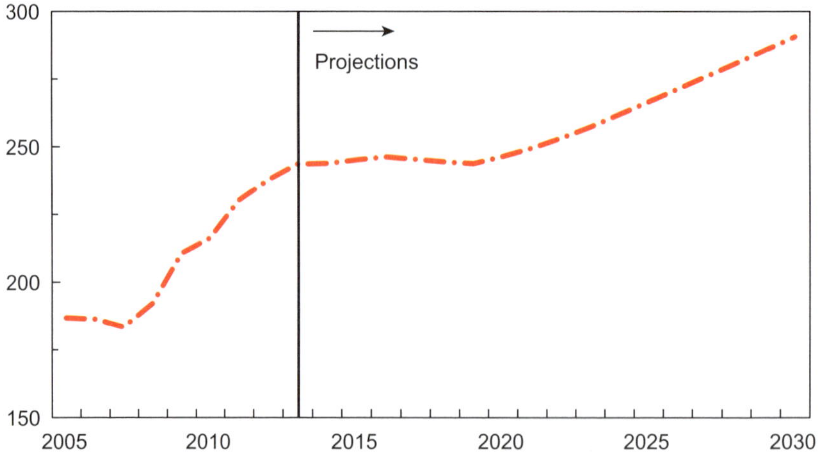

Sources: Cabinet Office; IMF staff estimates and projections.
Note: Gross debt of the general government including the social security fund; assumes automatic withdrawal of fiscal stimulus and a consumption tax increase to 10 percent in 2015.

introduced or another stimulus adopted, these would offset some of the improvement in the fiscal balance. Second, the Cabinet Office has two scenarios, namely the baseline and a reference scenario, but the former is based on relatively optimistic macroeconomic assumptions.[12] Third, given the primary deficit and 10-year JGB yields exceeding the nominal economic growth rate assumed in FY2023, the debt ratio is expected to eventually start to increase again. Finally, merely achieving the primary balance target by FY2020 may not be sufficient to put debt on a clear downward path, as argued below.

The IMF's (2014a) debt sustainability analysis projects a relatively stable debt-to-GDP ratio for the next five years (on a general government basis), but at high levels of about 240 and 140 percent of GDP on a gross and net basis, respectively (Figure 4.3). This is due to the planned consumption tax rate increase to 10 percent, favorable real and nominal growth rates, and only a modest and gradual pickup in interest rates. However, the gross debt ratio is projected to start rising again around the year 2020 and exceed 280 percent of GDP in 2030, suggesting that debt will remain unsustainable under current policies. The IMF's debt sustainability analysis assumes the second-stage increase of the consumption tax rate without revenue-eroding measures as in the Cabinet Office's projections. However, the IMF's macroeconomic assumptions are closer to the Cabinet Office's less optimistic scenario.[13]

---

[12]For example, the baseline assumes nominal growth of 3.6 percent in FY2016 and FY2020, which is significantly higher than the 2000–2007 average of 0.1 percent. Under the less optimistic reference scenario, the gross debt ratio increases to about 215 percent of GDP in FY2023, 30 percentage points higher than in the baseline.

[13]Two major developments, namely slower recovery after the consumption tax hike and the delay of the second-stage consumption tax increase, happened after the conclusion of the debt sustainability analysis and are expected to further worsen debt dynamics.

REVOLT OF THE INTEREST–GROWTH DIFFERENTIAL?

The IMF's long-term debt sustainability analysis is subject to a few important downside risks. The first factor relates to the assumption regarding interest rates on government bonds. The second stems from the possibility of lower growth in the absence of significant structural reforms if Abenomics fails. In combination, a higher interest rate–growth differential would worsen the debt dynamics. A third factor is the impact of demographic changes: pension and health care spending could rise more than currently assumed, as the next section will detail.

The interest rate–growth differential is a key concept in the debt sustainability analysis as the primary balance stabilizes the debt-to-GDP ratio if nominal interest rates equal nominal growth rates (Domar's theorem). The IMF's long-term debt sustainability analysis statically assumes that Japan's interest rate–growth differential converges to the average during the 2000s before the global financial crisis. This assumption is subject to two, interdependent, downside risks, namely higher interest rates and lower growth.

Tokuoka (2010) argues that Japan-specific factors, such as the large pool of household assets, strong home bias, risk averseness, and large and stable institutional holders (such as the Japan Post Bank, the Government Pension Investment Fund), the large financial surplus of the corporate sector, and the reduction in the Fiscal Investment and Loan Program,[14] have helped keep JGB yields low despite the increase in the general government's debt. He also finds that the impact of primary deficits on government bond yields is lower in Japan than in the other Group of Seven countries, and that the large net financial wealth of the household and corporate sectors and low share of foreign holdings have helped lower JGB yields.

Arslanalp and Lam (2013) analyze what explains Japan's low interest rates despite rising debt and whether this will continue. Looking at past studies, they list six common factors contributing to low and stable JGB yields: sustained deflation and low potential growth, expectations of future fiscal adjustments, external surpluses, a large private stock of savings, population aging leading to demand for safe assets, and a stable investor base. They empirically estimate the determinants of long-term interest rates using panel-data analysis covering 12 advanced economies and annual data for 23 years (1990–2012). The model specification is as follows:

$$E_t i_{t+\tau,j} = c_j + \beta_1 \, E_t EXT_{t+\tau,j} + \beta_2 E_t FIS_{t+\tau,j} + \beta_3 E_t DG_{t+\tau,j} + \beta_4 E_t y_{t+\tau,j} + \beta_5 E_t \pi_{t+\tau,j} + \beta_6 \, InvBase_{t,j} + \varepsilon_{t,j}$$

with variables expressing expectations at time t for τ periods ahead; j denotes a country. The dependent variable $E_t i_{t+\tau,j}$ is the nominal forward rate 5–10 years ahead (that is, 5-year forward of 5-year tenor rates). *EXT* and *FIS* are vectors of

---

[14] Outside of the general government and managed by the Fiscal Investment and Loan Program special account, which issues Fiscal Investment and Loan Program bonds (a type of JGB).

variables related to external and fiscal conditions both in terms of flows and stocks. Variables for external conditions include the current account balance and the net external balance as a percent of GDP. Fiscal variables include (1) the net government debt and/or public assets as a percent of GDP as stock variables; and (2) the primary balance or cyclical fiscal balance as a percent of GDP as a flow variable. A dummy variable is introduced to interact with fiscal variables to assess whether structural differences occurred after the global financial crisis given that sovereign bonds in some countries were perceived to be safe-haven assets. *DG* is the demographic factor measured by the (annualized) growth rate of the working-age population ratio. Variables y and π refer to real growth and inflation. The regression extends other empirical studies by analyzing the role of the investor base in affecting long-term sovereign yields: *InvBase* refers to the portion of sovereign bonds held by central banks, foreign nonofficial entities, or domestic financial institutions, depending on the specification.

Arslanalp and Lam (2013) find that (1) fiscal conditions are a key contributing factor to long-term sovereign yields across specifications in the panel; (2) stronger external conditions appear to lower long-term rates, but are seldom statistically significant; (3) inflation and growth expectations are also key factors in increasing long-term rates; (4) a reduction in the working-age population tends to reduce long-term interest rates; and (5) the composition of the investor base for government securities is important for long-term interest rates. They conclude that the upward pressure on long-term JGB yields from deteriorating fiscal conditions has been offset so far by other factors. These include a stable domestic investor base with a preference for safe assets and increased purchases by the BoJ, but these effects are likely to diminish over the medium term.

Using the estimation results, they forecast future interest rates in two scenarios (Figure 4.4). Based on current policies, deteriorating fiscal conditions over the medium term are likely to exert upward pressure on long-term interest rates, rising to 4½ percent by 2020 and to nearly 5½ percent by 2030, which are significantly higher than the assumed interest rates in the IMF's debt sustainability analysis. This represents a 4 percentage point increase in long-term yields from 2012 to 2030, to which deterioration in fiscal conditions would contribute 3½ percentage points. Inflation and higher growth would add another 2 percentage points and shrinking external surpluses a further ½ percentage point. These factors would be partially offset by population aging (−1¼ percentage points), BoJ purchases (−¾ percentage point), and other factors.

Abenomics could play a key role in preventing this rise in yields, provided medium-term fiscal consolidation succeeds in putting debt on a downward trajectory, while ambitious structural reforms lead to higher potential growth (IMF 2013). The analysis in Arslanalp and Lam (2013) also assumes the BoJ will not further ease monetary policy after it achieves its inflation target in a stable manner. In this regard, higher growth and lower BoJ purchases would push interest rates up slightly over the medium term, relative to the baseline, while near-term interest rates remain low and stable. Notably, lower public debt ratios, together with long-term primary surpluses, would keep nominal interest rates at stable

Figure 4.4 Decomposition of Long-Term Interest Rates

1. Current Policies

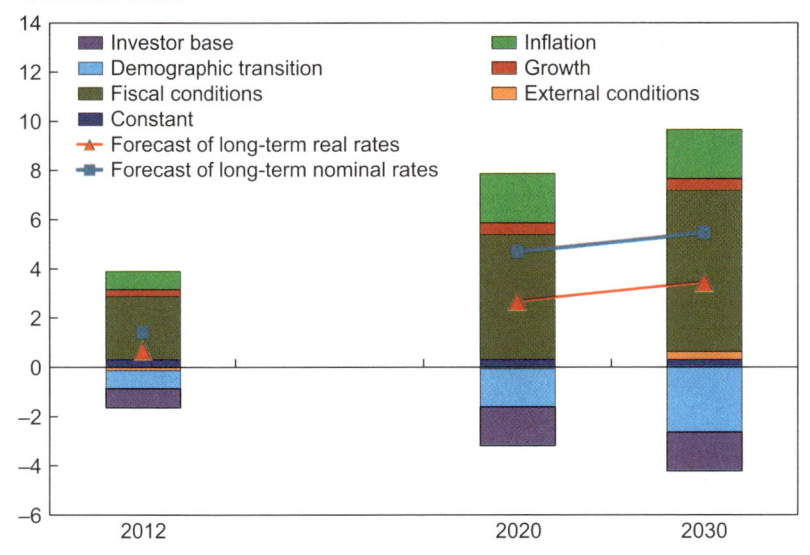

2. Complete Policies

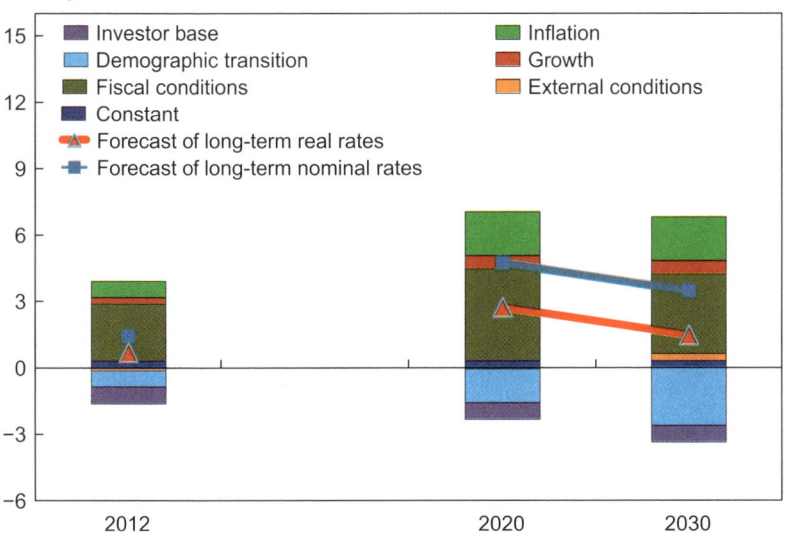

Source: Arslanalp and Lam (2013).

levels at about 3–4 percent over the long term, implying that real interest rates would be in the range of 1.2–1.9 percent.

The corporate sector will also feel the effects of Abenomics: the sector's saving may either flow into debt repayment or productive investment (rather than deposits that are invested in JGBs). Indeed, one of the main policy goals of

Abenomics is to promote investment. As Lam and Tokuoka (2011) point out, this does not necessarily lead to higher JGB yields, as it would happen in tandem with economic expansion, as seen in the 2003–07 recovery. If Abenomics fails, on the other hand, the corporate sector may see its profitability fall, resulting in smaller banking sector deposits without such favorable effects.

As discussed in more detail in Chapter 8, financial institutions, including not only the banking sector but also Japan Post Bank and the public and private pension funds, may change their portfolios away from JGBs. As noted in Lam and Tokuoka (2011), the reduction in banking loans amid rising deposits has increased banks' JGB holdings, but this may reverse under Abenomics as domestic credit growth expands. In fact, rebalancing from the JGB market to higher-yielding assets, including overseas, by banks is one of the key transmission channels under QQE. Also, public pensions, including the Government Pension Investment Fund, became a net seller of JGBs in 2012, partly because of the need to make transfers to the pension system, and the Government Pension Investment Fund has revised its portfolio allocation toward higher-yielding assets.

Currently Japan relies on foreign creditors only marginally: they held about 8 percent of JGBs as of end-June 2014. All considered, however, this favorable condition is not expected to continue forever. As the nonfinancial entities invest more, financial institutions move into higher-yielding assets, and the BoJ starts to unwind its liquidity support, the foreigners' share in the JGB market is expected to increase unless debt growth is contained. The above studies suggest that an increase in foreign holdings is correlated with higher government bond yields (see also Chapter 3). Also, Tokuoka (2010) points out that higher foreign ownership tends to increase volatility in sovereign yields.

Aside from these factors, external conditions could affect yields in Japan. For example, Lam and Tokuoka (2011) argue that global financial distress could have negative spillover effects on the JGB market through the banking system. They estimate the sensitivity of JGB yields to global risk factors and find that movements of U.S. Treasury securities and German bunds affect those of JGBs, but not in the opposite way. They also find that this relationship with U.S. Treasury securities strengthened at the height of the Great Recession,[15] and that uncertainty in the financial markets has a strong impact on JGB yields, lowering JGB yields through safe-haven flows, but these reverse as the global financial market stabilizes. As such, the JGB market remains subject to events in the global market.

Another downside risk stems from the rate of potential growth. Specifically, the IMF's debt sustainability analysis assumes that the real growth rate of 1.1 percent estimated for 2019 will remain for the rest of the projection period amid continued headwinds from a declining labor force. Population projections by the National Institute of Population and Social Security Research suggest that the

---

[15]More recently, JGB yields have remained low, while yields of U.S. Treasury securities have increased from their record low levels, reflecting the different monetary policy environments in both countries.

working-age population (age 15–64) will decline at an annual rate of 1.1 percent during 2010–19 and by 0.8 percent in the following decade. Although the annual reduction in the labor force during the 2010–2030 period is estimated to be smaller, at 0.3 percent, owing to an increase in labor participation of the working-age population, this remains substantially larger than the decline of 0.03 percent during the 2000s. In this regard, Hoshi and Ito (2012) argue that real growth from 2021 to 2030 could be as low as 0.28 percent if the annual growth rate of GDP per working-age population is about 1 percent, the average of 1994 through 2010. The IMF's debt sustainability analysis implicitly assumes that higher labor force participation and other factors will compensate for the declining labor force, which may not happen without significant structural reforms as envisaged under the third arrow of Abenomics. Also, the policy adjustment scenario in IMF (2014a) does not assume additional negative effects of medium-term fiscal consolidation on growth as enhanced confidence is expected to fully offset it, but this may not be the case.

Although a stronger-than-expected effort on the structural reform front and dividends from a sustained exit from deflation would help restore debt sustainability, these benefits are difficult to quantify. The simulations in IMF (2013) show that a complete Abenomics package—QQE, medium-term fiscal consolidation, and ambitious structural reforms—would achieve the 2 percent inflation goal, higher growth, and lower debt-to-GDP ratio quickly and sustainably. Compared to the baseline before the introduction of Abenomics, the successful package is estimated to reduce the debt-to-GDP ratio by about 20 percentage points by 2020.

An important channel for these strong effects stems from the interest rate–growth differential, which matters greatly for debt sustainability. An illustrative calculation shows that a differential of 2 percent (rather than 1 percent in the IMF's baseline) will add more than 20 percent of GDP of debt cumulatively by 2030. Fiscal consolidation is clearly important as it would reduce debt directly, mitigate underlying upward pressure on interest rates, and enhance growth through confidence effects over the medium term. In addition, ambitious structural reforms to enhance potential growth are essential. This is also indicated by debt sustainability analysis stress tests, with growth shocks the key driver of debt sustainability in the near term (Figure 4.5). This is more so than interest rate shocks, which will affect the outlook only gradually given the relatively long average maturity of outstanding JGBs (about 6.5 years), and notwithstanding the high gross financing requirement and potential repercussions through financial sector balance sheets (see Chapter 8).

The debt path is also subject to potential further shocks, which are captured by the sensitivity of the debt dynamics to macroeconomic assumptions in the stochastic version of the debt sustainability analysis. It is desirable that debt sustainability is secured with a reasonably high probability. IMF (2013) considers shocks to growth, inflation, and interest rates, based on historical patterns, in its stochastic simulations. It shows that, even with fiscal consolidation of about 10 percent of GDP over the next 10 years as recommended by the IMF

64 | Japan's Fiscal Risks

Figure 4.5 Japan: Public Debt Sustainability Analysis

1. Macro-Fiscal Stress Tests[1]

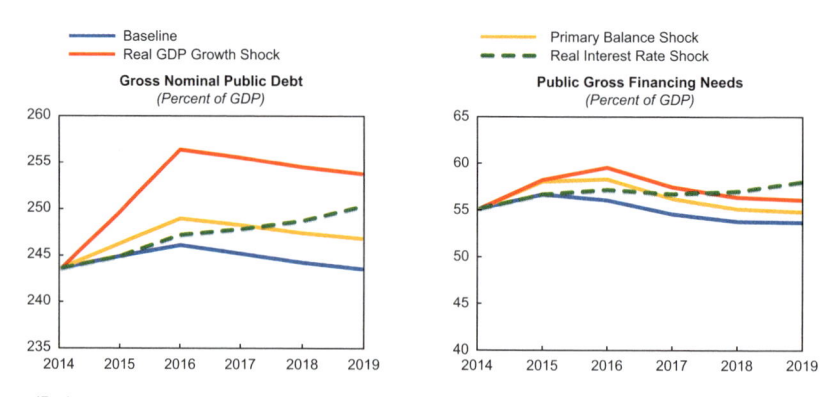

Legend: Baseline; Real GDP Growth Shock; Primary Balance Shock; Real Interest Rate Shock

Gross Nominal Public Debt (Percent of GDP)

Public Gross Financing Needs (Percent of GDP)

[1] Real output growth shock assumes growth lower by half of the 10-year historical average standard deviation of changes in growth, compared to the baseline, for two years starting in 2015. Primary balance shock assumes that the improvement in the primary balance underperforms by half of the 10-year historical standard deviation of changes in the primary balance compared to the baseline. Additional borrowing cost of 25 basis points per 1 percent of GDP worsening of the deficit is assumed. Interest rate shock assumes an increase of 200 basis points; this is assumed to happen in 2014 and remain for the rest of the projection period.

2. Additional Stress Tests

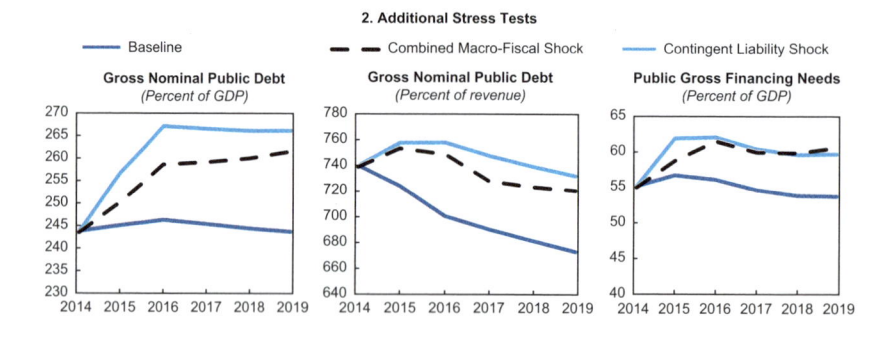

Legend: Baseline; Combined Macro-Fiscal Shock; Contingent Liability Shock

Gross Nominal Public Debt (Percent of GDP)

Gross Nominal Public Debt (Percent of revenue)

Public Gross Financing Needs (Percent of GDP)

3. Underlying Assumptions
(Percent)

Primary Balance Shock	2014	2015	2016	2017	2018	2019
Real GDP growth	1.4	1.0	0.7	1.0	1.0	1.1
Inflation	1.6	1.0	0.9	1.4	1.4	1.3
Primary balance	−6.4	−6.6	−5.4	−3.6	−3.4	−3.1
Effective interest rate	0.8	0.9	1.1	1.3	1.5	1.8

Real GDP Growth Shock	2014	2015	2016	2017	2018
Real GDP growth	1.4	−0.4	−0.7	1.0	1.0
Inflation	1.6	0.7	0.6	1.4	1.4
Primary balance	−6.4	−5.9	−5.3	−3.6	−3.4
Effective interest rate	0.8	0.9	1.0	1.3	1.5

Real Interest Rate Shock	2014	2015	2016	2017	2018	2019
Real GDP growth	1.4	1.0	0.7	1.0	1.0	1.1
Inflation	1.6	1.0	0.9	1.4	1.4	1.3
Primary balance	−6.4	−5.2	−4.0	−3.6	−3.4	−3.1
Effective interest rate	0.8	0.9	1.4	1.8	2.2	2.6

Real Exchange Rate Shock	2014	2015	2016	2017	2018
Real GDP growth	1.4	1.0	0.7	1.0	1.0
Inflation	1.6	1.7	0.9	1.4	1.4
Primary balance	−6.4	−5.2	−4.0	−3.6	−3.4
Effective interest rate	0.8	0.9	1.0	1.2	1.4

Combined Shock	2014	2015	2016	2017	2018	2019
Real GDP growth	1.4	−0.4	−0.7	1.0	1.0	1.1
Inflation	1.6	0.7	0.6	1.4	1.4	1.3
Primary balance	−6.4	−6.6	−6.0	−3.6	−3.4	−3.1
Effective interest rate	0.8	0.9	1.5	1.8	2.2	2.7

Contingent Liability Shock	2014	2015	2016	2017	2018
Real GDP growth	1.4	−1.7	−2.0	1.0	1.0
Inflation	1.6	0.4	0.3	1.4	1.4
Primary balance	−6.4	−8.6	−4.0	−3.6	−3.4
Effective interest rate	0.8	0.9	1.2	1.5	1.8

Source: IMF (2014a).

(see Chapter 5), the debt ratio may not decline, with a 25 percent probability. Instead, achieving a declining debt trajectory, with a 90 percent probability, requires an additional adjustment effort of 5 percent of GDP. Furthermore, although a tail risk, a jump in JGB yields could have a significantly adverse impact on the economy and debt dynamics: IMF (2012) estimates that an increase of 200 basis points would reduce output about 6–10 percent after ten years and increase the debt-to-GDP ratio about 15–30 percentage points at the peak. Other worrisome empirical evidence stems from the potentially nonlinear relationship between fiscal conditions and government bond yields (for example, Faini 2006) and the negative impact of debt on growth—the debt overhang (Reinhart and Rogoff 2010)—as Tokuoka (2010) and Arslanalp and Lam (2013) point out.

DOWNSIDE RISKS FROM AGING-RELATED SPENDING?

Social security spending has been a main driver behind the rapid rise in debt, as mentioned above. Public pension spending increased from 5.2 percent of GDP in FY1990 to 10.9 percent in FY2010, while public spending on health and long-term care increased from 4.1 percent to 8.3 percent of GDP during the same period. The combined increase of 9.8 percent is larger than the total increase in spending of 8.2 percent. The dependency ratio will continue to rise, putting further pressure on social security spending. Ueda, Yoneta, and Ota (2014) for example, estimate that the primary deficit of the general government will worsen after 2010–19 and reach about 11.5 percent of GDP in 2060, driven by age-related spending. The Daiwa Institute of Research (2013) assumes that the primary deficit of the central and local governments will deteriorate to 6.3 percent of GDP by 2036–40. In contrast, the IMF's debt projections discussed in the previous section assume mechanically that the primary deficit-to-GDP ratio in 2019 will remain constant for the rest of the projection period.

Japan introduced a fiscally sustainable scheme in the comprehensive pension reform in 2004 (also see Chapter 5). Pension benefits will be automatically adjusted (the so-called macroeconomic slide [indexing]), and contribution rates will be gradually increased and fixed from FY2017, for example at 18.3 percent of income for the second-tier (earnings-linked) pension. Pension finances are reexamined every five years to verify whether they remain sustainable for the next 100 years. Overall, this scheme is designed to prevent a rise in public pension spending in terms of GDP. Although macroeconomic indexing does not function well under a low-inflation environment and macroeconomic performance has been worse than the assumptions made in the 2009 examination of pension finances, it should nonetheless put a lid on pension spending.

Compared to pensions, Japan's health and long-term care system is less prepared in terms of securing long-term sustainability. Although Japan's health

Figure 4.6 Health Care and Long-Term Care Spending, 2010–60 *(Percent of GDP)*

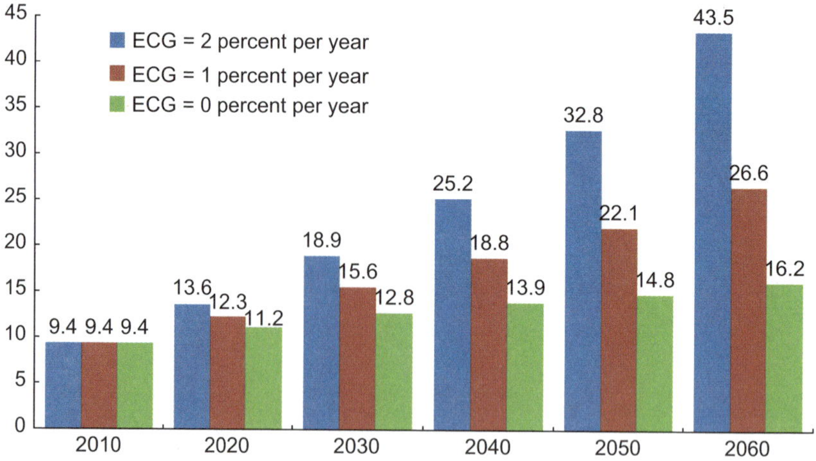

Year	ECG = 2 percent per year	ECG = 1 percent per year	ECG = 0 percent per year
2010	9.4	9.4	9.4
2020	13.6	12.3	11.2
2030	18.9	15.6	12.8
2040	25.2	18.8	13.9
2050	32.8	22.1	14.8
2060	43.5	26.6	16.2

Source: Kashiwase, Nozaki, and Saito (2014).
Note: ECG = excess cost growth.

spending has increased significantly for the past two decades, it remains broadly in line with international standards and has succeeded in promoting health and longevity. Specifically, total spending on health care and long-term care more than doubled in percent of GDP during the last two decades, with the share of public health spending to GDP currently around the average for Organization for Economic Co-operation and Development member countries. Nonetheless, it presents a risk to the debt outlook, not just from further aging, but also because health spending has been growing faster than per capita GDP growth, even after controlling for aging (excess cost growth, or ECG). Kashiwase, Nozaki, and Saito (2014) note that ECG has been on an upward trend since the late 1980s. ECG was –1.5 percent a year during the 1980s, but picked up to 0.6 percent a year in the 1990s and to 1.3 percent a year in the 2000s, reflecting the rising share of long-term care in total health care spending, which has higher ECG (Figure 4.6). This may reflect the cyclical downturn or lower labor force participation in the 2000s. However, after controlling for these effects, ECG for 2000–10 was still as high as 1.3 percent a year. In addition, high ECG was observed across the board for different age groups.

They next estimate that total health spending can increase about 6 percentage points of GDP in the next two decades, based on demographic changes and the past trend of cost increases. The aging of the population contributes 3.5 points and ECG the rest to this increase. They show that out of the increase, the government should finance 3.5 percentage points. Although these estimates are subject to considerable uncertainty, particularly as changes in ECG are difficult to project, including because a larger share of the population will enter the group of the very old (85 years and above), they pose an additional fiscal risk (see Chapter 5 for possible pension and health care reform options).

CONCLUSION

Japan has accumulated public debt quite rapidly for the past two decades, coinciding with the unprecedented pace of aging and significant economic challenges from weak growth and persistent mild deflation. Fiscal stimulus and automatic stabilizers during shocks played a key role as well, including after the bursting of the bubble, the Asian financial crisis, the global financial crisis, and the Great East Japan Earthquake in 2011. Under Abenomics, the government has provided further stimulus to jump-start the recovery, while making some headway with structural fiscal adjustment, including the April 2014 consumption tax increase.

Nonetheless, debt remains unsustainable under current policies. Furthermore, this baseline scenario is subject to important downside risks, including from possible further shocks, higher interest rates as the financing base for JGBs could change, lower-than-expected growth because of population aging, as well as potentially greater-than-expected aging-related pension and health care costs. As such, a spike in JGB yields remains a key medium-term tail risk, especially in light of the strong sovereign–financial sector nexus. This could have a potentially important impact on the rest of the world (see Chapter 10 on spillovers). Hence, it will be critical to reverse course and get debt on a downward trajectory. The next chapter discusses policy options to achieve this.

REFERENCES

Arslanalp, S., and R.W. Lam. 2013. "Outlook for Interest Rates and Japanese Banks' Risk Exposures under Abenomics." IMF Working Paper No. 13/213. International Monetary Fund, Washington, DC.

Arslanalp, S., and T. Tsuda. 2014. "Tracking Global Demand for Advanced Economy Sovereign Debt." *IMF Economic Review*, 62 (3). International Monetary Fund, Washington, DC.

Cabinet Office. 2012. "What Impacts Did the Fixed Amount Cash Benefit Have on Household Consumption?—Analysis Based on Individual Data of the Household Spending Survey." Policy Issue Analysis Series 8, Tokyo.

Daiwa Institute of Research. 2013. "30-Year Outlook of Super-Ageing Japan." Report on Economic and Social Structure Analysis. Tokyo.

Faini, R. 2006. "Fiscal Policy and Interest Rates in Europe." *Economic Policy*, 21 (47): 443–89.

Hori, M., C. Hsieh, K. Murata, and S. Shimizutani. 2002. "Did the Shopping Coupon Program Stimulate Consumption?—Evidence from Japanese Micro Data." ESRI Discussion Paper Series No. 12, Tokyo.

Hoshi, T., and T. Ito. 2012. "Defying Gravity: How Long Will Japanese Government Bond Prices Remain High?" NBER Working Paper 18287. National Bureau of Economic Research, Cambridge, Massachusetts.

Ihori, T. 2010. "Fiscal Consolidation and the Consumption Tax, as Well as Macroeconomic Activities." Presentation Material to the Fiscal System Council, May 18.

International Monetary Fund. 2012. "2012 Spillover Report." IMF Policy Papers, July 9, International Monetary Fund, Washington, DC.

———. 2013. "Japan: 2013 Article IV Consultation." IMF Country Report No. 13/253. International Monetary Fund, Washington, DC.

———. 2014a. "Japan: 2014 Article IV Consultation." IMF Country Report No. 14/236. International Monetary Fund, Washington, DC.

———. 2014b. *Fiscal Monitor: Public Expenditure Reform—Making Difficult Choices* (April). International Monetary Fund, Washington, DC.

Kashiwase, K., M. Nozaki, and I. Saito. 2014. "Japan's Health and Long-Term Care System: Fiscal Projections and Reform Options." IMF Working Paper No. 14/142. International Monetary Fund, Washington, DC.

Keen, M., M. Pradhan, K. Kang, and R. de Mooij. 2011. "Raising the Consumption Tax in Japan: Why, When, How?" IMF Staff Discussion Note 11/13. International Monetary Fund, Washington, DC.

Lam, R.W., and K. Tokuoka. 2011. "Assessing the Risks to the Japanese Government Bond (JGB) Market." IMF Working Paper No. 11/292. International Monetary Fund, Washington, DC.

Reinhart, C.M., and K.S. Rogoff. 2010. "Growth in a Time of Debt." *American Economic Review, Papers & Proceedings* 100 (2): 573–578.

Tokuoka, K. 2010. "The Outlook for Financing Japan's Public Debt." IMF Working Paper No. 10/19. International Monetary Fund, Washington, DC.

Ueda, J., Y. Yoneta, and I. Ota. 2014. "Size of Fiscal Adjustments Required for Fiscal Management in Japan—Quantitative Analysis of Dynamic Fiscal Imbalance," Ministry of Finance, Policy Research Institute, *Financial Review* 117 (1), Ministry of Finance, Tokyo.

CHAPTER 5

Options for Fiscal Consolidation in an Aging Society

Ikuo Saito

The previous chapter argued that Japan needs substantial fiscal consolidation to put debt on a downward trajectory. This chapter tries to answer a more difficult question—how to bring about such a large fiscal adjustment sustainably and equitably without unduly hurting growth and the nascent exit from deflation? After all, fiscal consolidation would harm aggregate demand, at least in the short term, as some crowding in through higher investment should be expected over the medium term. Also, fiscal consolidation generally has implications for intra- and intergenerational equity (IMF 2014a; Tokuoka 2012), which in turn has implications for the political support for it and thus its feasibility.

The size of the adjustment needed to put debt on a downward trajectory is unprecedented. IMF (2014b) argues that the planned fiscal adjustment of 1 percent of GDP in 2014 and 2015 strikes the right balance between establishing fiscal policy credibility and preserving the recovery.[1] However, policy discussions in Japan are bypassing long-term fiscal issues, with discussions on a medium-term plan expected to start only after the fiscal year (FY) 2015 budget has been formulated. The analysis in Chapter 4 highlighted that fiscal risks have remained largely unchanged under Abenomics as new stimulus has broadly offset the benefits of a wider growth–interest rate differential. After the April 2014 consumption tax hike, a further adjustment of 8.5 percent of GDP is needed over the medium term to put the debt ratio on a downward trajectory (Figure 5.1). About a quarter of the needed adjustment is identified from the next consumption tax hike, the waning of stimulus, and some expenditure restraint. This leaves a gap of more than 6 percent of GDP in yet-to-be-identified measures to restore fiscal sustainability, options and considerations for which will be discussed in this chapter. As the previous chapter noted, the debt outlook and, thus, the adjustment need are subject to a number of downside risks, but would benefit greatly from higher potential growth. Structural reforms are important, as such reforms would increase the chance of successful fiscal adjustment by offsetting its negative impact on growth and poverty. The next chapter discusses the broad contours of the structural reform agenda.

The pace of fiscal consolidation, in addition to its size and composition, matters as well. Given its growth impact, it should ideally proceed gradually in the

---

[1]The consumption tax increase to 10 percent in October 2015 was assumed.

Figure 5.1 Japan's Gross Public Debt[1] *(Percent of GDP)*

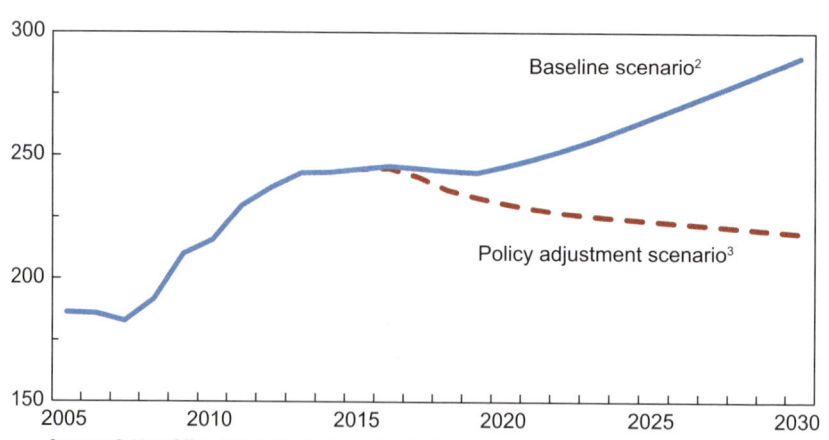

Sources: Cabinet Office; IMF staff estimates and projections.
[1]Gross debt of the general government including the social security fund.
[2]Automatic withdrawal of fiscal stimulus and a consumption tax rate increase to 10 percent are assumed.
[3]Policy adjustment scenario assumes an 8.5 percent of GDP improvement (baseline scenario + 6¼ points) in the structural primary balance between 2015 and 2020.

context of a medium-term framework if warranted by economic conditions and permitted by financing conditions (IMF 2012). On the surface, Japan seems to have the luxury of being able to undertake a gradual adjustment as the Japanese government bond market is calm and regarded as a safe haven so far. But the previous chapter revealed that this should not be taken for granted in the future. In addition, delaying fiscal consolidation is expected to increase its cost and exacerbate intergenerational inequality and potentially raise exit risks, including from fiscal dominance concerns, for the Bank of Japan once the two percent inflation target has been achieved in a stable manner as the primary deficit at that time would still be elevated.[2] Thus, the right balance needs to be struck between gradualism and making sufficient up-front adjustment to maintain credibility in the longer-term fiscal objectives. In this regard, Abenomics would benefit from quickly formulating a concrete medium-term fiscal strategy, as it is currently lacking specifics other than the two-stage consumption tax rate hike, which was designed under the previous government, and, as argued above, by itself would be insufficient to put debt on a downward trajectory.

In terms of composition, spending cuts are generally regarded as superior to tax increases as the former are more likely to be permanent, while the latter create greater economic distortions. IMF (2013a) finds that during past, large, and sustained improvements in the primary balance, more than 75 percent was driven by a reduction in primary expenditure. However, given that Japan's tax revenue-to-GDP ratio is one of the lowest among the Organisation for Economic

---

[2]For example, Keen and others (2011) compare the cases of immediately starting a consumption tax rate hike and of delaying it by two years. Tokuoka (2012) argues that delaying fiscal consolidation could be costly and worsen intergenerational imbalances.

Co-operation and Development (OECD) countries and its population is aging most rapidly, securing revenue should also play an important role.[3] This is why the IMF has recommended action on both spending and revenue equally to put debt onto a declining path (IMF 2014b).

We argue that, regarding revenue measures, the consumption tax should play a larger role in the future (Keen and others 2011). Relatively speaking, it is growth friendly, excels in horizontal and intergenerational equity, has a large and broad tax base, and is simple to administer and comply with provided it has a unitary rate. In the context of a comprehensive and concrete consolidation package, room should be created to reduce tax rates on corporate and personal income. These taxes are generally seen as most harmful to the economy (OECD 2010), and hence reducing their rates would offer some relief from the overall negative impact of fiscal consolidation on growth. Nonetheless, while stimulating investment and growth, corporate income tax rate cuts are unlikely to be self-financing and hence need offsetting revenue measures (De Mooij and Saito 2014).

On spending, this chapter suggests that containing age-related spending is the first priority. Although social security spending is relatively small compared with other advanced economies (IMF 2014c), it still comprised more than 50 percent of total general government outlays in 2012. In addition, as alluded to in the previous chapter, the 2004 pension reform intended to contain the ratio of public pension spending to GDP may not have met its objectives, while health and long-term care spending is expected to continue to rise significantly based on demographic and past cost trends (Kashiwase, Nozaki, and Saito 2014). Efforts to contain or further reduce other expenses relative to GDP are nonetheless also critical.

Finally, as the consolidation is large and takes place over an extended period, the institutional setting is vital to success. In this regard, a key challenge will be to move toward a credible and flexible long-term fiscal framework. This should be grounded in independent and prudent long-term fiscal projections and policy recommendations. In addition, greater accountability (IMF 2013b), multiyear budget planning, and stricter rules on the use of supplementary budgets (IMF 2013a and 2014b) will also enhance the credibility of the adjustment efforts.[4]

In the remainder of the chapter, we first describe the recent trend and current profile of government expenditure and revenue. We argue that the consumption tax should play a central role in fiscal consolidation, while corporate income tax reform should only proceed as part of a comprehensive and concrete consolidation plan that puts debt on a downward path. We discuss options to reform the pension system and recommend ways to contain health and long-term care spending, while paying special attention to intergenerational equity.

---

[3]Moreover, IMF (2012) estimates that Japan's fiscal multiplier is higher for spending measures than for revenue ones.
[4]In addition, to reduce vulnerability, mitigating rollover risks through further extending maturity is also important (see Tokuoka 2010 and Lam and Tokuoka 2011).

WHERE DOES JAPAN STAND ON SPENDING AND REVENUE?

Japan recorded its last fiscal surplus in 1992. Since then, the spending-to-GDP ratio increased by 8.5 percentage points, with social security benefits increasing particularly sharply by 10.6 percentage points. The combination of increased longevity and birth rates well below the replacement level has resulted in a declining population with a rising old-age dependency ratio, which has increased demand on the government's redistributive policies (Figure 5.2).[5] Since 1992 revenue has declined by 0.7 percentage point. Notwithstanding this modest reduction in total revenue, Japan remains at the low end of general government revenue collection relative to other advanced economies (Figure 5.3). It also masks a stark difference between the performance of revenue from direct and indirect taxes on the one hand versus revenue from social security contributions on the other: during the same period the former declined by 3.4 percentage points of GDP, while the latter increased by 3.9 percentage points (property income declined by 1.2 points). In combination, the rise in spending and sluggish revenue collection resulted in a deficit of 8.7 percent of GDP in 2012.

Revenue from each tax source has fluctuated significantly. For example, at a central government level, personal income tax peaked at 5.6 percent of GDP in FY1991 around the bursting of the bubble and declined to 3.0 percent in FY2012; corporate income tax similarly fell from 4.7 percent of GDP in FY1988 to 2.1 percent in FY2012. These reductions were due to the economic slowdown

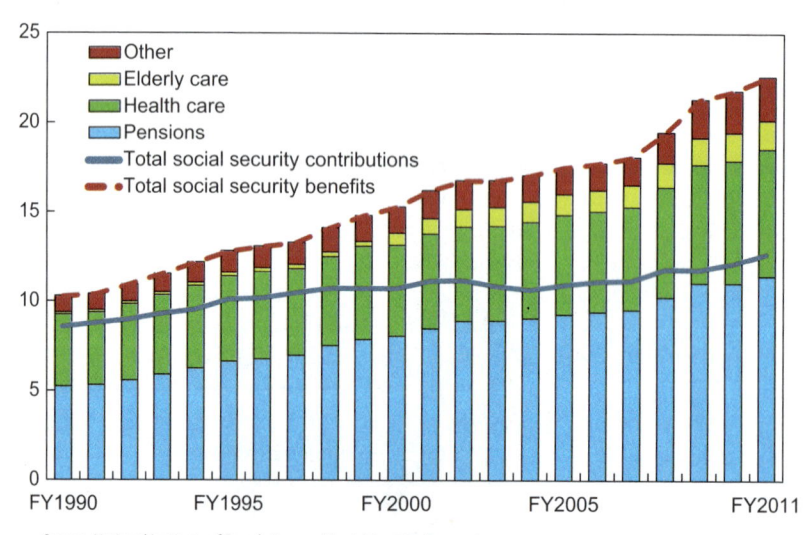

Figure 5.2 Social Security Benefits and Contributions *(Percent of GDP)*

Source: National Institute of Population and Social Security Research.

---

[5]The ratio of the population aged 65 or above to the working-age population (20–64) is the highest in the world and is expected to rise from 38 percent in 2010 to 57 percent in 2030.

Figure 5.3 General Government Tax and Social Security Revenue, 2012 *(Percent of GDP)*

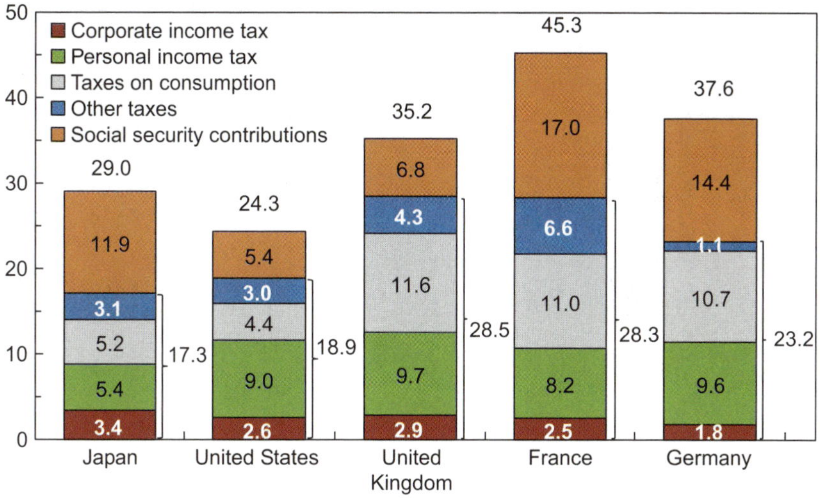

	Japan	United States	United Kingdom	France	Germany
Total	29.0	24.3	35.2	45.3	37.6
Social security contributions	11.9	5.4	6.8	17.0	14.4
Other taxes	3.1	3.0	4.3	6.6	1.1
Taxes on consumption	5.2	4.4	11.6	11.0	10.7
Personal income tax	5.4	9.0	9.7	8.2	9.6
Corporate income tax	3.4	2.6	2.9	2.5	1.8
Tax subtotal	17.3	18.9	28.5	28.3	23.2

Sources: Organisation for Economic Co-operation and Development and IMF, World Economic Outlook database.

as well as to discretionary tax reductions. On the other hand, revenue from the consumption tax increased to 2.2 percent of GDP in FY2012 owing to the tax hike from 3 percent to 5 percent in April 1997.[6]

The significant increase in social security spending can be broken down between pension outlays (5.7 percentage points during FY1990–2010) and spending on health and long-term care (4.2 percentage points). Also, spending on the social assistance system almost tripled, potentially reflecting aging and the "working-poor" problem.[7] On the other hand, other spending declined as a percent of GDP. The central government's spending on public works (general account) declined from 2.8 percent of GDP in FY1993 to the recent bottom of 1.2 percent of GDP in FY2010 because of the Koizumi reform and the previous government's "from concrete to human" policy, which was partly reversed under Abenomics. Interest payments declined from 3.6 percent of GDP to 2.0 percent during 1990–2010 despite the rapid debt accumulation owing to declining bond yields. As a result, Japan's ratio of non–social security spending to GDP is one of the lowest among OECD countries (Figure 5.4).

So what should Japan do specifically to close the large financing gap? The discussion above suggests that the large deficit is not due to a spending spree, but rather to a failure to secure sufficient revenue to prepare for an aging society. The next sections take a closer look at important components of a growth-friendly and equitable fiscal consolidation strategy, including reform of the consumption tax, the corporate income tax, pension spending, and health care spending.

---

[6]The consumption tax, Japan's value-added tax (VAT), replaced the excise taxes in April 1989.
[7]The share of nonregular workers increased from 20 to 37 percent during the 1990–2013 period.

Figure 5.4 OECD: Spending Excluding Social Security and Interest, 2013 *(Percent of GDP)*

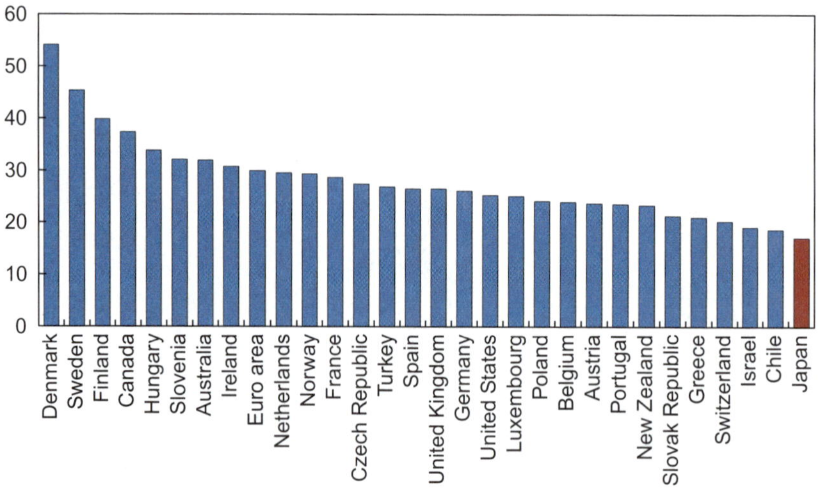

Source: IMF, World Economic Outlook database.
Note: General government basis. Organisation for Economic Co-operation and Development (OECD) countries with missing data (for example, Italy) are not reported here.

WHY THE CONSUMPTION TAX?[8]

As noted, additional revenue should play an important role in efforts to restore Japan's fiscal health. Keen and others (2011) argue that raising the consumption tax rate is the most appealing option. First, it is less distorting compared with taxes on income. A simulation using the IMF's Global Integrated Monetary and Fiscal Model in Keen and others (2011) shows that the negative growth impact is smaller for a consumption tax hike compared with an increase in the corporate or personal income tax rate, and that raising the consumption tax rate dampens growth initially, but this could be offset over time by improved confidence in the fiscal outlook (Figure 5.5).

Keen and others (2011) also point out the following reasons in favor of the consumption tax: even when it increases to 10 percent, it will remain among the lowest in the world (Figure 5.6) and because it is broad based, by international standards, there is ample scope for raising additional revenue by raising the rate. Additionally, provided a unitary rate is maintained, it is relatively easy to administer. Furthermore, it is a stable source of revenue in an aging society (consumption being smoother than income, for instance). Finally, raising the consumption tax rate may be fairer than raising other taxes in helping offset the imbalance in the distribution of lifetime benefits across generations (ensuring that the retired pay a fair share).

The Japanese government also views the consumption tax as a primary source of additional revenue. It increased the tax rate from 5 percent to 8 percent in April 2014

---

[8]This section is based on Keen and others (2011).

Figure 5.5 Impact of a Permanent Tax Hike of One Percent of GDP *(Percent of GDP)*

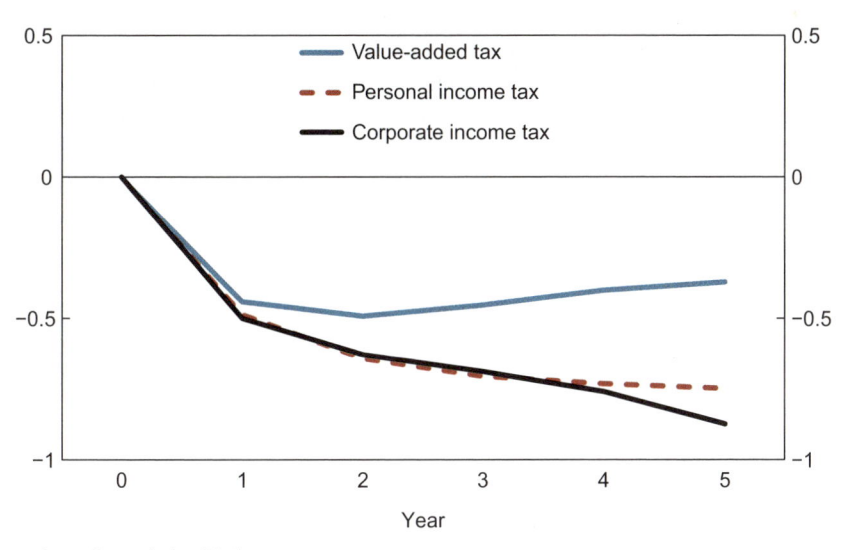

Source: Keen and others (2011).
Note: GDP impact measured as deviation from baseline.

Figure 5.6 Value-Added Tax Rates *(Percent, standard rates)*

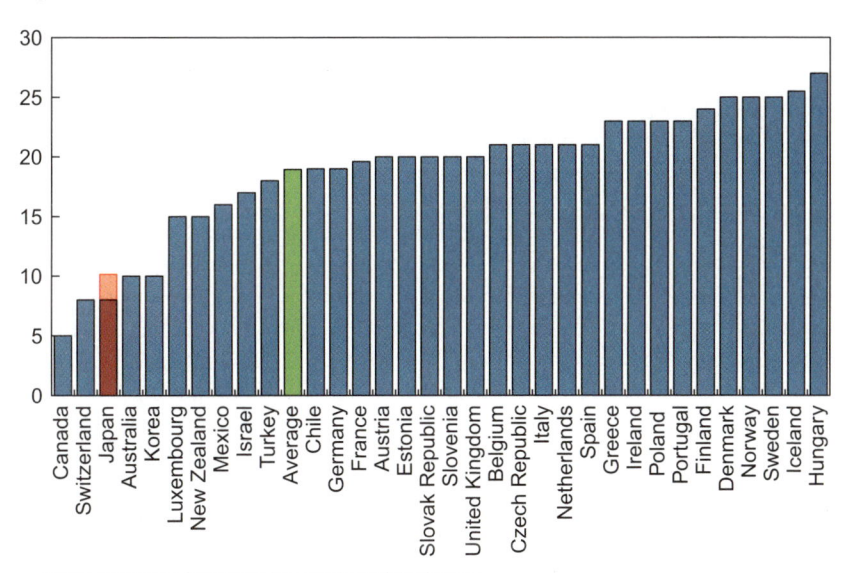

Source: Organisation for Economic Co-operation and Development.
Note: All countries, except Chile and Japan, have multiple tax rates.

and plans to increase it further to 10 percent, which was originally scheduled to occur in October 2015 but this has now been delayed. On revenue potential, Japan applies a uniform rate, although some goods and services are exempted, including health and financial services, education, and rents. As a result, the country's

C-efficiency is one of the world's highest at nearly 70 percent.[9] Specifically, each percentage point of the consumption tax produces roughly 0.5 percent of GDP. Thus, a further 5 percentage point hike from 10 percent to 15 percent would contribute close to one-half of Japan's unidentified adjustment need of 6¼ percent of GDP until 2020. A tax rate of 15 percent would still be modest by OECD standards. To fully utilize revenue potential, and avoid distortions as well as administrative and compliance complexities, maintaining a uniform rate system would be preferable.

A potential shortcoming of the consumption tax is its perceived regressivity. In Keen and others (2011), a simple static analysis using micro-level household data suggests that tripling the uniform consumption tax rate from 5 percent (at the time) to 15 percent in Japan will increase the tax burden for households in the bottom 20 percent of the income distribution by 9 percent of their current income, compared with only 4½ percent for those in the top 20 percent. However, such snapshots of the impact on a cross-section of households are widely recognized as misleading, since a household's income at any particular time is likely to be an imprecise indicator of its members' lifetime well-being. Young graduates may have high earnings prospects, for instance, that are reflected in their current consumption much more than in their current income, and the retired elderly may be able to finance high consumption even though their current income is relatively low. This is particularly relevant in Japan, which has a seniority-based wage structure. So differences in the apparent impact of a consumption tax increase across income groups largely reflect differences in saving rates. For instance, the average saving rate of the bottom 20 percent of households is only 5 percent, while for the top 20 percent, it is about 50 percent. As saving is just postponed consumption, the impact of a tax increase viewed over the lifetime of a household is less regressive than indicated by just looking at the static effects: indeed, a broad-based consumption tax would simply be a proportional tax on lifetime consumption.

Although the government could still consider introducing support measures for low-income households to address remaining equity concerns, doing so through multiple rates is a highly inefficient form of income support, creating various challenges. Household-level analysis shows that consumption tax rate differentiation could play only a very limited role in addressing equity concerns. Specifically, in Japan, setting a lower tax rate on food and offsetting the revenue loss by a higher standard rate does almost nothing for households in the bottom 20 percent of the income distribution. This is because the benefits of the lower tax rate on food products—quite small in the event, as the share of food in household budgets does not vary dramatically across income groups—are largely offset by the higher standard rate. It is thus questionable whether changing relative prices and shifting demand to lower-tax food products would address equity concerns. Moreover, rate differentiation makes implementation more costly for both taxpayers and tax authorities.

Keen and others (2011) argue that an important lesson from the experience of other countries is that rate differentiation, once conceded, is extremely hard to

---

[9]Revenue from the VAT divided by total consumption times the standard rate, which is a crude indicator of how far a VAT is from the benchmark of a single rate levied on all consumption.

reverse or even to contain. Instead, a uniform tax rate combined with targeted transfers to low-income households would be more effective and efficient. Such transfers would, of course, reduce the net gain from a higher rate, but—for any given impact on the poor—much less so than a reduced consumption tax rate for specific goods. Indeed, this is exactly what the Japanese government did at the time of the hike in April 2014. Keen and others (2011) illustrate this point by considering applying a reduced tax rate on food of 5 percent instead of a rate of 10 percent. In Japan, annual food consumption for households at the top and bottom 20 percent of the income distribution is on average about 1 million yen and 0.4 million yen, respectively. Hence, the reduced rate saves 50 thousand yen for the rich and 20 thousand yen for poor households annually, representing a substantial budgetary cost for the government. Instead, the government could compensate the poor by transferring to them an equivalent 20 thousand yen while maintaining a uniform rate of 10 percent, and save the cost of the implicit transfer of 50 thousand yen to the top 20 percent.

They also argue that, although a consumption tax increase places a greater burden on older generations than an income tax, this may be fair given the imbalance in the distribution of lifetime benefits across generations. First, elderly households typically own large assets. Second, on a lifetime basis the current and soon-to-be elderly in Japan are significant net beneficiaries under the social security system; that is, their benefits are higher than their lifetime tax payments and past contributions. In contrast, the younger generations have been and will likely remain net contributors to the system, reflecting the pay-as-you-go pension system and shrinking population (Cabinet Office 2005). So a higher consumption tax, which in part raises revenue from the past savings of the current cohort of the elderly, may help restore the balance of intergenerational fairness.

Finally, Keen and others (2011) discuss the pace of raising the consumption tax rate. Their simulation shows that a faster tax increase dampens growth more in the short term, although it would eventually lead to higher growth and lower debt. Given relatively low potential growth in Japan, estimated currently at about 0.5 percent, a sharp rise in the tax rate should be avoided to mitigate and instead smooth the impact on growth, even though steep hikes would reduce debt more quickly.

In conclusion, Keen and others (2011) propose that raising the consumption tax rate in Japan should follow what they call the four Ss. It should (1) start *sooner* rather than later, (2) be done in *steps*, (3) be *sustained* for some time, and (4) be *simple* in design.

COMPREHENSIVE CORPORATE INCOME TAX REFORM[10]

Japan has reformed its corporate income tax in recent years, but the statutory rate (35.6 percent in Tokyo) remains among the highest in the OECD and Asia

---

[10]This section is based on De Mooij and Saito (2014).

Figure 5.7 Corporate Income Tax Statutory Rates: Selected OECD Economies *(Percent)*

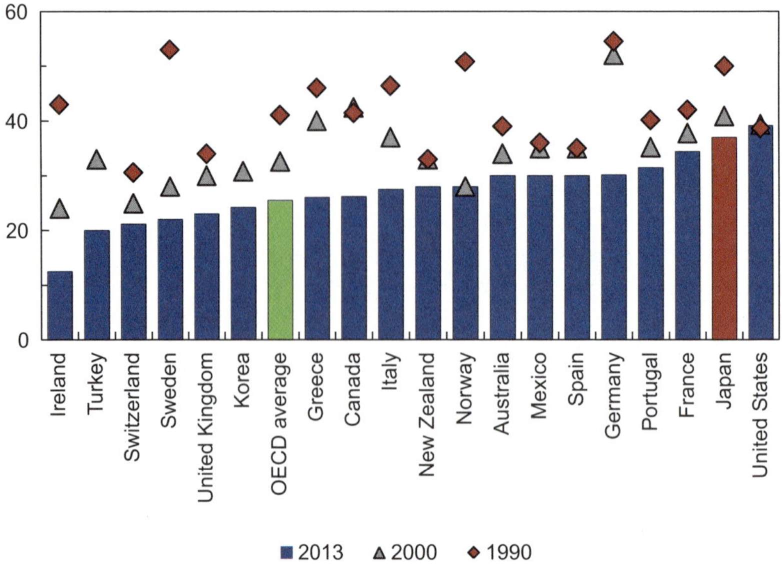

■ 2013   ▲ 2000   ◆ 1990

Source: Organisation for Economic Co-operation and Development (OECD).

(Figure 5.7),[11] and several other distortions remain. Among taxes, the corporate income tax is generally seen as the most harmful to growth. To stimulate the economy and attract more investment to the country, the Japanese government announced its intention to reduce the statutory rate to below 30 percent in a few years. Japan's high fiscal risk, however, requires careful analysis of the economic and fiscal impacts of corporate income tax reform.

Japan's corporate income tax system is relatively distortionary and complex, which warrants comprehensive reform. The country's rate varies by firm size, income level, and region, while most countries apply a single corporate income tax rate. The effective tax rates, which decide investment distortions, are also high in Japan. Differences in treatment between debt and equity financing (Figure 5.8) and incorporated and unincorporated firms are large and lead to distortions and arbitrage.[12] The proliferation of special tax incentives has reduced transparency and added distortions and complexity.

Corporate income tax reforms since 2009 have reduced some distortions and improved the competitive position of Japanese firms abroad. The move toward an exemption system for foreign dividends in 2009 has increased outbound foreign

---

[11]The average in 2014 of 11 Asian economies (China, Hong Kong, India, Indonesia, Japan, Malaysia, Philippines, Singapore, South Korea, Thailand, Vietnam) is 25 percent.

[12]Wage earners can claim the standard deduction that rises with income up to a certain threshold and the deduction is substantially higher than actual expenses and compared to other countries. This large wage income deduction creates incentives for small and medium-sized enterprises (SMEs) to become incorporated and distribute profits through directors' wages, which could reduce corporate income tax liabilities (Tajika and Yashio 2005).

Figure 5.8 Cost of Capital by Financing Measures, 2012 *(Percent)*

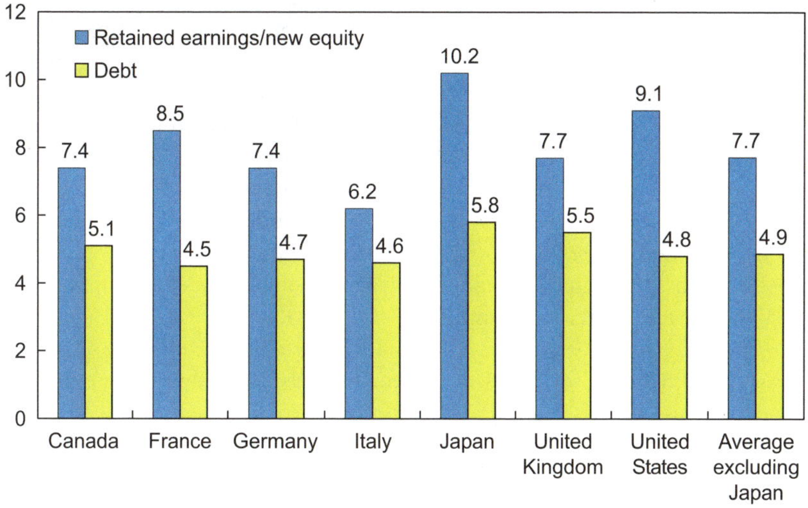

Country	Retained earnings/new equity	Debt
Canada	7.4	5.1
France	8.5	4.5
Germany	7.4	4.7
Italy	6.2	4.6
Japan	10.2	5.8
United Kingdom	7.7	5.5
United States	9.1	4.8
Average excluding Japan	7.7	4.9

Source: Center for European Economic Research.

direct investment (FDI) and encouraged foreign affiliates to repatriate profits to their Japanese parent companies. Yet, Japan may have incurred some fiscal costs in terms of revenue foregone from repatriation taxes and may have become more vulnerable to income shifting by multinationals as foreign tax rates are now final taxes. The 2009 reform might therefore have made it more difficult for Japan to sustain its high corporate income tax rate, although it has strengthened anti-avoidance measures. Since 2012, it has also reduced the corporate income tax rate by 5 percentage points.[13]

A further cut to the rate could have a positive yet limited impact on investment, including through higher inward FDI. A large body of international literature suggests that a 5 percentage point cut may increase investment by some 2–3 percent. However, Japan-specific estimates point to potentially smaller effects. For example, Uemura and Maekawa (2000) find that the corporate income tax rate cut in 1999 increased investment by 0.2 percent per 1 percentage point cut. Moreover, the meta-analysis of De Mooij and Ederveen (2008) finds that a five-point reduction in effective corporate income tax rates increases the stock of FDI, on average, by 15 percent. However, given that inbound FDI is relatively small in Japan and more than half of FDI in advanced economies is, in fact, mergers and acquisitions rather than greenfield, this effect may not be as large. All in all, investment is expected to expand about 0.4 percent for each percentage point that the statutory corporate tax rate is reduced in Japan.

A corporate income tax rate cut is unlikely to be self-financing. The elasticity of taxable income is key to estimating the dynamic impact on the fiscal balance. Past studies suggest that income and debt shifting by SMEs and multinational

---

[13] The government plans to further reduce the tax rate by 3.3 percentage points (2.5 percentage points in FY2015 and an additional 0.8 percentage point in FY2016).

corporations increases taxable income with an elasticity of –0.3, although the gain by SMEs comes at the expense of personal income tax revenue. In addition, micro evidence suggests that the elasticity for an average firm is in the range of –0.1 and –0.3. All considered, the initial, static, revenue loss following a corporate income tax cut—approximately 0.1 percent of GDP for every percentage point reduction in the rate—may be mitigated by perhaps 10–30 percent, far from fully offsetting its impact. With the possibility of a smaller response of investment to a corporate income tax rate cut in Japan, as mentioned above, the offset may be closer to the lower bound. Of course, higher economic growth or higher (expected) inflation as a result of a corporate income tax rate cut would improve the debt dynamics through a denominator effect, although such effects will depend also on how interest rates will change.

Revenue gains from base broadening seem limited, but streamlining tax incentives, including those for SMEs, is needed. Tax incentives come at an estimated overall revenue loss of 0.2 percent of GDP at the central government level. Some of these incentives may be justified on efficiency grounds, including for stimulating research and development, and eliminating them will partly undo the overall positive impact of a rate cut on investment. The number of tax incentives in Japan is very large, however, and not all seem effective, particularly those applicable to SMEs, including special reduced rates, which can, in fact, be distortionary. On the other hand, the generosity of depreciation allowances and loss carry forward provisions is not high compared with peer countries.

The IMF (2014b) has been advocating lowering the corporate income tax rate as part of a comprehensive fiscal adjustment package that would achieve debt sustainability. Although such a rate cut would raise the burden on taxes or expenditure savings, it would make the overall adjustment package more growth friendly. In addition to base broadening, two other options warrant consideration to contain fiscal risks. First, a gradual approach to lowering rates would reduce tax relief on past investments and thus fiscal costs. Second, consideration could be given to introducing an incremental allowance for corporate equity to stimulate investment, which has minimal fiscal costs in the short run. This would directly reduce the cost of equity financing, boosting incentives to invest. Moreover, it would also eliminate debt bias, which gives incentives for excessive debt accumulation, making firms more vulnerable to shocks. If an allowance for corporate equity is applied only to new equity, as recently introduced in Italy, revenue losses will be incurred only gradually. Alternatively, strengthening limitations on interest deductibility to bring them closer to those in Germany and France, for example, could also mitigate debt bias and would broaden the tax base but, by raising the cost of debt finance, risk lowering investment.

OPTIONS FOR PENSION REFORM[14]

Social security spending has been a main driver behind the rapid rise in debt as seen above. Within this category, public pension spending has played a large role:

---

[14]This section is based on Kashiwase, Nozaki, and Tokuoka (2012).

it increased from 5.2 percent of GDP in FY1990 to 10.9 percent of GDP in FY2012. This increase and further aging in store prompted the Japanese government to embark on comprehensive pension reform, which was adopted in 2004.

Pension benefits will be automatically adjusted to changes in real wages and demographic structure (that is, rises in the dependency ratio and longevity) in the future—or so-called macroeconomic slide (indexing).[15] On the other hand, contribution rates will be gradually increased and fixed from FY2017, for example at 18.3 percent of income for the second-tier (earnings-linked) pension.[16] Also, the Government Pension Investment Fund (GPIF) has invested around 130 trillion yen (as of end-September 2014) to contribute to pension finances. Finally, the 2004 reform increased the ratio of the government subsidy to the basic pension benefit by about one-half percent of GDP. All these factors are expected to contribute to securing the sustainability of the pension system, which is examined every five years for the next 100 years. Overall, this scheme is designed to contain public pension spending in terms of GDP—IMF (2014c) assumes that the pension-spending-to-GDP ratio would decline by 0.3 percentage point from 2014 to 2030.

However, macroeconomic indexing does not function well under a low price/wage increase environment.[17] Inflation was expected in both the 2004 reform and in the 2009 reexamination to rise to 1.0 percent, which did not happen. In addition, the indexing has never been activated as "excessive" payouts, caused by the fact that pension benefits were nominally maintained in FY2010–2012 despite price declines. Only recently did the government decide to reduce benefits in line with past price declines, and the first adjustment to the excessive payouts happened in October 2013 and the second in April 2014 (with a final adjustment planned for April 2015). The reexamination of pension finances was published in June 2014, which could urge the government to adjust the 2004 plan, and result in additional reductions in benefit levels or increases in public spending. Against this background, Kashiwase, Nozaki, and Tokuoka (2012) suggest further reforms to the pension system.

They analyze various reform options for their impact on fiscal consolidation, equity,[18] and economic growth. They argue that increasing the pension eligibility age is the most attractive option in light of high and rising life expectancy. Other attractive options include improving targeting by "clawing back" a small portion of pension benefits from wealthy retirees, reducing preferential tax treatment of pension benefits, and collecting contributions from dependent spouses of employees covered by the employment-based pension system. In contrast, across-the-board cuts in the replacement ratio and higher pension contributions are less desirable. Separately, raising returns of public pension funds, including through further diversifying investments, could help enhance the sustainability of the

---

[15]For details, see Box 1 in Kashiwase, Nozaki, and Tokuoka (2012).
[16]Equally split between employers and employees.
[17]Macroeconomic indexing allows the increase in pension benefits to be smaller than price or wage increases to contain pension spending. However, when prices or wages decline, pension benefits cannot be lowered by more than the decrease in prices or wages.
[18]The public pension plays an important role in helping reduce old-age poverty, as the system has a redistributive nature.

pension system.[19] Kashiwase, Nozaki, and Tokuoka (2012) propose that fiscal savings from these reforms could be used to reduce pension contributions, which could stimulate the economy by improving incentives to work.

The pension eligibility age is being raised to 65 by FY2030, although the pace is somewhat different among pension programs and between sexes. Kashiwase, Nozaki, and Tokuoka (2012) argue that taking account of rising, healthy life expectancy will give scope to increase the eligibility age further. The gap between life expectancy and the pension eligibility age is larger in Japan than in most other countries, which have been increasing the eligibility age in line with increased longevity. Raising the pension eligibility age would also have a positive effect on economic growth and could be fairer from an intergenerational perspective as it would promote the continued labor force participation of older-aged workers and raise consumption through improved lifetime earnings. Unlike the option of raising the contribution rate, the burden would be more equally shared between younger and older generations (Tokuoka 2012). They also note that an increase in the pension eligibility age should be accompanied by an expansion of the safety net, especially for those with disabilities.

The 2004 reform included a plan to lower the pension replacement ratio.[20] Kashiwase, Nozaki, and Tokuoka (2012) argue that a further reduction in the replacement ratio should be well targeted rather than across the board. Although the latter could have a positive economic impact and help correct intergenerational imbalances, it could worsen old-age poverty as the current level of the basic pension benefit is not so generous and reductions might result in a higher demand for social assistance, offsetting fiscal savings. There are opportunities for improved targeting by introducing a claw-back, as the government currently subsidizes half of the basic pension benefit payments, regardless of the income level of retirees.

A higher contribution rate, on the other hand, would have a negative growth effect and aggravate intergenerational imbalances. Instead, the authors propose collecting pension contributions from dependent spouses. Dependent spouses of employees covered by the employment-based pension insurance are eligible for basic pension benefits without paying contributions. Because benefits for them are paid out of contributions from both single and married employees, they are effectively cross-subsidized, raising concerns about fairness. This preferential treatment also creates a disincentive to work, because a spouse is qualified only if his or her annual earnings are lower than 1.3 million yen. This reform option

---

[19]The GPIF announced on October 31, 2014, a substantial portfolio rebalancing from domestic bonds to equities and foreign securities, bringing the new portfolio benchmarks in line with targets used in other countries. The rationale for the reallocation, which had been planned since late 2013, has been threefold: (1) to prepare the GPIF for higher inflation: reducing the portfolio of JGBs limits potential capital losses once nominal interest rates rise while increasing returns on assets; (2) to provide more risk capital to the economy by infusing funds into private assets; and (3) to strengthen its governance structure.

[20]Defined as a pension benefit for a representative couple divided by the average wage of the working-age population.

should be pursued in tandem with a similar one in health care (mentioned below) as these two systems adopt the same dependency threshold.

Finally, Kashiwase, Nozaki, and Tokuoka (2012) point out that eliminating the preferential tax treatment of pension income would generate sizable fiscal savings. At present, a substantial part of the public pension benefit is deducted from taxable income when calculating personal income tax liability. On an aggregate level, about three-fourths of pension benefit income is exempt from taxable income, which benefits wealthy retirees as well. Other countries, such as France and New Zealand, do not exempt pension benefits from taxable income (OECD 2010). The authors estimate that, all combined, the above reforms could reduce the annual government subsidy by up to 1¼ percent of GDP by 2020.

OPTIONS FOR HEALTH CARE REFORM[21]

Although public health care spending is still around the average of advanced economies, it is rapidly increasing, with measures to contain spending yet to be formulated. Total health and long-term care spending hovered at about 4–5 percent of GDP during the 1980s, but more than doubled during the last two decades, from 4.5 percent in 1990 to 9.5 percent in 2010. The introduction of a public long-term care insurance system in 2000 seems to have contributed to this increase. At the same time, public health spending has rapidly increased from 4.1 percent of GDP in FY1990 to 8.3 percent in FY2012.

Kashiwase, Nozaki, and Saito (2014) estimate that two-thirds of the spending increase over the last two decades resulted from population aging and the rest from excess cost growth, which is the growth differential between health spending and GDP per capita after controlling for the aging factor. Aging matters as per capita health spending is significantly higher for the elderly,[22] while excess cost growth is typically due to the higher share of health services consumption with rising income and technological advances. They argue that this trend will continue. Specifically, they estimate that total health spending can increase by about 6 percentage points of GDP in the next two decades, based on demographic changes and the past trend of excess cost growth, with each contributing about half of the increase.[23]

Kashiwase, Nozaki, and Saito (2014) further estimate that out of the 6 percentage points of GDP increase, about 3.5 percent of GDP should be financed by the government. They argue that the younger generations (0–64) would likely see their contribution rate rise more than older generations, resulting in an increasing imbalance between spending and contributions for different age cohorts.

Finally, Kashiwase, Nozaki, and Saito (2014) quantify potential fiscal savings through alternative reform options. Although Japan's health care system is highly

---

[21]This section is based on Kashiwase, Nozaki, and Saito (2014).
[22]In Japan, a person aged 80 or above spends about 19 times as much as a person aged 40–44 on health; this ratio is the highest among the OECD countries, whose median ratio is 6.2.
[23]Assumptions are taken from the National Institute of Population and Social Security Research.

valued, it shows some inefficiencies relative to the OECD average, including a large number of beds per capita, long hospitalization stays, and a relatively large amount of expensive equipment. Based on past studies, they estimate that cost savings from addressing these inefficiencies including through introducing budget caps and gate-keeping and strengthening supply constraints could amount to 0.7 percent of GDP by 2030. Moreover, more use of generic drugs and focus on preventing lifestyle-related diseases are estimated to save 0.4 percent of GDP.

In addition, they argue for raising copayment (out-of-pocket payment) rates, which is expected to produce a double dividend of increasing revenue while reducing excess demand. Raising effective copayment rates by 5 percentage points for people aged 70 and older in the health care system and for all users in the long-term care system could add revenue equivalent to 0.6 percent of GDP by 2030. Another potential option is increasing copayment rates on expenses above the monthly cap and for medical services provided under the social assistance program.[24] Although higher out-of-pocket payments would also contribute to reducing excessive demand, such payments may need to be accompanied by further differentiation of copayment rates based on income levels or means-testing to ensure fairness.

Kashiwase, Nozaki, and Saito (2014) also argue for collecting contributions from dependent spouses, which could increase revenue and reduce disincentives for second earners to work. Under the current system, as is the case with pensions, dependent spouses of employees are exempted from paying premiums if their annual earnings are below 1.3 million yen. This creates a disincentive to work beyond this threshold. Moreover, this special treatment of dependent spouses may be unfair vis-à-vis couples with both earning beyond the threshold and families of self-employed. They estimate that collecting contributions from dependent spouses could add revenue of 0.3 percent of GDP in 2030.

However, the total savings of up to 1.9 percentage points of GDP from raising copayment rates, more efficient use of health resources, and higher reliance on generic drugs, is smaller than the projected increase in government health spending of 3.5 percentage points of GDP. Fully offsetting the increase would require more radical reforms, such as further increases in copayment rates; increases in contribution rates, including by introducing a completely proportional contribution scale under the employment-based insurance;[25] and a review of government-controlled prices of health and long-term care services. Thus, containing health spending is a key policy area that could be used to restore fiscal sustainability.

INTERGENERATIONAL EQUITY

This section looks at the intergenerational impact of fiscal consolidation based on Tokuoka (2012). Intergenerational resource imbalances matter, as older generations

---

[24]The social assistance program provides free medical care. The cost more than doubled to 0.3 percent of GDP in 2010 from the recent low in 1991.

[25]Currently the monthly contribution amount is fixed beyond a certain threshold of monthly income, which makes the contribution scale regressive.

may not transfer their net benefits to younger generations, and such transfers—if made—may not exactly match the net burden of each individual. Intergenerational inequality in resource allocation in Japan is already significant, even without accounting for future fiscal consolidation. The pay-as-you-go social security system has widened intergenerational resource inequality substantially because of rapid aging. The Cabinet Office (2005) estimates that, based on government policy at the time, the present discounted value of the lifetime net burden for future generations would be 100 million yen per household (about 20 times household annual disposable income) more than that for those aged 60 years or older.[26] Therefore, implementing fiscal consolidation while minimizing further deterioration in intergenerational inequality is important.

Tokuoka (2012) analyzes the intergenerational implications of fiscal consolidation and concludes that combining social security spending reforms and revenue measures in a balanced manner would be the fairest way to distribute the burden of fiscal consolidation across the generations. However, an excessive reliance on these measures, in particular reducing pension benefits for current pensioners, would have a serious impact on the welfare of seniors.

In addition, his simulations show that delaying consolidation would exacerbate intergenerational imbalances. On the one hand, fiscal consolidation generally worsens intergenerational inequality compared with the level implied by existing policy, as the young have a longer remaining lifetime and would therefore feel the impact of fiscal consolidation for a longer period. However, a lack of fiscal consolidation would eventually lead to an increase in interest rates, which would lower output and reduce welfare substantially. In such a case, young generations would be hit harder, further aggravating intergenerational imbalances.

Specifically, Tokuoka (2012) uses a standard lifecycle overlapping generation model with perfect foresight, but without uncertainty about income or life length or heterogeneity within each generation (one representative agent in each generation). The model consists of the household, corporate, and government sectors. He calculates the lifetime resource burden from the following five measures, yielding 0.5 percent of GDP as a part of the 10 percentage point structural adjustment needed in Japan: (1) reducing the pension replacement ratio (while maintaining the pension eligibility age); (2) raising the pension eligibility age; (3) raising the pension contribution rate; (4) containing non-pension social security benefits; and (5) raising the consumption tax rate (beyond 15 percent already assumed).

He finds that reducing the pension replacement ratio or raising the pension eligibility age would keep the burden for young generations relatively low, with the former having a greater impact in correcting intergenerational inequality, as the latter would impose a zero burden on generations 65 years of age or older. The

---

[26]Tokuoka (2012) points out that intergenerational imbalances are worse than indicated by Cabinet Office estimates, as they do not take into account future fiscal consolidation, which this and previous chapters argue is unavoidable. He cites the results of Kotlikoff and Leibfritz (1999), which show that once needed expenditure cuts or future tax increases are considered, Japan is the most unequal economy in the world from an intergenerational perspective.

aggregate economic impact implied by the overlapping generation simulations is very similar for both measures.

Relative to reducing the pension replacement ratio, raising the pension contribution rate or the personal income tax rate would worsen the existing intergenerational imbalance as these would increase the lifetime burdens on younger generations. In addition, output would be lower, given the greater distorting impact of an increase in the pension contribution rate on labor supply and capital accumulation. The author argues that this finding is consistent with the empirical observation for OECD economies that growth is moderately, but negatively, correlated with social security contributions and the employee income tax.

Containing non-pension social security benefits would distribute the lifetime burden more equally across generations than reducing pension benefits or raising the pension contribution rate. The implications for intergenerational inequality of raising the consumption tax rate are similar to an adjustment of non-pension social security benefits. A consumption tax hike would also dampen aggregate output, but less than an increase in the pension contribution rate, because the latter has a larger negative effect on labor supply.

Next Tokuoka (2012) compares a gradual fiscal consolidation scenario with a delayed one. Under the latter, the lifetime burden would be smaller for all generations and the level of GDP would be higher initially relative to the former, owing to the lower (net tax) burden. However, as deficits and public debt remain elevated for longer, this would eventually crowd out investment through higher interest rates, implying higher cumulative output losses under a delayed adjustment scenario. These results may underestimate the costs of crowding-out, because they do not factor in the possibility of a nonlinear interest rate response to debt.

Assuming an eventual reduction in the ratio of debt to GDP to the same level, the overall adjustment would need to be larger by about 1 percentage point of GDP in the delayed scenario owing to accumulated interest expense. As a result, the increase in the lifetime burden for the younger generations would be larger, while it would be substantially smaller for senior generations, exacerbating the intergenerational resource imbalance. From a political economy perspective, the finding that delaying fiscal consolidation could lower the burden for older generations highlights the challenge faced by policymakers to implement fiscal consolidation early.

Finally, Tokuoka (2012) examines policy options to correct intergenerational imbalances. First, allowing greater immigration could correct the intergenerational resource imbalance. Assuming a constant size of new-born generations, instead of the annual decline of 0.75 percent under the baseline, reduces the per household lifetime burden of those currently aged 20 for financing pension benefits by 20 percentage points of current wage income per household (before taxes) relative to a no-immigration case, because a larger working population supports the public pension system. Since greater immigration would also reduce the debt-to-GDP ratio faster by boosting labor supply and the level of GDP, it could reduce young (and other) generations' burden further by lowering the size of the needed fiscal adjustment for a given debt target. Second, raising productivity growth through structural reforms could similarly reduce young generations' burden and help correct the intergenerational resource imbalance by trimming the size of the fiscal adjustment need. Third, expanding transfers to young generations, such as public education spending and child allowances, would help mitigate intergenerational imbalances, but the fiscal space for such policies may be limited. In this regard, raising the inheritance tax rate could be an option to secure revenue for financing larger education and family spending.

CONCLUSION

Japan faces the formidable task of steadily putting the debt-to-GDP ratio on a declining path. It needs to do so in a flexible and calibrated manner, contingent on economic conditions and progress in raising inflation, while maintaining financial stability. Structural fiscal adjustment of about 8.5 percent of GDP is needed to restore fiscal sustainability, with only about a quarter identified through the next increase in the consumption tax rate to 10 percent, the waning of stimulus, and plans for restraining expenditure, leaving a gap of more than 6 percent of GDP in yet-to-be identified measures.

Japan needs to take the aging of its population into consideration in deciding on the pace and content of fiscal consolidation as it is a primary driver behind the rapid rise in fiscal risks, sluggish growth, and the widening of intergenerational imbalances. In this chapter we examined specific measures on both the revenue and spending fronts for their impact on the government's financial requirement, growth, and equity where possible.

On the revenue side, we suggested that a further hike in the consumption tax rate is promising as it has large revenue potential in an aging society, is relatively growth friendly, and enables fairer burden sharing among generations. On the other hand, reforming the corporate income tax would provide benefits by stimulating investment and could be considered an element of a comprehensive fiscal reform package that ensures fiscal sustainability in a growth-friendly manner.

We discussed specific reforms to the social security system to contain spending in a manner that supports growth and intergenerational equity. Among various pension reform options, raising the pension age should be the first priority. Other measures include a partial claw back of pension benefits from wealthy retirees and reducing the preferential tax treatment of pension incomes. Collecting contributions from dependent spouses is another option and should proceed simultaneously in both the pension and health care systems. Raising copayment rates for medical and long-term care services would reduce excess demand. Also, there seems to be room for more efficient use of health resources.

There are important synergies between these different measures. For example, an increase in the consumption tax rate can be coupled with well-targeted transfers to low-income households rather than a multiple rate system. Revenue losses from a reduction in the corporate income tax rate should be offset by fiscal savings elsewhere. Pension reform leading to a reduction in benefits can be accompanied by measures to address old-age poverty.

Steady progress with structural fiscal adjustment is needed to avoid incurring additional costs and exacerbating intergenerational imbalances. However, given that Abenomics also aims to raise aggregate demand and inflation, economic conditions may warrant combining such permanent consolidation with temporary and well-targeted stimulus. As adjustment will have to take place over an extended period of time, Japan should review its fiscal institutions, considering other countries' experiences.

All in all, fiscal consolidation should be as growth friendly and equitable as possible. A credible and concrete medium-term framework to restore fiscal sustainability would also free up fiscal space in the near term to respond to downside risks when they emerge. By being concrete and credible, fiscal risks would be contained and such a plan would raise growth in the near term through confidence effects, supporting the exit from deflation. The fiscal sector could get a big boost from higher growth, which would lower the overall adjustment need. The next chapter discusses the structural reform agenda in detail.

REFERENCES

Cabinet Office. 2005. "Annual Report on the Japanese Economy and Public Finance—No Gains without Reforms V." Tokyo.

De Mooij, R., and S. Ederveen. 2008. "Corporate Tax Elasticities: A Reader's Guide to Empirical Findings." *Oxford Review of Economic Policy* 24: 680–97.

De Mooij, R., and I. Saito. 2014. "Japan's Corporate Income Tax: Facts, Issues, and Reform Options," IMF Working Paper No. 14/138. International Monetary Fund, Washington, DC.

International Monetary Fund (IMF). 2012. *Fiscal Monitor: Balancing Fiscal Policy Risks*. International Monetary Fund, Washington, DC.

———. 2013a. *Fiscal Monitor: Fiscal Adjustment in an Uncertain World*. International Monetary Fund, Washington, DC.

———. 2013b. "Case Studies of Fiscal Councils—Functions and Impact," IMF Policy Paper. International Monetary Fund, Washington, DC.

———. 2014a. "Fiscal Policy and Income Inequality," IMF Policy Paper. International Monetary Fund, Washington, DC.

———. 2014b. "Japan: Staff Report for the 2014 Article IV Consultation," IMF Country Report 14/236. International Monetary Fund, Washington, DC.

———. 2014c. *Fiscal Monitor: Public Expenditure Reform—Making Difficult Choices*. International Monetary Fund, Washington, DC.

Kashiwase, K., M. Nozaki, and I. Saito. 2014. "Japan's Health and Long-Term Care System: Fiscal Projections and Reform Options." IMF Working Paper No. 14/142. International Monetary Fund, Washington, DC.

Kashiwase, K., M. Nozaki, and K. Tokuoka. 2012. "Pension Reforms in Japan." IMF Working Paper No. 12/285. International Monetary Fund, Washington, DC.

Keen, M., M. Pradhan, K. Kang, and R. de Mooij. 2011. "Raising the Consumption Tax in Japan: Why, When, How?" IMF Staff Discussion Note 11/13. International Monetary Fund, Washington, DC.

Kotlikoff, L.J., and W. Leibfritz. 1999. "An International Comparison of Generational Accounts." *Generational Accounting around the World*, National Bureau of Economics Research Working Paper No. 6447: 73–102.

Lam, R.W., and K. Tokuoka. 2011. "Assessing the Risks to the Japanese Government Bond (JGB) Market." IMF Working Paper No. 11/292. International Monetary Fund, Washington, DC.

Organisation for Economic Co-operation and Development. 2010. "*Tax Policy Reform and Economic Growth*." OECD Tax Policy Studies No. 20. OECD, Paris.

Tajika, E., and H. Yashio. 2005. "Tax System and Choice on Business Form—Japanese Case." *Fiscal Research*, 1:177–194, Japan Institute of Public Finance.

Tokuoka, K. 2010. "The Outlook for Financing Japan's Public Debt." IMF Working Paper No. 10/19. International Monetary Fund, Washington, DC.

———. 2012. "Intergenerational Implications of Fiscal Consolidation in Japan." IMF Working Paper No. 12/197. International Monetary Fund, Washington, DC.

Uemura, T., and S. Maekawa. 2000. "Investment Activities by Industry and Corporate Income Tax—Empirical Analysis by the Tax-Adjusted Q Using Corporate Financial Data." *Japan Economic Research* 41: 45–70, Japan Center for Economic Research.

CHAPTER 6

Japan's Growth Challenge: Needs and Potential

STEPHAN DANNINGER AND CHAD STEINBERG

Potential growth steadily declined over the past two decades as the effects of Japan's shrinking labor force outweighed the contributions from solid productivity gains. The average GDP growth rate of 0.8 percent in the 2000s was below that of France, Germany, the United States, and many other developed economies. Deflation, lingering effects of the asset bubble burst in the late 1980s, and structural constraints in domestic markets are commonly thought of as the main culprits. Yet, economic fundamentals have also been less favorable than in other countries; in particular, faster and earlier population aging weighed on growth (see Chapter 3).

But higher growth is needed to bring down Japan's high debt-to-GDP ratio and sustain stable inflation at the Bank of Japan's 2 percent target. This chapter poses three questions in this regard. Does Japan have a growth problem? How much faster can Japan grow based on international experience? And how can Japan raise growth?

International evidence indicates that comprehensive structural reforms can raise potential growth by up to 1 percentage point over the course of a decade. In this chapter we find that Japan's productivity growth has been comparable to that in other countries, but the decline in the labor force has been a major drag on overall GDP growth. Considerable scope therefore exists for raising trend growth, although macroeconomic policies can only play a limited role. As previous chapters discuss, necessary fiscal consolidation will quite likely depress growth for some time, while the zero interest bound constrains conventional monetary policy. A key avenue for increasing potential growth is to pursue mutually reinforcing structural reforms (Abenomics' third arrow) aimed at raising labor supply, opening up domestic sectors for greater competition and corporate dynamism, creating an environment for new growth sectors to flourish (such as energy, environment, and health care services), establishing a more growth-supporting financial sector, and integrating further with Asia.

DOES JAPAN HAVE A GROWTH PROBLEM?

The significant deceleration of growth in Japan stands out compared with that in other advanced economies (Figure 6.1). Potential growth fell precipitously from

Figure 6.1 Real GDP Growth, G7 Countries *(Percent; year-over-year change)*

Source: IMF, World Economic Outlook database.
Note: G7 = Group of Seven.

Figure 6.2 Japan: Potential Annual Growth Rate *(Percent; year-over-year change)*

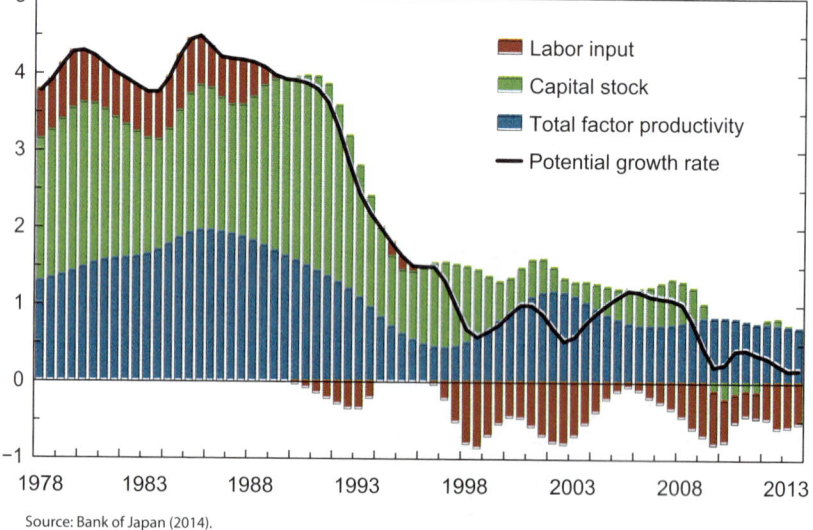

Source: Bank of Japan (2014).

an average of 4 percent in the 1980s to less than 1 percent in the 2000s. Trend growth also declined in other large advanced economies, but the decreases were more modest.

A decomposition of long-term growth shows that the slowdown in Japan occurred in two waves (Figure 6.2). In the early 1990s—the first decade after the asset bubble burst—growth fell by over 2 percentage points, primarily as a result of a rapid deceleration in capital formation and a reduction in total factor productivity (TFP) growth. In the second phase, beginning in the late 1990s, TFP growth began to recover, but its effects were offset by declining labor input and weak investment growth. More recently, the effects of the global recession in 2008–09 have depressed investment, as in many other countries.

The main reasons for the decline in trend growth during the last two decades were:

- *A drawn-out resolution of Japan's banking crisis and balance sheet repair.* Following the collapse of asset prices in the late 1980s, banks and nonfinancial corporations were slow in addressing balance sheet problems (including sizable bad debt and high leverage). Low nominal interest rates allowed banks to roll over credit to nonviable "zombie" firms, and a muted policy response facilitated the accumulation of bad debt on banks' balance sheets (Hoshi and Kashyap 2010). With lending constrained because banks needed to rebuild capital buffers, private investment declined and growth fell, requiring repeated fiscal stimulus to keep the economy going (see Chapter 4). Only after decisive financial sector reforms in the early 2000s under then-Prime Minister Junichiro Koizumi did credit conditions ease again.

- *Demographic changes.* Population aging accelerated in the mid-1990s and the shrinking labor force reduced potential growth (Chapter 3). The growth penalty from population aging has been larger than in other advanced economies (OECD 2010) and will remain a headwind. The aging effect is projected to level off in the 2020s as the old-age dependency ratio approaches 50 percent in 2030 compared with about 35 percent now.

- *Mild deflation.* For over a decade, mild deflation lowered growth expectations and slowed private investment by raising real levels of debt and higher-than-warranted real interest rates. By lowering tax revenue and raising real social spending (as many benefits are not adjusted for falling prices), deflation also aggravated fiscal problems (Chapter 4).

On the upside, government spending and labor market reforms supported growth. Public infrastructure spending after 1995 boosted the public capital stock, although the impact on trend growth has likely been small owing to declining marginal productivity gains (Doi and Ihori 2006). Amendments to the dispatched labor law in 1999 and 2003 eased employment conditions for temporary and part-time workers and created new employment opportunities. Indeed Ono (2010) finds that, although job mobility remains considerably lower in Japan than in other advanced economies, the prevalence of lifetime employment has steadily decreased. He also finds evidence that the economic stagnation of the 1990s disproportionately affected women and younger workers. These effects of government spending and labor market reforms were most visible in the manufacturing sector, where labor's contribution to growth increased (Hoshi and Kashyap 2010).

Stripping out the effects of population aging, Japan's growth was solid until the global financial crisis. During the 2000s, growth per capita was at par with the United States and TFP growth was comparatively high and at similar levels to Germany. The global recession interrupted this overall positive development, hitting Japan particularly hard. Demand for high-end consumer durables and capital

TABLE 6.1

Potential Growth in Japan

	2007	2014	Medium-term[1]
Potential GDP growth	1.4	0.5	1.0
Contributions from:			
Labor	0.1	0.0	−0.2
Capital	0.7	−0.2	0.4
TFP[2]	0.7	0.7	0.8

Source: IMF staff estimates.
[1] Under current policies.
[2] Total factor productivity.

goods were especially affected and a sharp decline in investment and labor supply reduced potential growth to an estimated ½ percent in 2012 (Table 6.1). This is far below the 2 percent growth widely considered the threshold for Abenomics to become successful.

Lifting the potential growth rate to 1 percent over the medium term is already a major task as it requires a strong acceleration of private investment and steady productivity growth. Raising it even further requires a broad and ambitious effort amid headwinds from further declines in the working-age population. Possible dividends from a sustained exit from deflation are a difficult-to-quantify upside risk. Given the uncertainty about potential growth, estimates of the output gap vary widely. Most estimates suggest a relatively modest gap at end-2014, as evidenced by the relatively tight labor market conditions.

Although productivity growth is high, Japan could grow faster given several favorable factors. The country has close ties to Asia, the world's fastest-growing economic region; strong balance sheets among large corporations; and a steady current account surplus. About 50 percent of exports go to Asia, and businesses are well placed to meet the needs of a growing middle class in the region. Innovation has remained an important driver of growth as a result of comparatively high spending on research and development (Figure 6.3).

HOW MUCH FASTER CAN JAPAN GROW BASED ON INTERNATIONAL EXPERIENCE?

Sustained increases in potential growth over a decade are rare among advanced economies, but not unprecedented. Using the IMF's World Economic Outlook database, we find eight country cases since the 1980s in which real trend GDP growth increased by more than 1 percent over a decade and the increase was sustained over at least five years (Table 6.2). Several of these growth improvements came after a deep economic crisis—as in Finland, New Zealand, and Sweden, for instance—which triggered broad-based growth reforms.

The factors behind the potential growth gains differ substantially across the eight country cases. A decomposition of the growth accelerations by contributing factors shows that the main sources of growth were TFP gains and increases in the

Figure 6.3 Research and Development Spending *(Percent of GDP)*

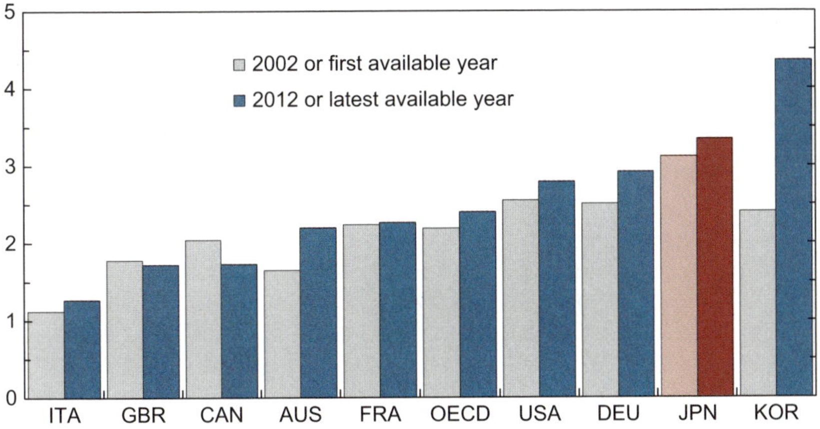

[Bar chart showing R&D spending for 2002 or first available year and 2012 or latest available year, for countries: ITA, GBR, CAN, AUS, FRA, OECD, USA, DEU, JPN, KOR]

Source: Organisation for Economic Co-operation and Development (OECD).
Note: AUS = Australia; CAN = Canada; DEU = Germany; FRA = France; GBR = United Kingdom; ITA = Italy; JPN = Japan; KOR = Korea; OECD = OECD country average; USA = United States.

TABLE 6.2

Sustained Potential Growth Rate Increases *(Percent)*

	Decade	Potential rate Initial	End of decade
Canada	1988–98	2.9	3.9
Finland	1987–97	2.1	3.2
Greece	1985–95	0.7	2.5
Iceland	1987–97	2.3	3.3
Ireland	1983–93	1.7	4.1
Netherlands	1982–92	1.2	2.9
New Zealand	1985–95	1.9	3.4
Sweden	1989–99	1.7	3.5

Source: IMF staff estimates.
Note: For advanced economies only. Defined as a 1 percent increase in the growth rate over one decade sustained for five years.

contributions from labor (Figure 6.4). But the winning formula was quite different across countries. Much of the improvement in New Zealand, for instance, was the result of labor market reforms that raised labor force participation (Brooks 1990). In the Netherlands and Sweden, where reforms stand out as having been particularly durable, the improvements came from greater labor contributions and higher productivity growth. A deep recession in the Netherlands (1980–82) and a banking crisis in Sweden (1990–92) triggered a change in macroeconomic policies and supply-side reforms. Public expenditure-to-GDP ratios were reduced significantly, allowing a reduction of large fiscal deficits and high tax levels; labor markets were made more flexible with increased incentives to work; and product markets were reformed to boost competition. As a result, Sweden

Figure 6.4 Growth Accelerations and Sources of Increase *(Percentage difference in potential growth rates over a decade)*

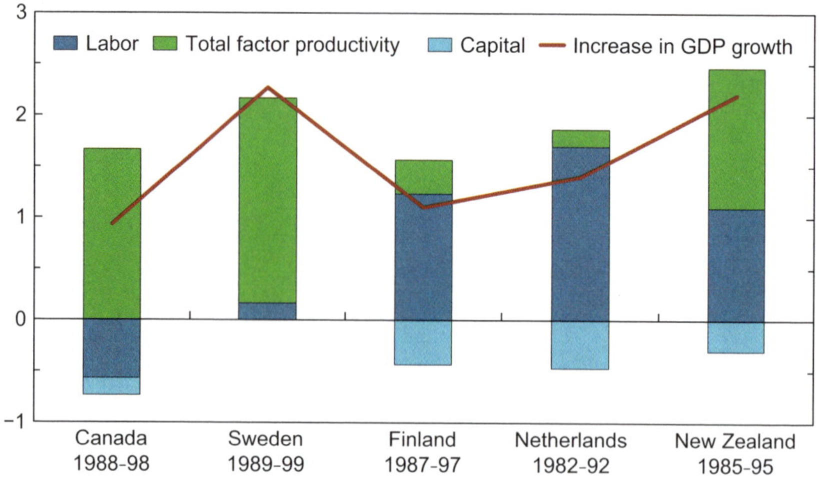

	Canada 1988–98	Sweden 1989–99	Finland 1987–97	Netherlands 1982–92	New Zealand 1985–95

Legend: Labor, Total factor productivity, Capital, Increase in GDP growth

Source: Organisation for Economic Co-operation and Development (2010); and IMF staff estimates.

experienced two decades of rapid growth and the Netherlands became known for its employment miracle.

HOW CAN JAPAN RAISE GROWTH?

To raise potential growth significantly, Japan's growth reforms will most likely need to proceed simultaneously on multiple fronts. The government needs to proceed with measures under the first and second arrows of Abenomics—ending deflation and restoring fiscal sustainability—to establish macroeconomic conditions supportive of higher growth (Figure 6.5).

For the third arrow, however, there appears to be no single measure that could raise growth substantially and quickly. But there are well-defined areas for reform that are essential to make a growth strategy successful. These include:

- Labor reforms to increase employment and make labor markets more efficient to counter the effects of a shrinking labor force resulting from population aging (see Steinberg and Nakane 2011, 2012);
- Reforms that promote competition by opening up protected sectors and easing regulations to enhance productivity and investment;
- Financial sector reforms to raise the provision of risk capital to foster business creation, new investments, and productivity increases;
- A more dynamic business sector spurred by corporate governance and tax reform; and
- Stronger regional economic integration to take advantage of Asia's growth potential.

Figure 6.5 The Three Arrows of Abenomics

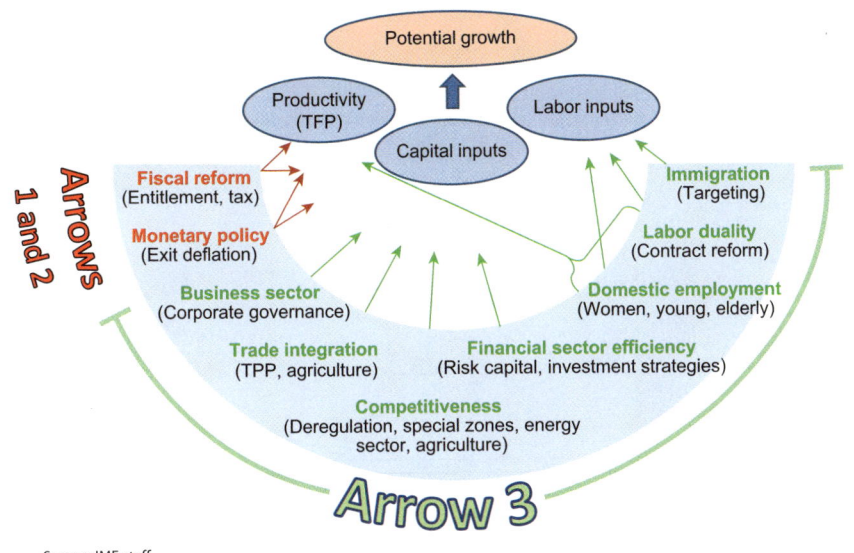

Source: IMF staff.
Note: TFP = total factor productivity; TPP = Trans-Pacific Partnership.

Important synergies exist between aggressive monetary easing, medium-term fiscal consolidation, and structural reforms. In the structural sphere, growth will only increase if complementarities are exploited. These exist between deregulation efforts aimed at developing new markets and greater domestic and foreign labor supply in aging-related services, between providing risk capital for new investment and opening of markets to greater competition, and between trade agreements and efforts to spur greater business dynamism. Indeed, Berger and Danninger (2007) explore the effects of labor and product market deregulation on employment growth. Their empirical results, based on an Organisation for Economic Co-operation and Development (OECD) country panel from 1990–2004, suggest that lower levels of product and labor market regulation foster employment growth, including through sizable interaction effects. The rest of this chapter briefly reviews key structural reforms that, in combination, could have a measurable impact on growth. Following chapters will have a fuller discussion of many of these issues.

More Foreign Labor

Given the decline in the labor force, increasing participation needs to be an integral part of any growth strategy for Japan. There is much the country can still do to mitigate the decline in the size of its workforce relative to other OECD countries, since both immigration and female labor force participation are low (Figure 6.6). Chapter 7 discusses options for raising labor force participation and the efficiency of labor markets, including by reducing the duality between workers with regular and nonregular employment contracts.

Figure 6.6 Immigration and Female Labor Participation *(Percent share of foreign labor and percent share of women in labor force)*

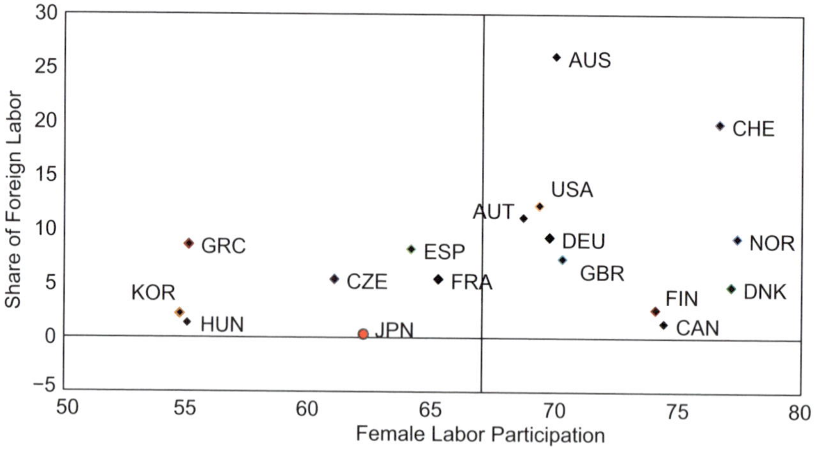

[Scatter plot: X-axis "Female Labor Participation" from 50 to 80; Y-axis "Share of Foreign Labor" from -5 to 30. Data points: AUS (~72, 25), CHE (~78, 20), USA (~68, 14), AUT (~67, 11), GRC (~55, 8), ESP (~63, 7), DEU (~68, 7), NOR (~76, 7), GBR (~69, 5), CZE (~61, 5), FRA (~64, 5), DNK (~76, 5), KOR (~54, 4), FIN (~73, 3), HUN (~56, 2), CAN (~74, 1), JPN (~64, 0).]

Sources: Organisation for Economic Co-operation and Development; and International Migration Database.
Note: AUS = Australia; AUT = Austria; CAN = Canada; CHE = Switzerland; CZE = Czech Republic; DEU = Germany; DNK = Denmark; ESP = Spain; FRA = France; FIN = Finland; GBR = United Kingdom; GRC = Greece; HUN = Hungary; JPN = Japan; KOR = Korea; NOR = Norway; USA = United States.

A complementary reform option is to raise the level of foreign labor.[1] In 2013, the government introduced a points-based, preferential immigration treatment system to attract highly skilled foreign professionals. Broadening eligibility criteria to include a spectrum of different skill sets could overcome employment bottlenecks in nontradable sectors such as construction, childcare, and long-term care for the elderly. Substantial scope exists to increase the percentage of foreign-born workers, currently about 1.7 percent of the total work force.[2]

Highly skilled immigrants could also be an important source for innovation in traditional sectors. Kerr and Kerr (2011) report that, in the United States, immigrants represented almost one half of the engineering workforce based on the 2000 census and several studies connect high-skill immigration to growth in innovation in cities or states. Foreign labor has also become a key in providing long-term care for aging populations. The vast majority of studies suggest that immigration does not exert significant effects on native labor market outcomes, either on employment or earnings. Japan could consider a more ambitious, targeted immigration policy for high-skilled workers and implement it within the newly established special economic zones.

---

[1] Raising potential growth by ½ percent would require additional employment of ½–1 million (out of an 80 million person labor force) per year.
[2] The actual share is likely much lower, with second-generation Japanese and long-term Korean residents accounting for a significant part of this number.

With the aging of the population and associated fiscal costs, one advantage cited in other economies is the positive impact of immigration on public finances. In Japan, this would be particularly relevant. Although new immigrants improve public finances by raising output and paying taxes, they also consume social services, and so the net effect is difficult to quantify, with most recent studies showing mixed results (Kerr and Kerr 2011).

Potential labor market displacement effects may also emerge because of an increase in the labor supply. In general, this should put downward pressure on overall wages, with the impact largest on relative wages or employment of natives for whom immigrants are close substitutes. This overall effect on wages needs to be weighed against the benefits from higher aggregate demand and stronger growth (see Chapter 3). In the health and old-age care industry, where wages are already 25 percent lower than other industries, there is a strong concern that immigration would put further downward pressure on wages or at least prevent them from rising. International evidence of these effects, however, is mixed, with the majority of studies unable to substantiate a significantly large impact (Kerr and Kerr 2011). Boubtane, Coulibaly, and Rault (2011) empirically examine the interaction between immigration and host-country economic conditions. They use a large annual dataset on 22 OECD countries over 1987–2009 and provide evidence of migration contributing to host economic prosperity (positive impact on GDP per capita and negative impact on aggregate unemployment, native- and foreign-born unemployment rates). They also find that migration is influenced by host economic conditions (migration responds positively to host GDP per capita and negatively to the host's total unemployment rate).

Beyond increasing the size of the labor force, immigration can also have nontraditional positive impacts on the economy. Saiz (2007) has shown that immigration raised housing prices in the United States, and an emerging literature is linking immigration to increased entrepreneurship (OECD 2011). In addition, although recent immigrants tend to have lower earnings than natives, the increasing use of point systems—in, for example, Australia, Canada, and the United Kingdom—raises the skill level of immigrants. Finally, immigration can boost entrepreneurship through self-employment and job creation.

One specific sector that would benefit substantially from greater immigration relates to the provision of long-term care for the aged. Long-term care is a small but growing sector globally (Figure 6.7). The OECD (2010) estimates that, in 2008, average long-term care expenditure accounted for 1.5 percent of GDP among its member countries. Spending will quite likely more than double over the coming decades and could exceed 4 percent of GDP in Japan by 2050. Since long-term care is labor intensive, labor demand will probably grow rapidly in line with rising demand for these services.

Long-term care programs globally have steadily evolved and are increasingly shifting to cash benefits with more user choice. There are many different arrangements, but the trend is to move away from fully covered institutional care—which is costly—to more flexible, at-home care arrangements. New cash-for-care programs provide consumers with more choice and control over services (OECD

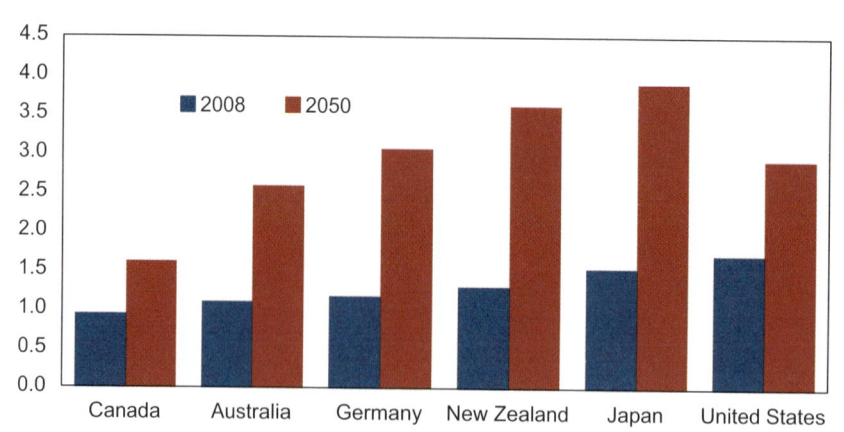

Figure 6.7 Projected Demand for Long-Term Care Workers *(Percent of labor force)*

[Bar chart showing 2008 and 2050 values for Canada, Australia, Germany, New Zealand, Japan, United States]

Source: Organisation for Economic Co-operation and Development.
Note: As a percentage of full-time nurses and personal caregivers to total projected working population.

2010). Recent reforms in Austria, Finland, and Germany, for instance, provide cash benefits for targeted groups, such as disabled elderly, which they then can use to hire home-care help from private providers. Services vary and usually imply some private cost sharing.

Because of domestic shortages, many countries rely on immigration to supply long-term care services. In Europe, labor mobility within the European Union and simplified licensing requirements provided a boost for such activities. From a growth perspective, a flexible long-term care program can raise growth by:

- Freeing up captured labor or preventing family caregivers from dropping out of the labor market, while providing employment for the underemployed. The availability of qualified in-home care for the elderly reduces demands on family members, mostly women, to provide care. A study on Australia estimates the opportunity cost of forgone earnings as a result of unpaid family care of the elderly as equivalent to nearly 10 percent of the total expenditure on formal health care in the country (Manaaki 2009). In several countries, trained foreign workers meet the growing service need, but this could also be a source of employment for underemployed domestic labor.

- Creating a new private service market. Country experiences, such as in Austria, show that long-term care programs with cash benefits, adequate choice, and quality control address a rising unmet demand (Riedel and Kraus 2010). Although the funding for these services still comes primarily from the public sector, they reduce the demand for more costly institutional care and increase private spending. A well-functioning market could draw in private household saving and generate a new services market that could in turn produce substantial employment and income.

Competitiveness Reforms: Opening Protected Sectors and Easing Regulations

Japan's domestic-oriented sectors account for more than 80 percent of activity. Comparisons of productivity levels across countries, especially of services, are unreliable and differences in preferences (such as for more labor-intensive services) may play a role. But time-series data show that productivity growth in Japan's tradable sector has been much higher than in services (Ogawa, Saito, and Tokutsu 2012) (Figure 6.8). One reason for the slower productivity growth in services could be the lingering effects of past public support policies—for example, exemptions and weak penalties in the Antimonopoly Act—which have limited competition. Promising initiatives include:

- *Special economic zones.* The designation in 2014 of large parts of the Japanese economy for these zones, including nine regions in Tokyo and Osaka, could accelerate deregulation and enhance dynamism. The small size of areas dedicated to pilot projects or an ineffective decision-making process have hampered past efforts to reduce red tape. The government's new approach of exploiting economies of scale could overcome these problems, although it will take time to assess whether this will be successful and be used as a laboratory for nation-wide reforms.

- *Reforming the agricultural sector.* Although affecting only a small share of the economy, reforming the agricultural sector could have an important catalytic effect for broader reforms. To promote land consolidation, the government in late 2013 approved a bill setting up a land consolidation bank for each prefecture. The establishment of land banks could help consolidate

Figure 6.8 Japan Labor Productivity Index *(2000 = 100)*

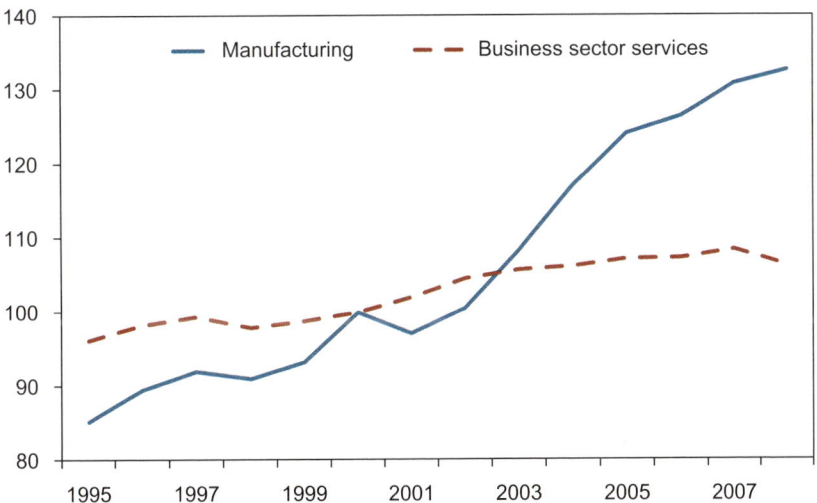

Source: Organisation for Economic Co-operation and Development.

farmlands by allowing renters to combine plots through leasing them. The government is also phasing out subsidies that provide incentives to maintain small land plots. While it is difficult to assess the overall economic impact of these reforms, productivity increases within the agricultural sector could be substantial. Naomasa (2013) estimates that productivity improvement from greater economies of scale could exceed 60 percent, based on estimates derived by comparing TFP rates across regions with different average agricultural plot sizes.

- *Reforms in the energy sector.* These have proceeded swiftly. Legislation passed in late 2013 and early 2014 laid out a road map for opening the electricity grid to other suppliers, tariff regulation, and an eventual separation of the network from electricity production. The new legislation is a fundamental departure from the past structure of Japan's energy market. It aims to infuse more competition into the sector and promises substantial efficiency gains if protected areas can indeed be opened up.

The growth benefits of deregulation could also be seen in downstream industries. Reforms would not only generate efficiency gains in the directly affected sectors, but also have positive spillover on sectors that use services as inputs. A recent cross-country study finds that greater service sector competition is associated with greater output growth, productivity gains, and exports in downstream sectors (Barone and Cingano 2011). Across industries, the effect is more pronounced in energy provision and through regulation of professional services. In terms of the size of firms, there is a particular need to reform the small and medium-sized enterprise (SME) sector, including restoring incentives for corporate restructuring to facilitate firm entry and exit (see Chapter 8 for a fuller discussion).

Financial Sector and Corporate Governance Reform

More effective financial intermediation and a greater willingness to allow SME restructuring could foster innovation, raise investment, and help generate new markets. The availability of credit appears ample, but the pervasive risk aversion of financial institutions and underdeveloped risk management tools have constrained financing for more risky investments in new growth areas. At the same time, a reluctance to let nonviable zombie firms fail and government involvement in credit intermediation (for example, through credit guarantees) have weakened credit assessment capacity, limited SME turnover, and kept corporate debt levels among SMEs high. Chapter 9 discusses how financial sector policies can help promote growth.

Japanese companies have high savings compared with other Group of Seven countries and comparable tax rates on dividend income (Figure 6.9). But the preference for holding large amounts of cash prevents them from increasing wages (Chapter 7) and investment (Chapter 9), holding back aggregate demand and potential growth. This view is consistent with Shinada (2012), who uses Japanese firm-level data for 1980–2010 to analyze the impact of cash holdings on business performance. His results suggest that conservative cash management—regardless

Figure 6.9 Composite Taxation on Dividend Income, 2014 *(Percent; corporate plus individual tax rate)*

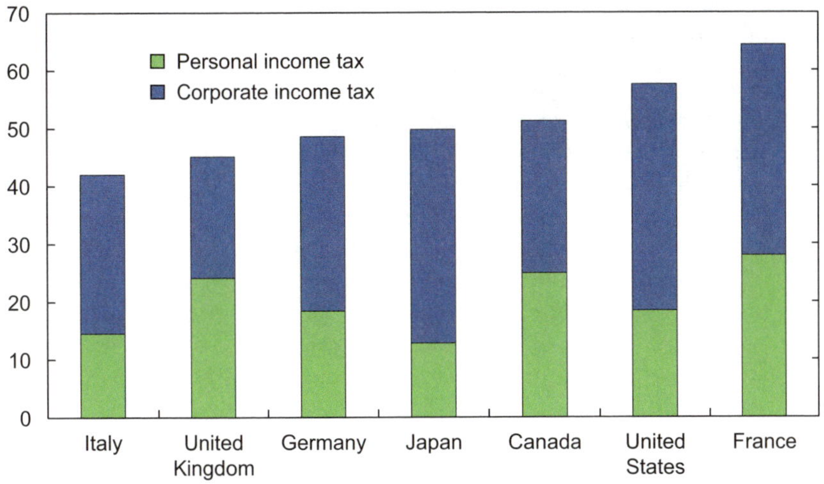

Source: Organisation for Economic Co-operation and Development.

of large investment opportunities—increases "side-line" cash and firms cannot fully utilize investment opportunities to maximize return on assets.

The existing literature suggests that corporate governance is a significant determinant of cash holdings and that Japan fares worse compared with other Group of Seven countries on firm-level governance attributes; for example, boards, audits, shareholder rights, ownership, and compensation. Aoyagi and Ganelli (2014), using a panel of Japanese companies, suggest that improving corporate governance—proxied in the regression by an index summarizing company disclosure of governance data—could reduce corporate cash holdings and contribute to the recovery. Reform options include complementing the recently introduced stewardship code for institutional investors with a corporate governance code for firms, and expanding the use of outside directors.

As noted in the previous chapter, taxation might also play a role in affecting corporate cash holdings since Japan has one of the highest statutory corporate tax rates among advanced economies. Reducing the corporate tax rate could help stimulate investment demand but, given high public debt, fiscal implications need to be taken into account. Tax reforms also need to take incentives for debt financing into account, which could keep firms cash holdings high. Kunieda and Shibata (2005) argue that higher corporate taxes make debt financing more attractive than other means of financing, thus reducing free cash flows.

Tapping into Regional Dynamism

On the international stage, Japan has not taken full advantage of its growth potential in a number of areas. During the last decade, export market shares have declined and inward foreign direct investment is low, which has reduced gains from technology spillover and limited competition in domestic sectors. According to the OECD, Japan had the lowest import penetration rate for services in 2003 and the lowest growth rate of service imports during 1997–2005. Taking advantage of Asia's economic dynamism should therefore be a centerpiece of growth reforms. Measures to better tap into overseas growth potential include:

- *Pursuing free trade or economic agreements.* Japan has lagged in signing trade agreements, especially with the United States, the euro area, China, and Korea. It did, however, make a breakthrough in 2014 with a new trade deal with Australia. The most promising development on the multilateral front has been Japan's decision to join membership negotiations of the Trans-Pacific Partnership free trade agreement. This is envisioned as a high-standard, twenty-first century trade agreement that includes commitments covering all aspects of trade and investment. It includes many regional trading partners like the United States, Canada, and Mexico. As such the partnership is seen as a starting point for a broader free trade area in Asia and the Pacific.

  The Trans-Pacific Partnership requires unfettered market access for foreign companies to domestic markets, including agriculture and services, potentially triggering domestic reform and efficiency gains. The immediate economic effects from lowering tariffs are estimated to be 0.2–0.3 percent of GDP based on estimates derived from the Global Trade Analysis Project model. The analysis is static in the sense that it only captures the economic efficiency impact of a tariff removal, but no allowance is made for more dynamic adjustments, such as incorporating the impact of capital accumulation and productivity improvements. The main economic gains may be substantially larger (see Schott, Kotschwar, and Muir 2013) and come from efficiency increases associated with the opening of domestic markets by fostering more competition and innovation. Any such gains will quite likely accrue gradually, in line with the usually extensive phase-in periods of trade agreements.

- *Promoting inward foreign direct investment.* This should be pursued by reducing legal and nonlegal impediments, especially in services, and strengthening the business environment. Trade agreements could help with the harmonization or mutual recognition of licenses. Agreeing on common standards and qualification requirements would also substantially enhance market integration and reduce setup costs of foreign firms.

CONCLUSION

Japan's growth performance over the past two decades has been robust if population aging is excluded. However, higher growth is needed to bring down the high debt-to-GDP ratio and sustain stable inflation. International evidence shows that comprehensive reforms can raise potential growth up to 1 percent over the course of a decade, but only few advanced economies have achieved this. Attaining higher growth requires raising labor supply—to counter the effects of a declining population—complemented by deregulation to increase competition and innovation, a greater supply of risk capital to fund new activities, corporate governance reforms, and closer economic and trade integration with the region to take advantage of Asia's high growth momentum. Since these reforms will take time, steady progress on the third arrow of Abenomics is needed. Only then can Japan overcome its growth challenge.

REFERENCES

Aoyagi, C., and G. Ganelli. 2014. "Unstash the Cash! Corporate Governance Reform in Japan." IMF Working Paper No. 14/140. International Monetary Fund, Washington, DC.

Bank of Japan. 2014. "Toward the Early Achievement of the 2 Percent Price Stability Target and Sustainable Growth of Japan's Economy." Speech at the Keizai Doyukai (Japan Association of Corporate Executives) Members' Meeting in Tokyo delivered by Haruhiko Kuroda, Governor of the Bank of Japan.

Barone, G., and F. Cingano. 2011. "Service Regulation and Growth: Evidence from OECD Countries." *Economic Journal* 121 (555): 931–57.

Berger, H., and S. Danninger. 2007. "The Employment Effects of Labor and Product Market Deregulation and Their Implications for Structural Reform." *IMF Staff Papers* 54 (3): 591–619.

Brooks, R. 1990. "Male and Female Labour Force Participation in New Zealand 1978–1988." Discussion Paper G90/3. Wellington: Reserve Bank of New Zealand.

Boubtane, E., D. Coulibaly, and C. Rault. 2011. "Immigration, Unemployment, and GDP in the Host Country: Bootstrap Panel Granger Causality Analysis on OECD Countries." CEPII Working Papers No. 2011-29. Paris: CEPII Research Center.

Doi, T., and T. Ihori. 2006. "Soft-Budget Constraints and Local Expenditures," CIRJE F-Series CIRJE-F-422. Tokyo: Center for International Research on the Japanese Economy.

Hoshi, T., and A. Kashyap. 2010. "Why Did Japan Stop Growing?" Report prepared for the National Institute for Research Advancement.

International Monetary Fund. 2011. *Regional Economic Outlook: Asia and Pacific*. April, Washington.

———. 2014. "Japan: Staff Report for the 2014 Article IV Consultation." IMF Country Report No. 14/236, Washington.

Kerr, S.P., and W.R. Kerr. 2011. "Economic Impacts of Immigration: A Survey." NBER Working Papers No. 16736. Cambridge, Massachusetts: National Bureau of Economic Research.

Kunieda, T., and A. Shibata. 2005. "Credit Constraints and the Current Account: A Test for the Japanese Economy." *Journal of International Money and Finance* 24 (8): 1261–77.

Manaaki, T. 2009. "How Should We Care for the Careers, Now and into the Future?" National Health Committee of New Zealand. Wellington: Ministry of Health.

Naomasa, E. 2013. "Economies of Scale and the Total Factor Productivity of Japanese Agriculture: Quantitative Analysis with Prefecture-Level Data." Unpublished. International Monetary Fund, Washington, DC.

Ogawa, K., M. Saito, and I. Tokutsu. 2012. "Japan Out of the Lost Decade: Divine Wind or Firms' Effort?" IMF Working Paper No. 12/171. International Monetary Fund, Washington, DC.

Ono, H. 2010, "Lifetime Employment in Japan: Concepts and Measurements." *Journal of the Japanese and International Economies* 24 (1): 127.

Organisation for Economic Co-operation and Development (OECD). 2010. *Going for Growth*. Paris: OECD.

———. 2011. *Help Wanted? Providing and Paying for Long-Term Care*. Paris: OECD.

———. 2013. *OECD Tax Statistics*. Paris: OECD.

Riedel, M., and M. Kraus. 2010. "The Austrian Long-term Care System." ENEPRI Research Report No. 69. Brussels: Centre for European Policy Studies.

Saiz, A. 2007. "Immigration and Housing Rents in American Cities." *Journal of Urban Economics* 61 (2): 345–71.

Schott, J.J., B. Kotschwar, and J. Muir. 2013. *Understanding the Trans-Pacific Partnership*. Washington, DC: Peterson Institute for International Economics.

Shinada, N. 2012, "Firms' Cash Holdings and Performance: Evidence from Japanese Corporate Finance." RIETI Discussion Papers 12-E-031. Tokyo: Research Institute of Economy, Trade and Industry.

Steinberg, C., and M. Nakane. 2011. "To Fire or to Hoard? Explaining Japan's Labor Market Response in the Great Recession," IMF Working Paper No. 11/15. International Monetary Fund, Washington, DC.

———. 2012. "Can Women Save Japan?" IMF Working Paper No. 12/248. International Monetary Fund, Washington, DC.

CHAPTER 7

Labor Market Reform: Vital to the Success of Abenomics

CHIE AOYAGI AND GIOVANNI GANELLI

Japan's labor market has traditionally been characterized by the lifetime employment system, under which employers refrain from firing workers and workers implicitly commit not to switch employment until retirement. The lifetime employment system served the country well during the high-growth decades by facilitating the accumulation of firm-specific human capital and building trust between employer and employee. The image of the Japanese "salaryman," who returns home from work late at night after long hours in the office is legendary. Such devotion has been traditionally rewarded by employers, who in Japan tend to feel personally responsible for the welfare of employees and their families and are very reluctant to lay off workers. Even during 2009–10, as Japan felt the impact of the global economic crisis, unemployment was just slightly above 5 percent, compared with 8 percent on average in the Organisation for Economic Co-operation and Development (OECD).

Despite its advantages, the Japanese lifetime employment system has resulted in limited labor mobility and impaired broader economic restructuring. As a consequence, companies have responded to the lack of employment flexibility embedded in the traditional lifetime system by expanding their use of nonregular workers.

However, a closer look at Japan's labor market trends shows that labor market duality—a two-tier job market—has forcefully emerged over the last two decades. The traditional lifetime employment system, often referred to as regular employment, was challenged by declining job growth in the wake of the asset bubble collapse in the early 1990s, leading to the Lost Decade. The prolonged recession, together with labor law reforms, which made it easier to hire nonregular workers, gave firms incentives to explore alternative human resource practices. One result of these factors was to shut out a growing share of workers from the traditional lifetime employment model. As we discuss in more detail in this chapter, Japan's labor market duality has become excessive and is likely having a detrimental effect on labor productivity and potential growth.

The problems posed by the erosion of the lifetime employment system and the attendant rise in duality are not the only difficulties facing the country's labor market. Japan is also experiencing the sharpest labor force decline among the advanced economies through rapid population aging. As a result, policymakers

107

have been tasked with implementing reforms aimed at simultaneously increasing labor supply and labor productivity. In this chapter we argue that these reforms should include measures to increase labor participation of women, foreigners, and older workers, as well as contract reform to help reduce labor-market duality. But these reforms will unavoidably take time to design and to raise potential economic growth. Furthermore, while we expect the medium- and long-term impact of these reforms to be reflationary because of the higher growth that they will generate (see Chapter 3), some policies might have a deflationary impact in the short term depending on the precise timing of the boost to aggregate demand on the one hand and the reduction of average wages on the other.

With this in mind, it is important to note that in addition to the need to raise medium-term growth, there is also a need for shorter-term policies that could help get Abenomics off the ground, including measures to help exit deflation. Such policies should encourage the transition of Abenomics from its first phase, which has been driven mostly by monetary and fiscal stimulus, to a second phase which should be driven in a more sustainable way by the private sector (see Chapter 3). For this to happen, nominal wages need to start increasing. Higher wages would help break the deflationary spiral and establish a virtuous growth cycle. This chapter argues that key policy options to achieve this could include social "concertation" and tax incentives to encourage wage growth, and using the minimum wage as a policy tool to help increase the average nominal wage.[1]

Given that several advanced economies are facing rapid population aging and increasing labor market duality, the issues discussed in this chapter with reference to Japan could also provide some useful lessons for policymakers in other countries.

LABOR MARKET TRENDS

Japan's rapid population aging implies that the country is experiencing the sharpest labor force decline among advanced economies. According to current population projections, the working-age population (those aged 15–64) will fall from its peak of 87 million in 1995 to about 55 million in 2050. Population aging has obviously contributed to lowering potential growth. In principle, the drop in labor supply related to aging could be mitigated by immigration and increased labor participation of segments of the population under-represented in the labor market, such as women. As Steinberg and Nakane (2011) stress, however, Japan has lower immigration and female labor participation (FLP) rates than other advanced economies (see Chapter 6).

Although population aging has contributed to sluggish growth in Japan, the country fares well by international comparison on unemployment. The jobless rate has been low, albeit steadily increasing in the last three decades. The 10-year

---

[1]Social concertation refers to a process of continuous interaction between social partners, which can include, at the macro level, centralized agreements and, at the micro level, company-level consultation practices.

average unemployment rate rose from 2.5 percent in the 1980s to 3 percent in the 1990s and to 4.7 percent in the 2000s (Figure 7.1). This is remarkably low compared with other advanced economies. Even in the wake of the most recent global financial crisis, it increased only a modest 1 percentage point, compared with increases of about 5 percentage points in the United States and 2 percentage points in the United Kingdom.

Even so, the problem of skill mismatches in certain sectors might need special attention. Shibata (2013) finds that some occupation types (production processing, engineering; services; transportation; information and communication; defense; agricultural, forestry, and fishing), have a disproportionately higher share of hires relative to their corresponding shares of unemployed workers compared with others (such as clerks, sales personnel, and managers). Such occupational mismatches accounted for about 20–40 percent of recent increases in unemployment, suggesting that skill mismatches are as big an issue as in other advanced economies.

Steinberg and Nakane (2011) document the fact that in Japan the response of unemployment to output fluctuations (Okun's law) has been historically lower than in other advanced economies. They explain that, even though Japan's Okun's law coefficient has increased over time, the country managed to limit employment losses during the last crisis because of its quick implementation of an employment subsidy program—which provided incentives for firms to hoard labor during the crisis—and owing to downward nominal wage flexibility.

Despite this last fact, wages tend to be upwardly rigid and do not automatically increase during periods of labor market tightening. As a consequence, real wage growth has lagged productivity in Japan during the last two decades (Figure 7.2). Even during the economic revival of 2002–2008, real wage growth was

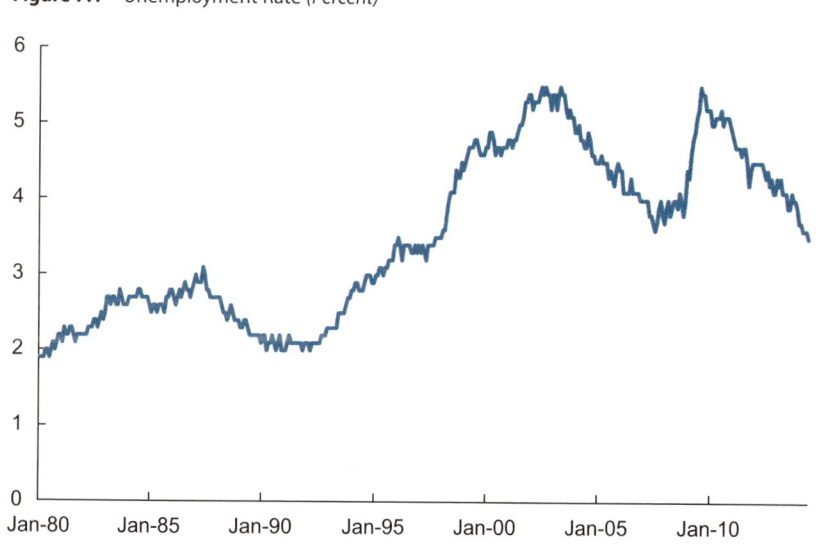

Figure 7.1 Unemployment Rate *(Percent)*

Source: Labor Force Survey Database.

Figure 7.2 Wages, Productivity, and Labor Share

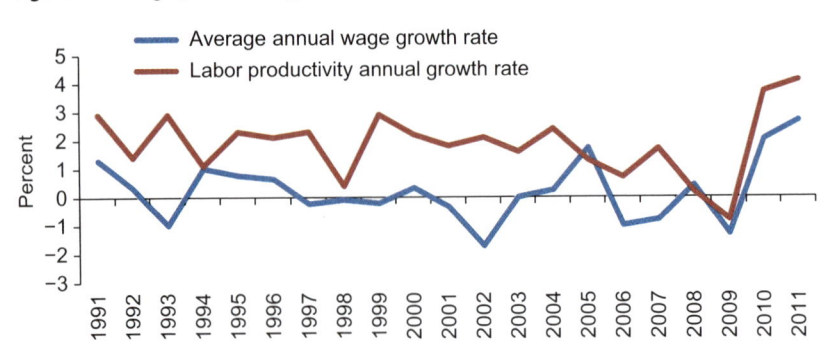

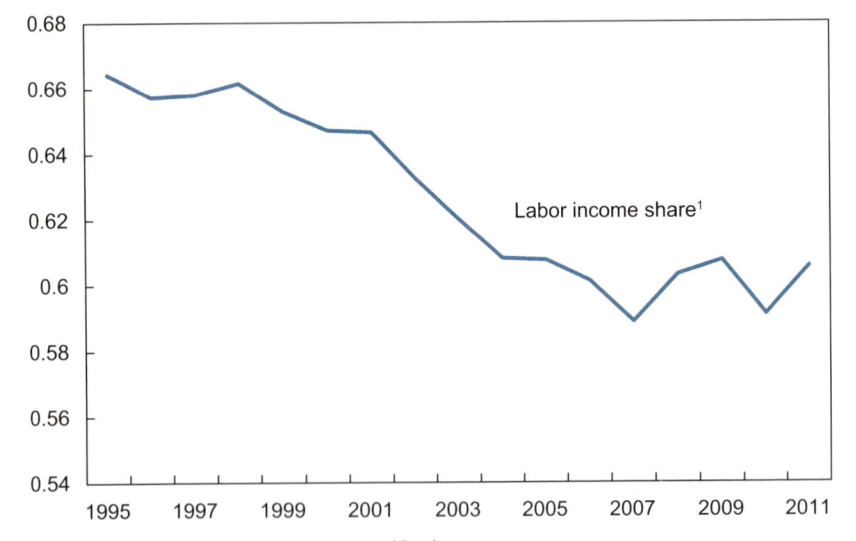

Source: Organisation for Economic Co-operation and Development.
[1] Calculated as total labor costs divided by nominal output.

slightly higher than productivity only in two years. In this regard, Japan also stands out among Group of Seven countries. These trends have resulted in a decline in labor's share of income (Figure 7.2).

Several explanations for Japan's sluggish wage growth, both cyclical and structural, have been offered; for example, by Sommer (2009) and Aoyagi and Ganelli (2014). These include:

- An emphasis on reducing costs related to the deflationary mindset;
- Competitiveness concerns;
- The waning influence of the coordinated spring wage negotiations (*shunto*) in affecting overall wages;
- Structural characteristics of Japan's labor market—such as low horizontal mobility of workers, intra-firm job rotation, and the seniority-based wage

system—which reduce incentives to increase wages to attract workers from competitors;

- A weak small and medium-sized enterprise sector, accounting for nearly 70 percent of employment, which may not have benefited from Abenomics because of higher energy costs as well as other intermediate imported goods costs caused by the weaker yen; and
- The increasing share in the labor market of nonregular workers, who have less bargaining power and lower wages (Figure 7.3).

The share of nonregular workers increased dramatically in Japan in the last two decades. Although nonregular workers accounted for less than 20 percent of total employment before the bubble burst in the early 1990s, their share has now reached 35 percent (Figure 7.3). In addition, microeconomic studies show that the probability of moving from a nonregular to a regular job in Japan— ranging from 1.7 to 10.3 percent—is very low compared with other advanced economies (for example, about 45 percent in Germany and 30 percent in the United Kingdom). As discussed in Aoyagi and Ganelli (2013), the net effect of the "duality" of the Japanese labor market on potential growth is likely to be negative because nonregular workers tend to be less motivated and less trained than regular ones.

Given the importance of increasing labor supply and labor productivity to boost potential growth, the rest of this chapter discusses policy options for labor market reforms that should be implemented as part of the growth strategy, the third arrow of Abenomics.

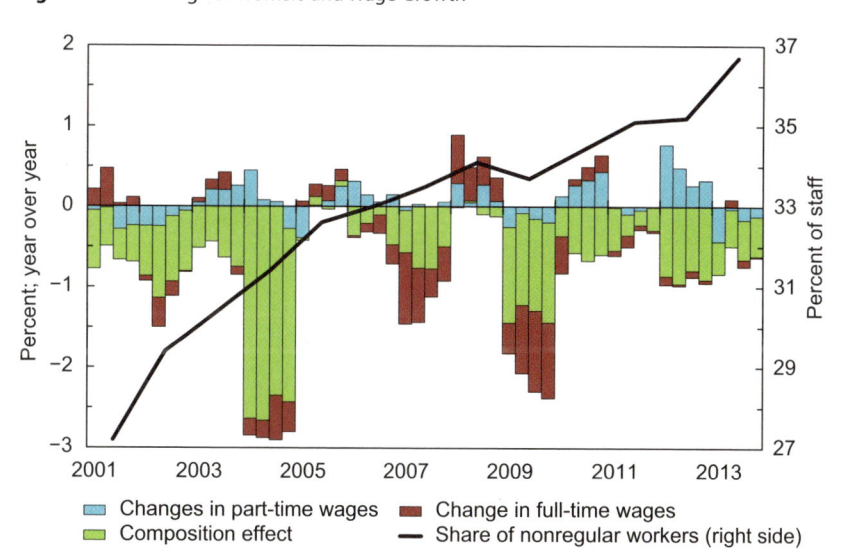

Figure 7.3 Nonregular Workers and Wage Growth

Sources: Haver Analytics; and IMF staff estimates.

OPTIONS FOR LABOR MARKET REFORM

Increasing Female Labor Participation

Given the low participation of women in Japan's labor market compared with other countries, any strategy aimed at raising labor supply will have to include measures to increase FLP. Steinberg and Nakane (2012), for example, estimate that if Japan were to raise its FLP ratio to the level of the Group of Seven (excluding Italy and Japan), GDP per capita would be about 4 percent higher. Their calculations are based on a rise in the FLP rate from 63 percent in 2010 to 70 percent in 2030. They also estimate that a further increase in FLP rates—for example to the level of northern European countries—could increase GDP per capita by an additional 4 percent (Figure 7.4). Under these two scenarios, Japan's potential growth would be 0.2 and 0.4 percentage point higher, respectively.

Steinberg and Nakane (2012) identify three main hurdles to higher FLP and provide policy recommendations to address them. The first is related to employment and promotion policies, which tend to relegate women to support positions, with little investment made in their human capital. This is reflected in the very low number of female managers in Japan compared with other advanced economies (Figure 7.5). To address this, Steinberg and Nakane (2012) suggest measures aimed at encouraging more equitable promotion policies and increasing the number of female role models; for example, by establishing rules for the minimum number of female directors on boards.

The second main hurdle to higher FLP is related to balancing family responsibilities with work. Japan has FLP rates similar to other advanced economies for women in their early twenties, but the participation rate drops off sharply from

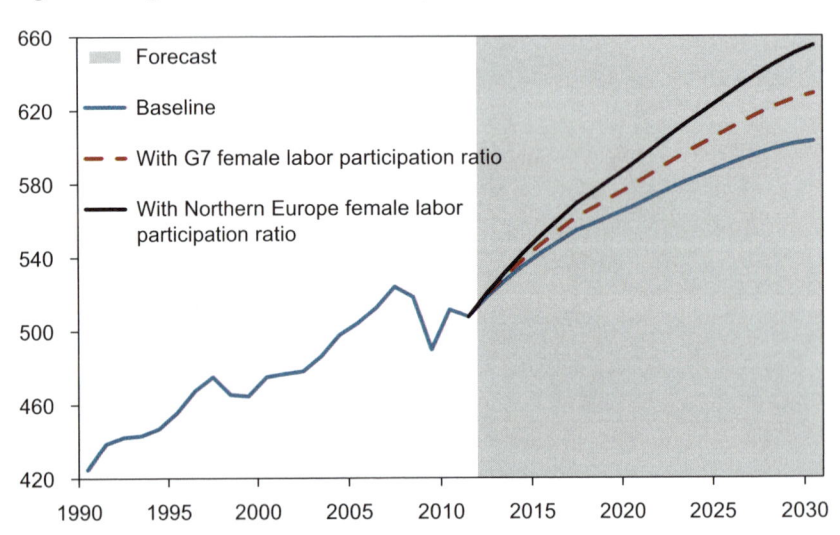

Figure 7.4 Higher Female Labor Force Participation and Real GDP *(Trillion yen)*

Sources: IMF, *World Economic Outlook*; and IMF staff estimates and projections.

Figure 7.5 Female Managers in Selected Economies, 2009 *(Percent of total managers)*

Source: United Nations Development Programme.

the late twenties, reflecting that some 60 percent of Japanese women quit work after giving birth to their first child (Figure 7.6). Steinberg and Nakane (2012) suggest that policies to address this should include extending the duration of parental leave, which in Japan is near OECD averages but generally less than in major European countries; encouraging men to take parental leave; and increasing

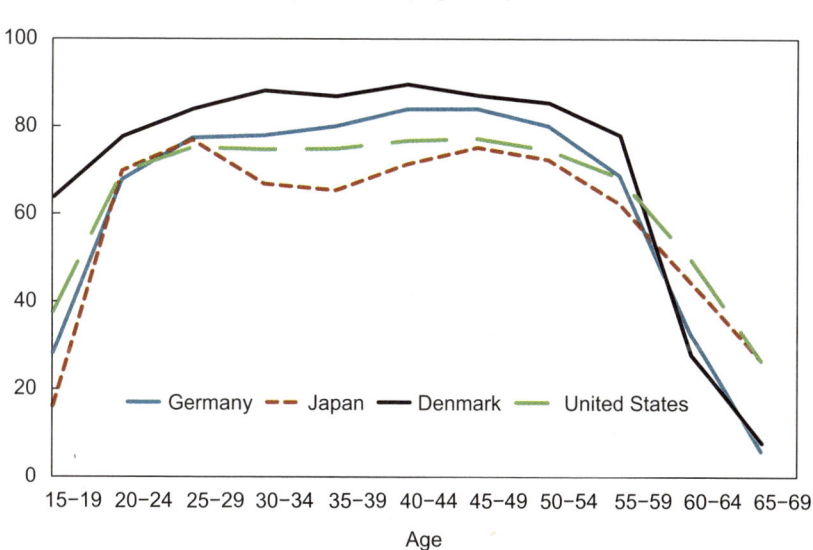

Figure 7.6 Female Labor Participation Rate by Age Group, 2009 *(Percent)*

Source: Organisation for Economic Co-operation and Development.

the availability of child care, for which demand largely outstrips supply. The authorities have recently put a lot of emphasis on the latter and have increased the budget for public provision of child care. This is clearly a welcome development, but removing bureaucratic obstacles to the private provision of child care would also be useful. Since deregulation of the sector in 2000, private companies have been allowed to operate publicly funded child care facilities, but the local authorities are cautious about choosing private operators and this model is not widespread. Reforms aimed at allaying local authorities' concerns could lead to a more significant private sector response.

The tax system is another important factor discouraging women from fully participating in the workforce. In Japan, a head of a household can claim a dependent exemption as long as the spouse's annual income is less than 1.03 million yen (see Chapter 5). This is often referred to as the "barrier to full-time female employment," in that households' second earners (which in most cases are female) tend to prefer part-time to full-time work so as not to exceed this threshold. Steinberg and Nakane (2012) point out that eliminating this tax distortion would encourage more married women to seek full-time employment, and they note that this monetary incentive could be especially important for low-income households.

Relaxation of Immigration Requirements

Relaxing immigration requirements should also be considered given substantial scope to increase the supply of foreign-born workers. The government recently introduced a points-based preferential immigration treatment system to attract highly skilled foreign professionals, as noted in the previous chapter, but a more ambitious targeted immigration policy for the highly skilled would be useful. Furthermore, given labor shortages, this measure could be broadened to include lower-skilled immigrants who could help eliminate employment bottlenecks in nontradable sectors, such as child care, long-term care for the elderly, and construction. While limited steps have been taken in this direction, especially in the construction sector in preparation for the 2020 Olympics, a more comprehensive approach would be desirable (see Chapter 6 for a more extensive discussion).

Increasing Labor Participation of Older Workers

The labor force decline caused by population aging can also be counteracted by measures promoting the continued participation of older workers in the labor force, particularly by increasing the standard retirement age, currently 65 years, and making early retirement possible at age 60 (see Chapter 5 for a discussion on the effects of pension reform options). Although a standard retirement age of 65 is not out of line with other advanced economies (the OECD average is 64.4 years), it is incongruous with Japan's high and rising longevity—which at 82.6 years is the highest in the OECD—and the high and improving health conditions of older people. A recent law that encourages firms to rehire productive workers aged 60–64 on nonregular contracts has helped to lift employment rates for workers in this age group from 53 percent in 2006 to 57 percent in 2010. Despite this, employment rates still fall significantly with age, from 75 percent in the 55–59 age group in 2010 to 57 percent of the 60–64 age group and 36 percent of the 65–69 age group (OECD 2011).

Increasing the average retirement age would not only increase labor participation, but also reduce cost pressures on the pension system, strengthening the medium-term fiscal outlook and lessening the need for contractionary near-term adjustment. However, raising the average retirement age under the current lifetime employment system may create inequities for younger generations by making it more difficult for new graduates to enter the labor market in regular jobs, because current workers retire later. Thus, achieving greater labor participation by raising the retirement age also requires a change from the current lifetime employment system to one that places greater weight on performance and flexibility.

Reducing Duality

Although the recommendations discussed here focus on increasing labor supply through the higher labor force participation of women, foreigners, and older workers, increasing the productivity of labor is also important to raise potential growth. To this end, Aoyagi and Ganelli (2013) argue that reforms aimed at reducing Japan's excessive labor market duality are necessary.

This duality has some positive aspects, for example, it can help satisfy demand for more flexible work arrangements and bring new "voluntary nonregular" workers into the workforce. But it also has potentially sizable economic costs, such as disincentives for workers to exert effort, which can reduce productivity. Female workers in particular comprise a disproportionate share of nonregular workers (Figure 7.7). Microeconomic survey studies show the majority of Japanese

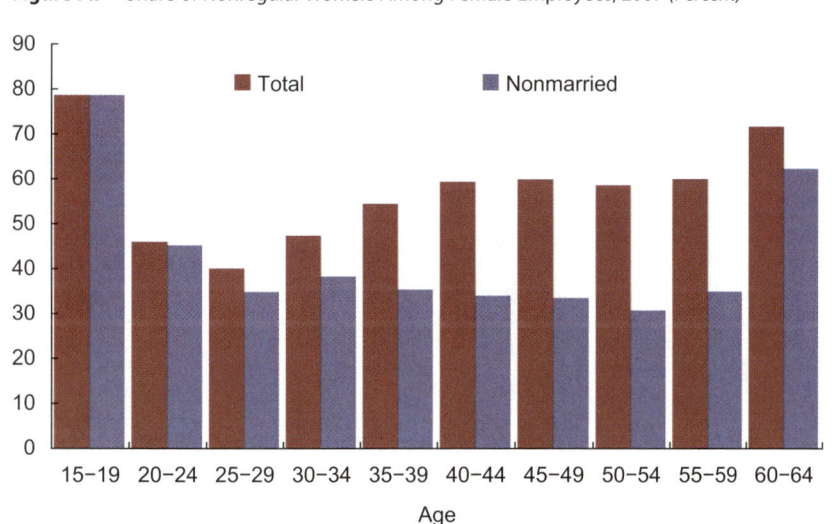

Figure 7.7 Share of Nonregular Workers Among Female Employees, 2007 *(Percent)*

Sources: Ministry of Internal Affairs and Communications; and IMF staff calculations.

nonregular workers would be willing to work as regular employees (Ohtake and others 2011). It is conceivable that working involuntarily as nonregular employees hurts morale and job effort, thus lowering labor productivity. Fukao and others (2007) estimate that Japanese part-time workers are 75 percent less productive than full-time ones.

Another economic cost of duality is related to limited training opportunities for nonregular workers, which also likely reduces productivity. IMF (2013) stresses that firms tend to invest little in their temporary workers in countries with dual labor markets. This is confirmed by a survey of 1,066 Japanese companies, which shows that while 92 percent of them provided training for regular workers, only 42 percent did so for nonregular workers (Kawaguchi and others 2006). A negative impact of duality on productivity in Japan is also supported by the observation that the share of nonregular workers is high in sectors in which labor productivity is low (Figure 7.8).

Aoyagi and Ganelli (2013) use econometric panel data techniques to assess how various economic, demographic, and policy factors affect the degree of labor market duality in OECD countries and investigate the implications of their results for Japan. A key finding is that an increase in the level of employment protection of regular workers (as measured by an OECD index) tends to increase labor market duality, but an increase in the level of employment protection of temporary workers has the opposite effect. One policy implication of these findings is that reducing the difference in the degree of protection between the two categories of workers can go a long way in reducing duality.

Aoyagi and Ganelli (2013) suggest that, for Japan, a reform that would reduce the level of employment protection of regular employees to levels similar to those

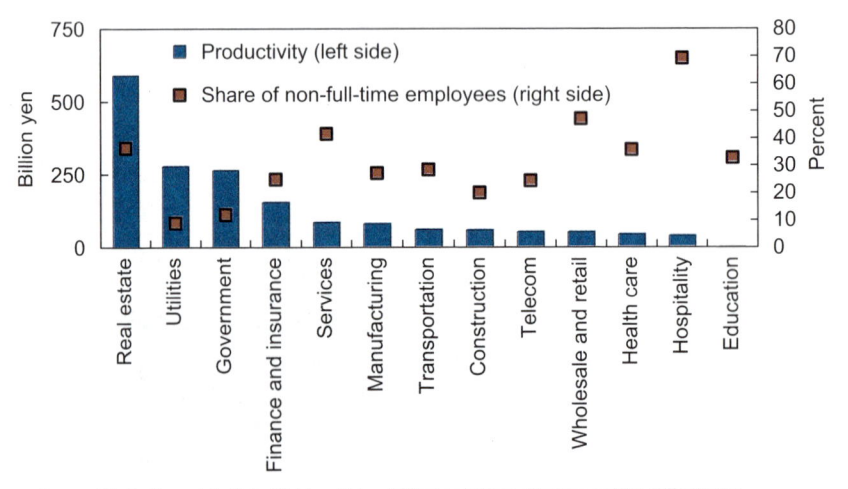

Figure 7.8 Labor Market Duality and Productivity by Sector

Sources: Mizuho Research Institute; Ministry of Internal Affairs and Communications; and IMF staff estimates.
Note: Productivity measured as value added per worker.

observed in Denmark or in the United Kingdom could bring the share of nonregular workers close to or below 30 percent. Their study stresses that these estimates are based only on, with other things being equal, first-round effects. If, as expected, the reduction in labor market duality results in higher growth, this would reduce unemployment and help with exiting deflation. Indeed, according to the econometric results presented in the study, a fall in unemployment and an increase in inflation would occur in a second-round effect of the initial reform, which in turn would further reduce duality. Since, in Japan, the share of nonregular workers is large among women and considerably larger for married women (see Figure 7.7), reducing duality would also increase the number of women in regular positions, creating synergies with reforms aimed at increasing FLP, which were discussed earlier in this chapter.

On the basis of their empirical analysis, Aoyagi and Ganelli (2013) suggest that an effective measure to reduce labor market duality could be replacing all regular and nonregular contracts currently offered to new hires with a single open-ended contract. Under this type of contract, employment protection would increase gradually and severance pay would rise with tenure. Implementing this reform would imply introducing a formal severance pay system, which currently does not exist in Japan. Introducing a single open-ended contract would therefore drastically reduce firms' marginal costs of converting nonregular to regular positions. This type of contract would strike a good middle ground by implying lower job security compared to current regular employment, but higher job security compared to current nonregular employment. Although no country has yet introduced a single open-ended contract, simulations carried out by García-Perez and Osuna (2011) for Spain suggest that it would significantly reduce labor market duality in that country.

A possible first step to implement the recommendations in Aoyagi and Ganelli (2013) could be a wider use of limited regular (*gentei seishain*) contracts. In Japan, employees who are classified as limited regular workers still enjoy regular worker status and benefits, but with limitations on one or more of the following: job content, working hours, and mandatory relocations. Contracts of this kind implicitly introduce lower job protection compared to regular workers, most notably in cases in which limited regular positions are cancelled for economic reasons. For nonregular workers, on the other hand, the possibility to transition to limited regular contracts would imply an improvement in employment protection as well as career and training prospects. The restrictions that the limited regular status puts on working hours, job content, and mandatory relocations would also improve work-life balance, which would be important to encourage FLP, since many female workers give up their regular worker positions after getting married or having their first child in their early thirties (Figure 7.9). An improved work-life balance would also facilitate acceptance of reduced employment protection compared with current regular employment, as discussed later in this section.

Although limited regular contracts already exist in Japan, most companies are reluctant to use them because of uncertainties in the legal framework, especially for dismissals. Reforms aimed at clarifying their legal framework would reduce uncertainties and encourage firms to move nonregular workers to limited regular

Figure 7.9 Number of Female Workers by Employment Type, 2014:Q1 *(In tens of thousands of workers by age)*

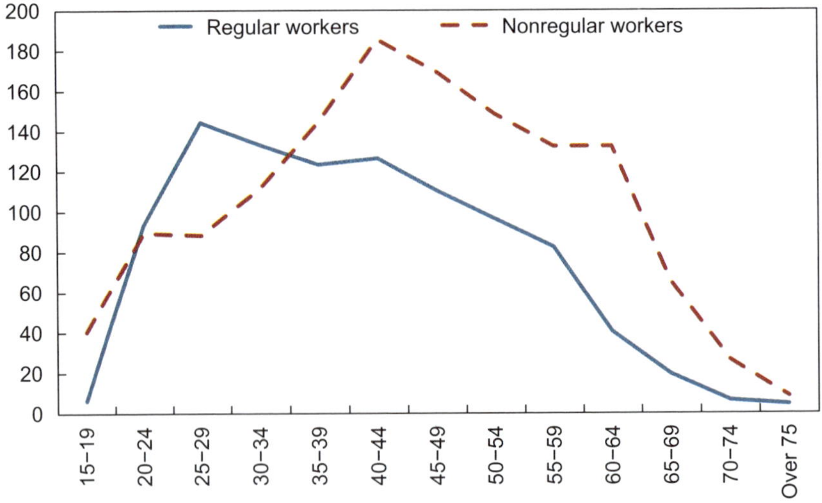

Source: Labor Force Survey.

status, helping reduce labor market duality. Tsuru (2014) argues that a major challenge in expanding the use of limited regular workers is the lack of an adequate explanation for the distinctions in the treatment of limited and regular employees through pre-employment documents, such as employment rules and labor contracts, as well as termination documents. Here, clarifying the distinctions between the two systems and raising the predictability of issues arising from the differences should be important components of reforms in this area.

Shifting toward "Flexicurity"

The introduction of a single open-ended contract or extending the use of limited regular contracts could be complemented by other measures aimed at reducing duality while also helping to build consensus for the reform package. One useful reform would be giving workers the right to choose between part-time and full-time work (after a certain tenure period) while maintaining the same hourly wage and legal rights. This would eliminate the incentive for employers to discriminate in favor of full-time workers in on-the-job training, because any full-time worker might at any time decide to switch to part-time work (and vice versa). Ultimately, part-time workers would no longer be considered nonregular workers. The Netherlands introduced a similar reform in 2000, contributing to a significant increase in FLP. Guaranteeing new hires the future right to choose between part-time and full-time work would facilitate social and political acceptance of the reduced employment protection (compared to current regular employment) implied by the single open-ended contract.

More generally, other elements of the so-called flexicurity model could also be considered in Japan. Reduced employment protection of regular workers could be complemented by measures to encourage more job mobility and to offer greater support to workers during periods of temporary unemployment, such as strengthening programs that help the unemployed to upgrade their skills and encourage job seeking. This would mark a shift away from the current Japanese labor market—characterized by excessive duality and lifetime employment for regular workers—to one more similar to the Danish flexicurity model, in which the focus is on protecting workers rather than jobs. One important measure in this regard would be increasing unemployment insurance benefits, which are low in Japan compared with Denmark and other countries that rely on the flexicurity model (Figure 7.10). As increasing unemployment insurance would likely entail fiscal costs, such a reform should only be considered as part of a comprehensive medium-term fiscal consolidation package that achieves debt sustainability (see Chapter 5 for a discussion on the key elements of such a package). According to the OECD (2013), Japan spends about 0.4 percent of GDP on unemployment insurance compared with the OECD average of 0.8 percent. Strengthening programs that help the unemployed upgrade their skills would also be important to reduce the aforementioned skill mismatches.

For the proposed package of reforms to work, "soft institutions" need to change. To make the reduction in employment protection of regular workers socially and politically acceptable, some negative aspects of regular work also need to be reformed. Options could include improving work-life balance, such as increased accessibility to annual leave, the right to refuse involuntary relocations, and reduction of overtime work. Working until very late (that is, a lot more than the typical 49-hour work week) among full-time workers is very common in Japan and anecdotal evidence suggests that the problem is more serious than in most

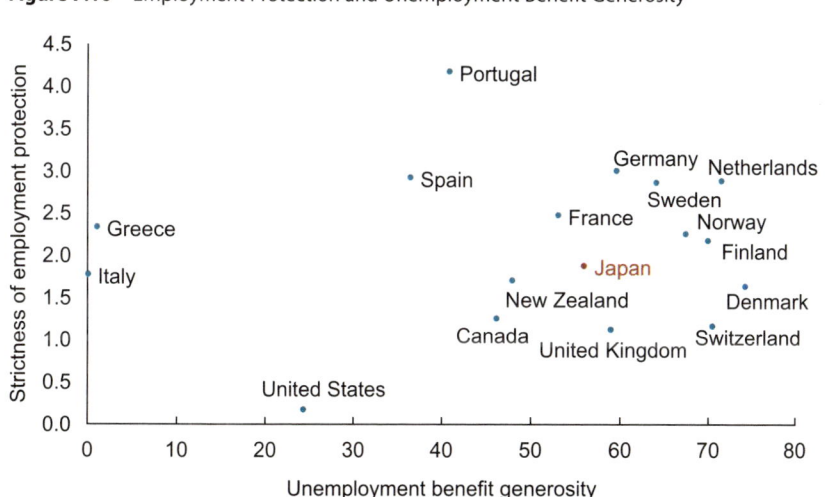

Figure 7.10 Employment Protection and Unemployment Benefit Generosity

Source: Organisation for Economic Co-operation and Development.
Note: Strictness of employment protection is measured as employment protection regulation for regular contracts (2007), unemployment benefit generosity is measured as net replacement rate over five years of unemployment (2007).

other advanced economies. One of the reasons for this is that it is cheaper for firms to ask regular workers to do overtime than to expand employment. The premium that employers have to pay for work outside statutory hours is only 25 percent of the regular hourly wage. Overtime also does not count toward bonuses, which comprise 20–30 percent of a worker's annual earnings in big firms. Measures aimed at eliminating these biases in favor of overtime would help, but a voluntary change in working practices by firms (soft institutions) would also be required.

Policies to Increase Nominal Wages

The policies discussed in this chapter are aimed at increasing labor supply and labor productivity to raise Japan's growth potential, but they may take time to be implemented and take effect. As noted earlier, nominal basic wages for many years have been declining despite generally tight labor market conditions. Real wages have also fallen despite solid productivity growth. As a result, the average Japanese worker has been dipping into savings to finance consumption growth. But there is a limit to how long this can continue. The saving rate as a percent of disposable income has declined from about 5 percent a decade ago to close to zero, leaving little further room for spending from saving, and this has happened amid continued high financing demand from the government, which still runs a sizable deficit (see Chapter 3).

Real wages are set to come under even greater pressure as underlying inflation increases. As such, higher wages are needed to help to break the deflationary spiral and establish a virtuous growth cycle. Insofar as wage increases are passed on to consumers by firms, higher nominal wages would allow the Bank of Japan to meet its inflation target more quickly and without overburdening monetary policy. Larger pay packets would also support aggregate demand and create favorable conditions for firms to raise their investment. Higher wages would also facilitate acceptance of reduced employment protection by regular workers from the suggested reforms to tackle labor market duality.

Even so, wages are just one ingredient for a successful transition to self-sustained growth. This also requires shaking off other remnants of the deflationary mindset. Financial institutions need to pursue new lending opportunities at home and abroad rather than accumulate excess reserves at the Bank of Japan (Chapter 8). And firms will need to put their retained earnings to good use, by raising investment and increasing dividend payments in addition to higher wages (Chapter 9). Exporters, meanwhile, need to take advantage of the weaker yen by striving to gain larger market shares (Chapter 10).

Compared with other countries, Japan stands out in having downward nominal wage flexibility and upward rigidity. It is indeed surprising that with the Bank of Japan's 2-percent inflation target gaining credibility and underlying inflation picking up markedly, wages appear to remain rather sluggish. As noted earlier, various structural impediments underpin the sluggish growth of nominal wages, which will need to be overcome through structural reforms (Chapter 6) and the labor market reforms discussed in this chapter. However, wage growth has also been hampered by the existence of a "coordination problem" in an economic environment in which people are only gradually shedding their deflationary mindset. Given Japan's history of low growth and deflation and lack of formal or de facto wage indexation, if firms believe that the recovery is not long-lasting and that other firms will not increase wages, they will be reluctant to raise wages as well. This coordination problem has been amplified by the declining importance of the annual, synchronized, spring wage-bargaining round, with firm-level profitability now playing a dominant role and bonuses and overtime payments comprising important shares of compensation, especially for larger firms.

To overcome this coordination problem and achieve the goal of increasing nominal wages, the government has been relying on a "moral suasion" strategy, by explicitly asking profit-making companies to increase wages. While at the current juncture it is appropriate for the government to have a role in wage negotiations, it is important to avoid the temptation to micromanage the process. In this regard, a wider social concertation framework, such as the one toward which the Abe administration moved by setting up the Tripartite Commission, is a more appropriate path. In addition, the government has introduced tax incentives for companies that raise wages and public sector wage cuts have been reversed.

As an additional measure, a larger-than-usual minimum wage hike could be considered to increase average wages. In Japan, the minimum wage applies to both regular and nonregular workers. Usually central and regional minimum wage councils decide on the amount of increase for regional minimum wages around August–September, with implementation around October–November. According to IMF (2013), virtually all studies that estimate the wage effect of minimum wage hikes find that formal sector wages rise with higher minimum wages. Aoyagi and Ganelli (2014) present some empirical evidence based on panel regressions carried out on Japanese prefectural data. Their analysis is somewhat supportive of the idea that increasing the minimum wage can contribute to higher average wages in Japan. Depending on the specific estimation techniques used, the impact of increasing the minimum wage on average wages is either not statistically significant or positive and statistically significant.

One additional argument in favor of this policy option is that Japan's minimum wage is one of the lowest among the OECD countries (Figure 7.11). This is partly because the introduction of the minimum wage in Japan was not originally meant to apply to principal household earners, but for a supplemental wage earner. In this context, Kambayashi, Kawaguchi, and Yamada (2010) argue that the minimum wage increase during 1994–2003 provided a wage floor for female workers, but this came at the cost of a moderate employment loss among low-skilled, middle-aged female workers. As Figure 7.12 shows, workers in low value-added service sector jobs and those with lower levels of education receive considerably lower average wages compared to other categories of workers. The former could be hurt if an increase in the minimum wage brings their wages above the "reservation wage." To limit the negative employment impact of a minimum wage increase, some categories of workers could be exempted. In practice,

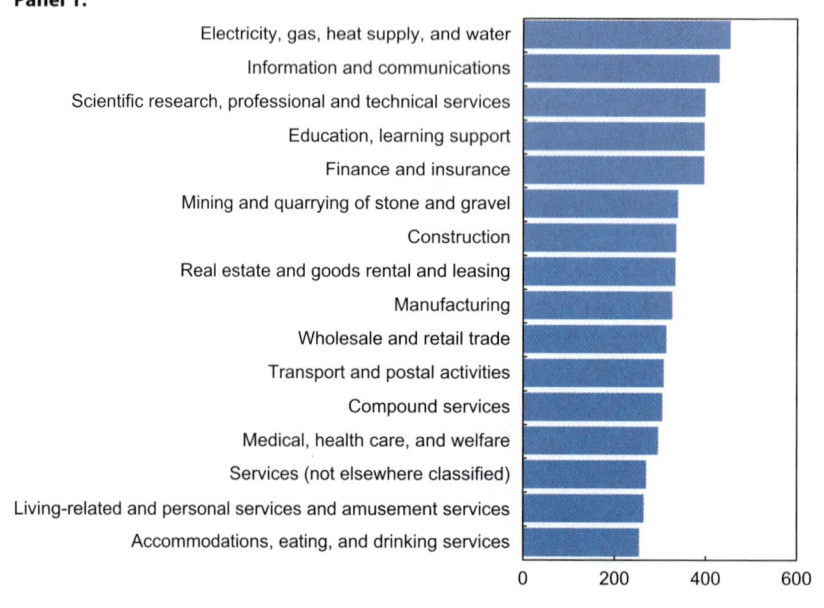

Figure 7.11   Median Wages Relative to Median Wages of Full-Time Workers

Country	Ratio
Turkey	~0.71
France	~0.60
New Zealand	~0.59
Slovenia	~0.58
Latvia	~0.57
Portugal	~0.57
Australia	~0.54
Greece	~0.52
Belgium	~0.51
Hungary	~0.50
Lithuania	~0.49
Romania	~0.48
Ireland	~0.48
Netherlands	~0.47
United Kingdom	~0.46
Slovak Republic	~0.45
Canada	~0.44
Poland	~0.44
Spain	~0.43
Luxembourg	~0.42
Korea	~0.41
Estonia	~0.39
Japan	~0.39
United States	~0.38
Czech Republic	~0.36

Source: Organisation for Economic Co-operation and Development.

Figure 7.12   Average Wage by Sector (Panel 1) and Educational Attainment (Panel 2)

Panel 1.

Sector	Wage
Electricity, gas, heat supply, and water	~480
Information and communications	~460
Scientific research, professional and technical services	~420
Education, learning support	~410
Finance and insurance	~410
Mining and quarrying of stone and gravel	~350
Construction	~340
Real estate and goods rental and leasing	~340
Manufacturing	~330
Wholesale and retail trade	~320
Transport and postal activities	~310
Compound services	~300
Medical, health care, and welfare	~290
Services (not elsewhere classified)	~270
Living-related and personal services and amusement services	~260
Accommodations, eating, and drinking services	~250

Figure 7.12 (continued)
Panel 2.

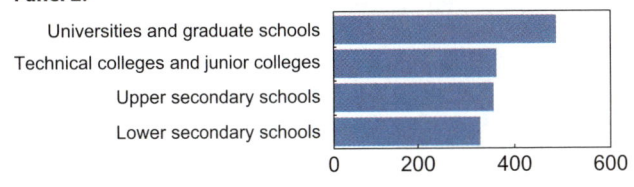

Universities and graduate schools	
Technical colleges and junior colleges	
Upper secondary schools	
Lower secondary schools	

0   200   400   600

Sources: Ministry of Health, Labour, and Welfare; and IMF staff calculations.

policies need to walk a thin line to avoid a significant negative impact on unemployment while at the same time ensuring that minimum wage increases have some effectiveness in raising average wages.

CONCLUSION

This chapter discusses options for reforming Japan's labor market to support raising potential growth and exiting deflation. Such reforms should be key components of Abenomics' third arrow of bold structural reforms. The labor market underwent dramatic changes in the course of the last two decades, including the erosion of the traditional lifetime employment system and the emergence of a dual labor market in which more than one-third of workers now have nonregular jobs. Such excessive duality harms labor productivity, contributing to lower medium-term growth potential. Japan is also experiencing the sharpest labor force decline among the advanced economies because its population is aging rapidly, further dragging on growth potential.

This chapter argues that measures aimed at increasing both labor productivity and labor supply should be put in place. On the first, labor contract reform to reduce duality is urgently needed, and should be complemented by a shift toward flexicurity and by a change in soft institutions. To increase the labor supply, measures aimed at encouraging the labor participation of women, foreigners, and older workers are also needed. These should include enhancing public and private childcare provision, reforming the tax system to increase incentives to work for households' second earners, relaxing immigration requirements for both high-skilled and lower-skilled workers, and pension reform to encourage the labor participation of older workers.

Although these measures will be useful to raise Japan's medium-term growth potential, they will take time to implement and impact the economy. To speed up implementation, Japan could take advantage of recent legislation that approved the establishment of special economic zones, which could be used to experiment with the reforms suggested in this chapter if their implementation at the national level takes longer.

Shorter-term measures to help get Abenomics off the ground and to end deflation are also needed. Measures to encourage wage growth would be appropriate and facilitate recovery from a policy-driven initial phase to the next level in which the private sector sustainably leads growth. Such measures could include well-targeted tax incentives for raising basic wages, social concertation, and a larger-than-usual minimum wage hike to help increase the average nominal wage.

REFERENCES

Aoyagi, C., and G. Ganelli. 2013. "The Path to Higher Growth: Does Revamping Japan's Dual Labor Market Matter?" IMF Working Paper No. 13/202. International Monetary Fund, Washington, DC.

———. 2014. "Options for Wage Policy to Exit Deflation." Unpublished. International Monetary Fund, Washington, DC.

Fukao, K., R. Kambayashi, D. Kawaguchi, H.U. Kwong, Y.G. Kim, and I. Yokoyama. 2007. "Deferred Compensation: Evidence from Employer-Employee Matched Data from Japan." Hi-Stat Discussion Paper Series No. 187. Tokyo: Hitotsubashi University.

García-Perez, J.I., and V. Osuna. 2011. "The Effect of Introducing a Single Open Ended Contract in the Spanish Labor Market." Unpublished. Pablo de Olavide University, Seville.

International Monetary Fund. 2013. "Jobs and Growth: Analytical and Operational Considerations for the Fund." IMF Policy Paper. Washington, DC. www.imf.org/external/np/pp/eng/2013/031413.pdf.

Kambayashi, R., D. Kawaguchi, and K. Yamada. 2010. "The Minimum Wage in a Deflationary Economy: The Japanese Experience, 1994–2003." IZA Discussion Papers No. 4949. Bonn: Institute for the Study of Labor.

Kawaguchi, D., R. Kambayashi, Y.G. Kim, H.U. Kwong, S. Shimizutani, K. Fukao, T. Makino, and I. Yokoyama. 2006. "Are Wage-tenure Profiles Steeper than Productivity-tenure Profiles? Evidence from Japanese Establishment Data from the Census of Manufacturers and the Basic Survey Wage Structure." Hi-Stat Discussion Paper Series No. 189. Tokyo: Hitotsubashi University.

Organisation for Economic Co-operation and Development (OECD). 2011. *OECD Employment Outlook*. Paris: OECD.

———. 2013. *OECD Employment Outlook*. Paris: OECD.

Ohtake, F., H. Okudaira, K. Kume, and K. Tsuru. 2011. "Life and Employment of Temporary Workers: Evidence from RIETI Survey." RIETI Discussion Paper No. 11-J-050. Tokyo: Research Institute of Economy, Trade, and Industry.

Shibata, I. 2013. "Is Labor Market Mismatch a Big Deal in Japan?" IMF Working Paper No. 13/196. International Monetary Fund, Washington, DC.

Sommer, M. 2009. "Why Are Japanese Wages so Sluggish?" IMF Working Paper No. 09/97. International Monetary Fund, Washington, DC.

Steinberg, C., and M. Nakane. 2011. "To Fire or to Hoard? Explaining Japan's Labor Market Response to the Great Recession." IMF Working Paper No. 11/15. International Monetary Fund, Washington, DC.

———. 2012. "Can Women Save Japan?" IMF Working Paper No. 12/248. International Monetary Fund, Washington, DC.

Tsuru, K. 2014. "A Farewell to Japanese Employment Practices: Why Is Regular Employment System Reform Necessary? Proposals Made by the Regulatory Reform Council." Japan Policy Forum. http://www.japanpolicyforum.jp/en/archives/economy/pt20140120140815.html.

CHAPTER 8

The Opportunities and Risks of Abenomics in the Financial Sector

SERKAN ARSLANALP, RAPHAEL LAM, AND MALHAR NABAR

Crucial to the success of the Abenomics program to shift the Japanese economy to permanently higher growth and inflation is the role of the financial sector. This chapter examines the risks and opportunities for the sector and highlights financial sector policies that could enhance the effectiveness of the policy framework.

The new policy framework could have a fundamental impact on the financial sector. The Bank of Japan (BoJ) expects its monetary easing program to affect the financial system and the economy through three channels (BoJ 2013). First, large-scale purchases of Japanese government bonds (JGBs) are expected to suppress long-term interest rates across the yield curve (the interest rate channel). Second, a clear commitment to achieve the new inflation target is expected to raise inflation expectations and boost private demand through a decline in real interest rates (the expectations channel). Third, investors and financial institutions investing in JGBs are expected to shift from these instruments to risk assets such as stocks and foreign-denominated bonds or to increase lending within their portfolios (the portfolio rebalancing channel).

In this chapter we explore how the domestic and cross-border balance sheets of Japanese institutions may change under the government's new policies. A key finding is that the impact is likely to depend on whether all three arrows of Abenomics are implemented together, as recommended in Chapter 3.

In this chapter, we first take stock of portfolio allocations and discuss the performance of the financial sector during the past decade. We next look at some of the opportunities that could arise from the implementation of a complete package of policies under Abenomics for the domestic and cross-border activities of Japanese financial institutions. We then examine new risks that may emerge, in particular from an incomplete package of policies under the program. We conclude with some policy options to help manage these risks, maintain financial stability, and support growth.

PORTFOLIO ALLOCATIONS TOWARD RISK CAPITAL

The success of Abenomics depends in part on whether Japanese financial portfolios rebalance away from large holdings of currency and government securities toward higher-yielding, riskier assets. Portfolio rebalancing is important for all three arrows: enhancing the transmission of monetary easing by lowering borrowing costs, providing an impetus for eventual fiscal consolidation by exerting market discipline on the government, and supporting the growth strategy by intermediating risk capital.

Over time, investment strategies across most major investor groups appear to have broadly adjusted to an environment with mild deflation and low nominal interest rates, in which safe and liquid assets have delivered steady, albeit low, real returns. Portfolio allocations across households, banks, pension funds, and insurance companies remain heavily weighted toward "safe assets," consisting of currency, deposits, and government securities.

While some rebalancing away from this mix of safe assets appears to be under way, the process has so far not advanced that rapidly. In most cases, the allocations to safe assets continue to be well above portfolio shares prior to the global financial crisis (Figure 8.1). Specifically, the portfolio share allocated to currency, deposits, and government securities declined during Abenomics' first year for households, public pensions, and other financial intermediaries, such as securities investment trust companies. Banks, insurance companies, and corporate pension funds, however, have maintained their overall allocation to risk-free assets. Although banks' holdings of JGBs have fallen since the launch of the quantitative and qualitative monetary easing (QQE) framework, the increase in their excess reserve holdings at the BoJ has offset this to maintain a broadly unchanged share of low-yield assets in bank portfolios.

In a bank-dominated financial system such as Japan's, the potential of the financial sector to provide risk capital is linked closely to the health of bank balance sheets. After a period of balance sheet repair and consolidation during the 1990s and early 2000s (necessitated by the collapse of the 1980s real estate bubble and the 1997–98 Asian financial crisis), the Japanese financial system fared well during the global financial crisis. Bank buffers and asset quality appear stronger now than during the last decade. Capital ratios have increased in aggregate across all categories of banks (city, regional, *shinkin*) (Figure 8.2) and loan-loss reserves are below levels seen during the last decade (Figure 8.3). The evidently healthy state of bank balance sheets suggests that there is room for banks to increase exposure to riskier projects either by funding new ventures directly or by investing in risk assets in capital markets. With lower funding costs under the QQE, supply constraints on risk capital allocation are arguably even lower now than was the case previously.

Portfolio rebalancing toward riskier assets, however, requires more than willingness and capacity on the supply side to shift exposures in that direction. Other actors in the economy have a role to play in this as well—intermediaries that help share risks by securitizing small business loans; institutional investors that take direct exposures in new ventures; and, ultimately, end-users.

Even prior to the global financial crisis, securitization activity in Japan was relatively low (less than 2 percent of GDP at its peak). Within this small envelope, securities were backed mostly by mortgages (Figure 8.4). Small business loans constituted a negligible underlying asset class used in securitization. Banks have

Arslanalp, Lam, and Nabar | **127**

Figure 8.1 Allocation to "Safe Assets" by Investor Type *(Percent of total assets)*

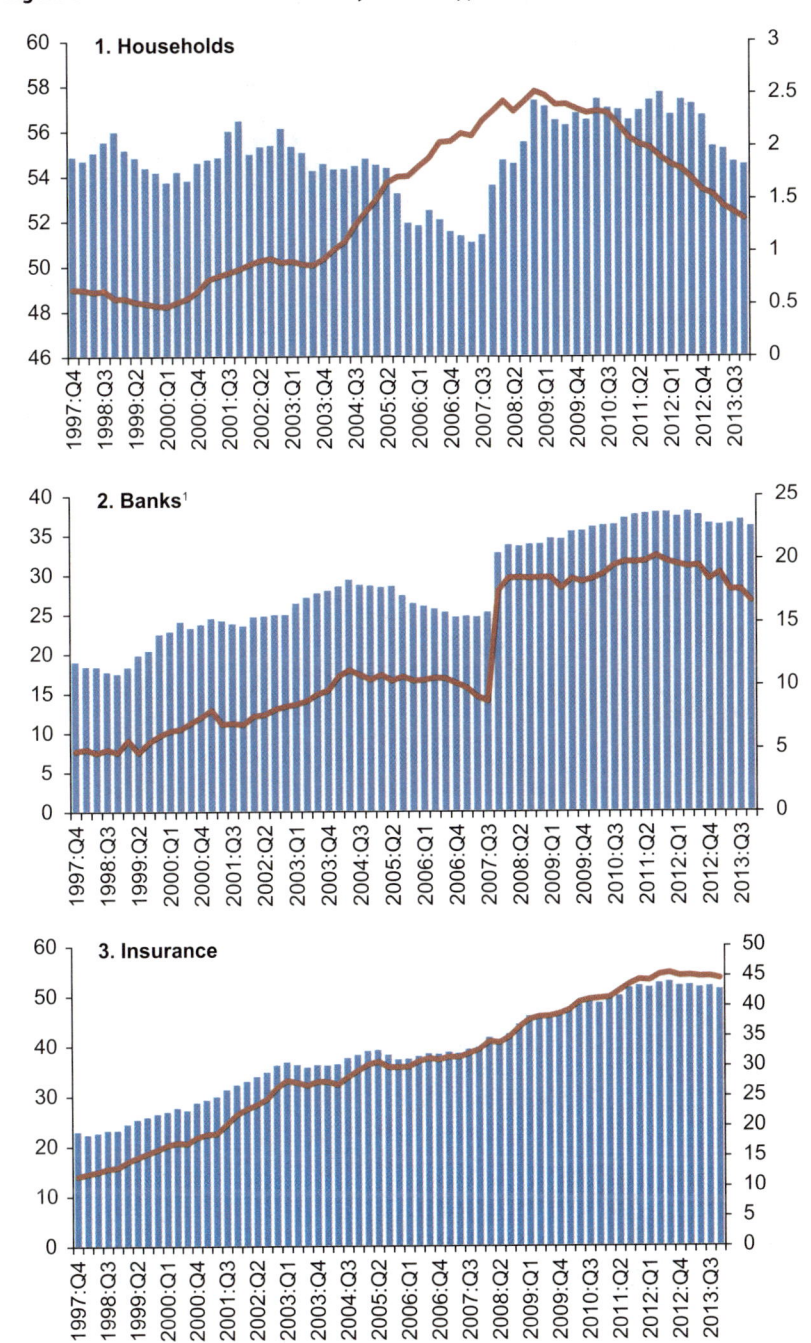

1. Households

2. Banks[1]

3. Insurance

128 The Opportunities and Risks of Abenomics in the Financial Sector

Figure 8.1 (continued)

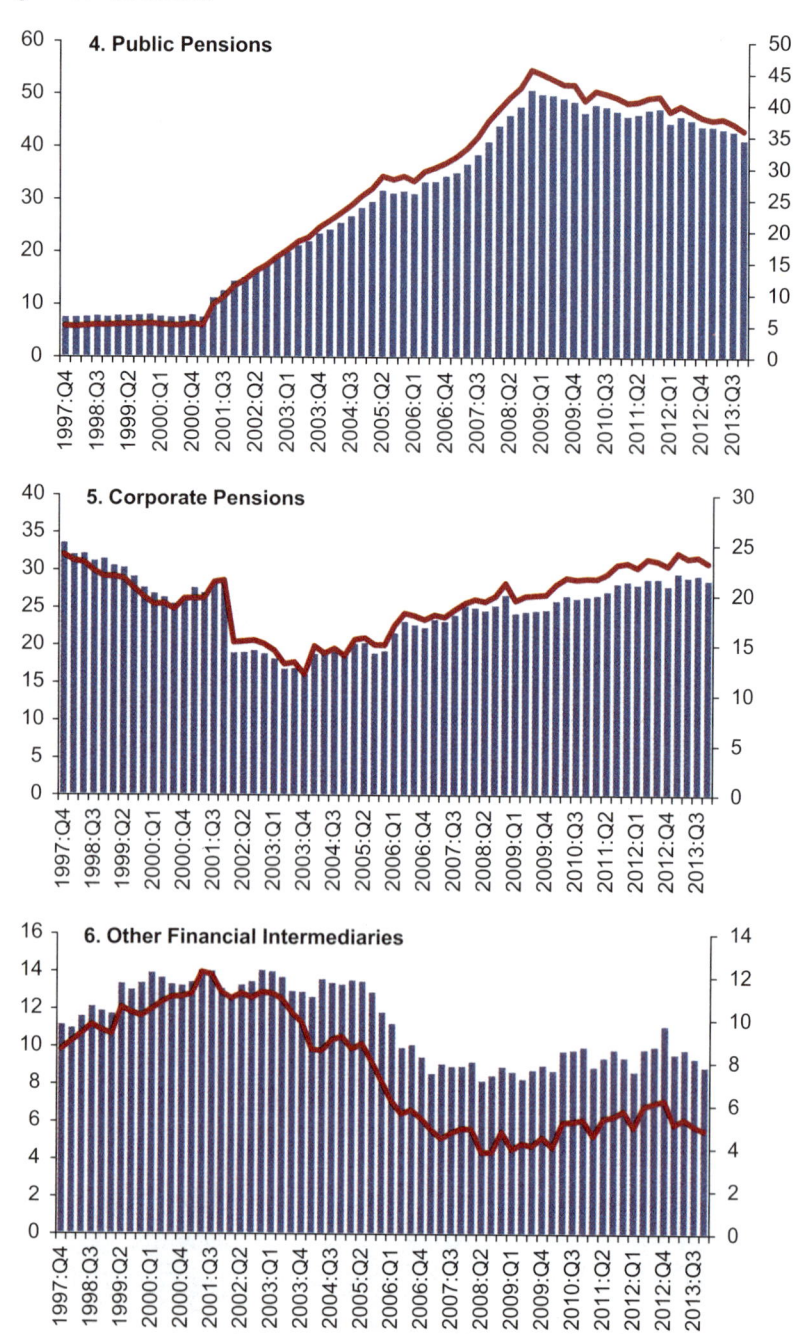

4. Public Pensions

5. Corporate Pensions

6. Other Financial Intermediaries

Sources: Bank of Japan, Flow of Funds; Haver Analytics; and IMF staff estimates.
Note: The bars in each panel represent the share of currency, deposits, and government securities, in percent (left-hand side). The line represents the share of Japanese government bonds, in percent (right-hand side).
[1] Starting in 2007:Q4, assets of postal savings are included under banks.

Figure 8.2 Regulatory Capital to Risk-Weighted Assets *(Percent)*

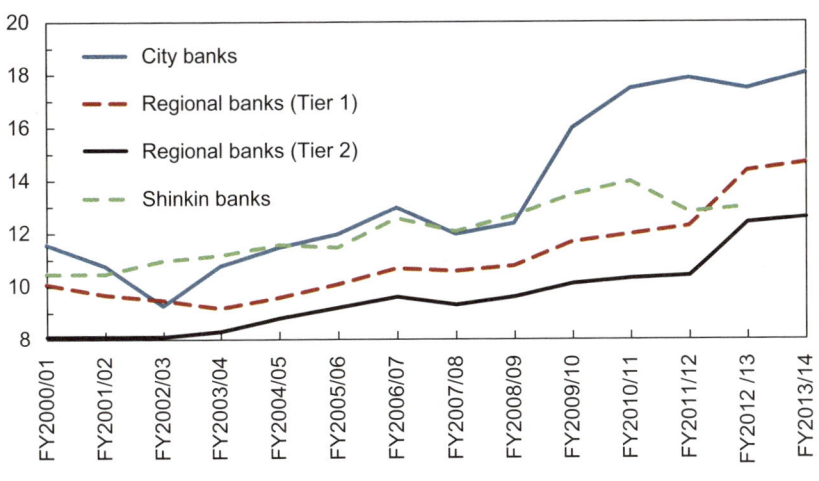

Source: Financial Services Agency.
Note: As of the end of the fiscal year (that is, end-March of the second of the two years) except in the case of FY2013/14, which refers to the half-year ending in September 2013.

Figure 8.3 Banks' Loan-Loss Reserves *(Percent of total loans, three-month moving average)*

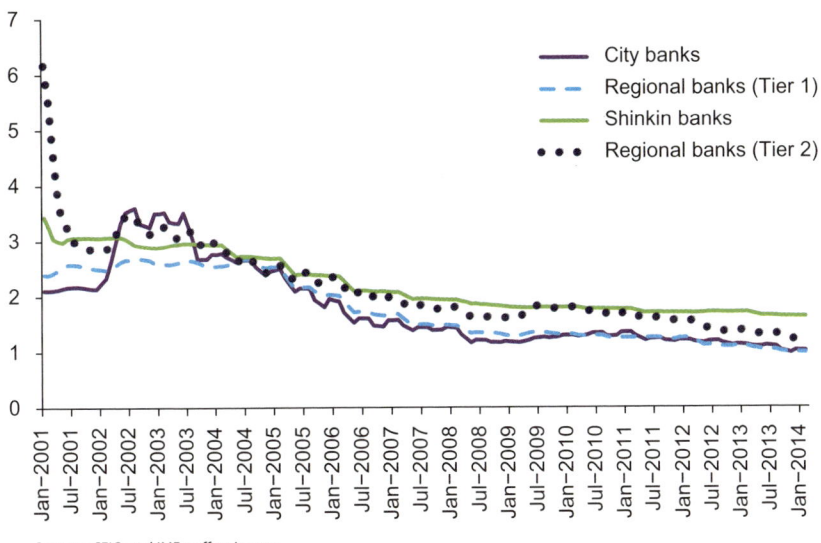

Sources: CEIC; and IMF staff estimates.

typically originated small business loans and maintained them on their books to maturity, rather than selling them off to institutional investors for securitization. This business model has led to a concentration of small-business-related credit risk on bank balance sheets, compared to a model in which a larger fraction of

Figure 8.4 Securitization Product Issuance by Underlying Assets *(Percent of GDP)*

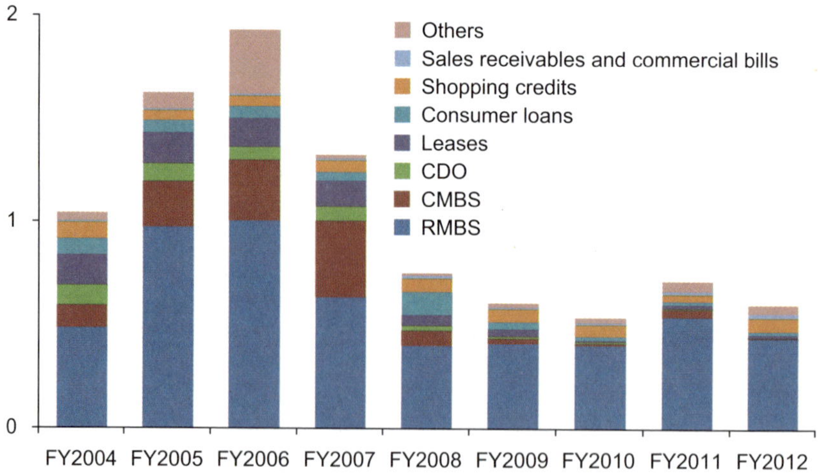

Sources: CEIC; Japan Securities Dealers Association; and IMF staff estimates.
Note: CDO = collateralized debt obligation, CMBS = commercial mortgage-backed security, RMBS = residential mortgage-backed security.

small business loans is originated for subsequent distribution, leading to a diffusion of credit risk across multiple intermediaries.

Other investors in small businesses such as venture capital firms have typically been less prominent in Japan than in other Organisation for Economic Co-operation and Development countries (Nabar and Syed 2011, Lam and Shin 2012). Linked to the low level of venture capital activity, initial public offerings—often used as exit routes for early investors to cash out their seed capital—are also relatively low in Japan. In 2013, when the stock market rose some 60 percent in local currency terms, capital raised through initial public offerings in Tokyo was closer to the levels seen in emerging markets and smaller advanced economies than to the amounts raised in New York or London (Figure 8.5).

Looking beyond intermediation infrastructure, increasing risk capital allocation ultimately depends on the demand for loanable funds. Loan officer surveys have typically pointed to tepid demand as the reason for slow credit growth. To the extent this reflects firms' perceptions of poor growth prospects and lack of new investment opportunities, efforts to boost risk capital allocation will need to focus more on take-up. There is some evidence from private nonresidential investment trends that firms have so far not been persuaded about a step shift in domestic growth prospects (Figure 8.6). In contrast, firms have continued to expand overseas, as seen in the pickup in outward foreign direct investment, even as domestic private capital expenditure softened in 2013.

Previous studies (Lam and Shin 2012, Caballero, Hoshi, and Kashyap 2008) have pointed to several underlying reasons for low demand, in many cases related to factors in the broader economy beyond the financial system. In the first instance, there is limited restructuring or exit of nonviable small and medium-sized enterprises

Figure 8.5 Global IPOs: Top Ten Exchanges by Capital Raised, 2013 *(Percent of total)*

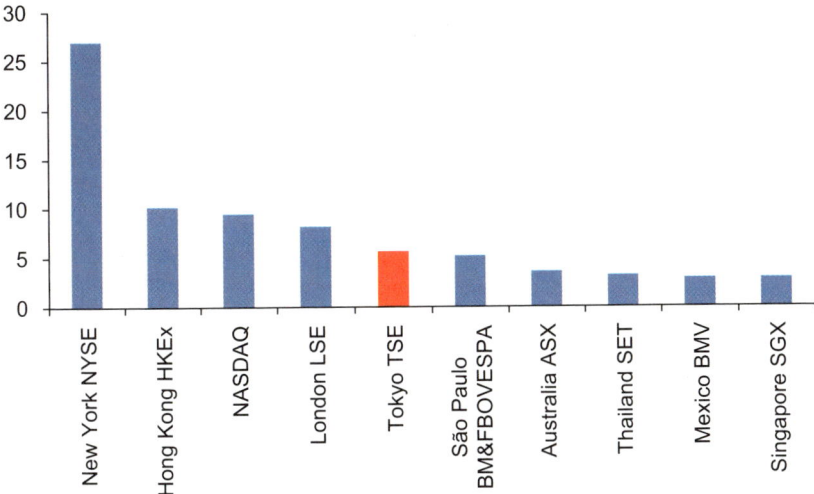

Sources: Ernst & Young, Global IPO Trends; and IMF staff estimates.
Note: ASX = Australian Securities Exchange, BM&FBOVESPA = Bolsa de Valores, Mercadorias & Futuros de São Paulo, BMV = Bolsa Mexicana de Valores, HKEx = Hong Kong Exchanges and Clearing Ltd., IPO = initial public offering, LSE = London Stock Exchange, NYSE = New York Stock Exchange, SET = Stock Exchange of Thailand, SGX = Singapore Exchange, TSE = Tokyo Stock Exchange.

Figure 8.6 Private Nonresidential Fixed Investment and Outward FDI *(Percent of GDP)*

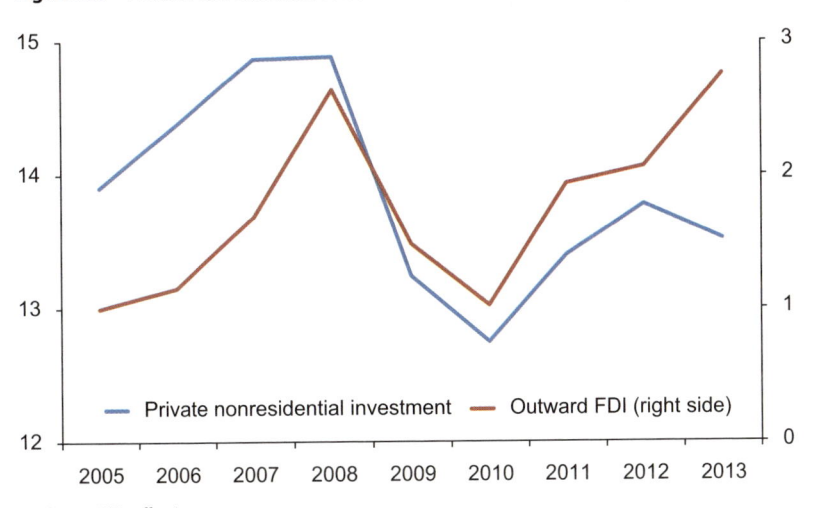

Source: IMF staff estimates.
Note: FDI = foreign direct investment.

(SMEs) because refinancing tends to be easily available and this has curtailed incentives for troubled borrowers to voluntarily enter into mergers and workouts (exit rates are about a third of those in other advanced economies, see Lam and Shin 2012). Furthermore, multiple creditors and wide use of personal guarantees create further barriers to workouts and business transfers.

The persistence of nonviable SMEs combined with regulatory barriers in several sectors deters entry (Lam and Shin 2012 also note that entry rates are roughly a third of those in other advanced economies). As Caballero, Hoshi, and Kashyap (2008) argue, the persistence of "zombie" borrowers has affected existing healthy firms and potential entrants in multiple ways. It has tended to reduce profits for healthy firms by driving down market prices while keeping wages higher than they otherwise would have been, slowed investment and employment growth among healthy firms, worsened collateral value and prevented solvent banks from lending to them, and deterred entry. The overall effect has been to block the needed structural transformation of the economy.

Over and above this, as Lam and Shin (2012) point out, public guarantees have further compounded the problem by facilitating rollovers and delaying repayments. These public guarantees have come in different forms: standard and special/emergency credit guarantees; safety-net lending by government-affiliated financial institutions; temporary SME financing facilitation; and relaxed Financial Services Agency's guidelines to classify restructured loans under the normal category, which means smaller loan-loss provisioning by banks.

In sum, amid weak growth prospects and a deflationary mindset, gaps in intermediation capacity (securitization, venture capital) and factors that impede demand for risk capital (insufficient SME restructuring, entry, and exit) appear to have contributed to skewing portfolio allocations toward safe and low-yielding assets. While potentially holding back the emergence of new growth areas, these distortions have also had serious implications for the financial sector. The banking system, in particular, continues to face challenges, such as the steady decline in the profitability of lending operations and large JGB holdings, which are a source of interest rate risk (discussed in more detail in the following section).

JAPANESE BANKING SECTOR: INTEREST RATE RISK

Large JGB holdings of Japanese banks imply that even a modest rise in interest rates can have important implications for financial stability (IMF 2012). The large issuance of JGBs over the past two decades has been financed mostly through the domestic financial sector, with banks' JGB holdings currently just over 15 percent of total assets, representing an important source of exposure to interest rate risk. If interest rates were to rise sharply, losses from such exposures could reduce capital ratios across a range of financial institutions. For instance, a 100 basis point parallel rise in domestic bond yields could lead to mark-to-market losses of 13 percent of Tier 1 capital for major banks and 21 percent for regional banks based on latest available data (BoJ 2013).

This section explores how the new policies under Abenomics could affect the interest rate risk of Japanese banks. In particular, it illustrates that their exposures could decline substantially during 2014–15 as the BoJ becomes a large buyer of JGBs. But this may rise again to current levels if structural and fiscal reforms disappoint over the medium term.

Throughout the exercise, we use three hypothetical scenarios based on IMF (2013): (1) a baseline pre-Abenomics scenario; (2) a complete Abenomics package under which the QQE, fiscal consolidation, and ambitious structural reforms lead to lower government funding needs and higher growth; and (3) an incomplete Abenomics package under which inflation expectations adjust in a sluggish manner, possibly because of the lack of a structural reform program, requiring further fiscal stimulus to close the output gap and boost inflation in the near term (Table 8.1).

Japanese banks have played a key role in the JGB market, essentially serving as the marginal buyers of JGBs given their role as primary dealers and market makers. Accordingly, Japanese banks' purchases of JGBs have been determined to a large extent by the following factors: (1) net issuance of JGBs, (2) social security fund net purchases of JGBs, (3) BoJ's net purchases of JGBs, and (4) foreigners' net purchases of JGBs. More specifically, the following stylized equation can explain most of the variation in Japanese banks' holdings of JGBs since 2000 (top and bottom charts of Figure 8.7).

$$B_t = B_0 + D_{0,t} - SSF_{0,t} - CB_{0,t} - FOR_{0,t} - \text{alpha}^* t$$

where B_t represent Japanese banks' JGB holdings at time t; $D_{0,t}$ represents the cumulative net issuance of JGBs between 2000 and t; $SSF_{0,t}$, $CB_{0,t}$, and $FOR_{0,t}$ represent the cumulative net purchase of JGBs by social security funds, the BoJ, and foreigners, respectively; and alpha represents a time trend that captures the secular purchase by other investors, in particular insurance and pension funds (that is, alpha is equal to ¥9 trillion).

It seems unusual at first glance that JGB yields or other macro variables do not enter into the equation, but the equation captures the dynamics because (1) it simply relies on the supply and demand balance in the JGBs market; (2) Japanese insurance and pension funds have had a historically stable demand for JGBs due to their asset liability matching policies, and (3) other domestic nonbanks, including mutual funds, are negligible buyers of JGBs (top chart of Figure 8.7).

TABLE 8.1

Alternative Scenarios

Scenario	Description
Baseline	The pre-Abenomics baseline is taken as the December 2012 forecasts in the IMF's *World Economic Outlook*.
Complete Policy Package	Ambitious structural reforms are taken to raise the trend long-term growth to 2 percent (IMF 2013).
	Inflation expectations are aligned to the inflation target quickly within the timeframe forecast by the Bank of Japan.
	Medium-term fiscal adjustments are undertaken to put debt on a downward trajectory.
Incomplete Policy Package	Long-term growth remains stagnant without structural reforms.
	Inflation expectations adjust in a sluggish manner and align only gradually with the target.
	Further fiscal stimulus is taken to stimulate near-term growth and inflation, but the lack of medium-term fiscal adjustment leads to a rising risk premium.

Source: IMF (2013).

Figure 8.7 Demand and Supply Balance in the JGB Market

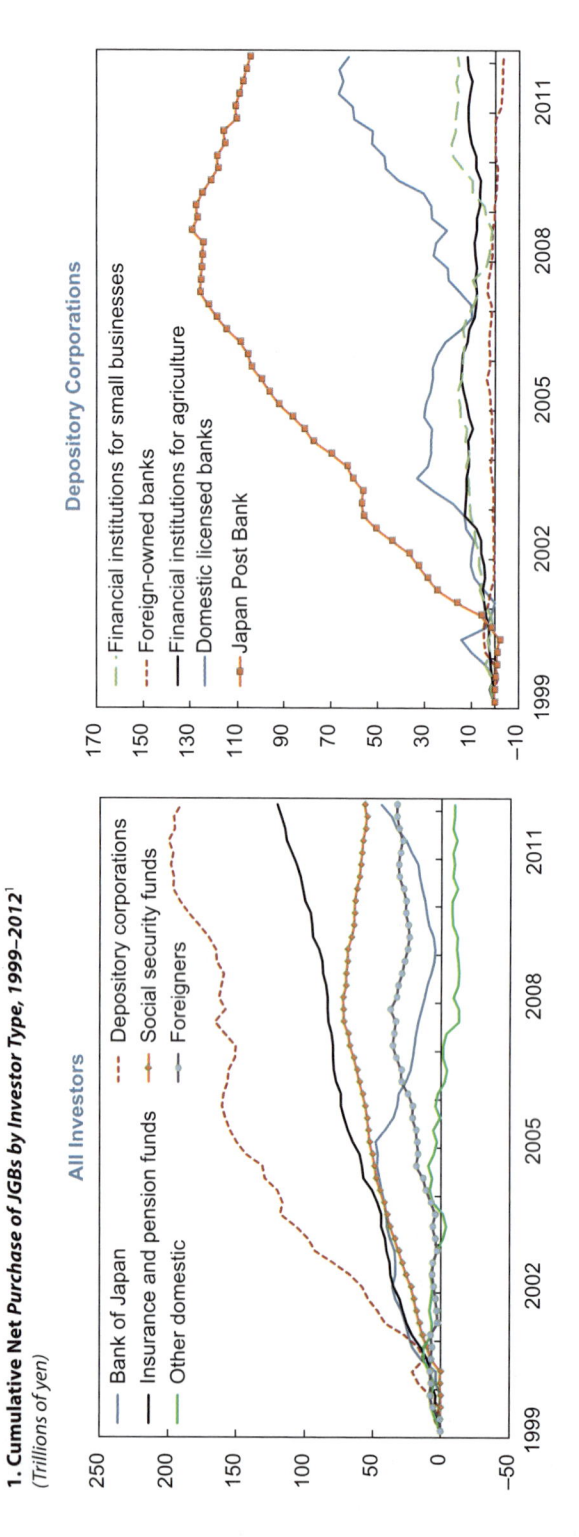

1. Cumulative Net Purchase of JGBs by Investor Type, 1999–2012[1]
(Trillions of yen)

2. Actual and Predicted Cumulative Net JGB Purchase by Depository Corporations[2]
(Trillions of yen)

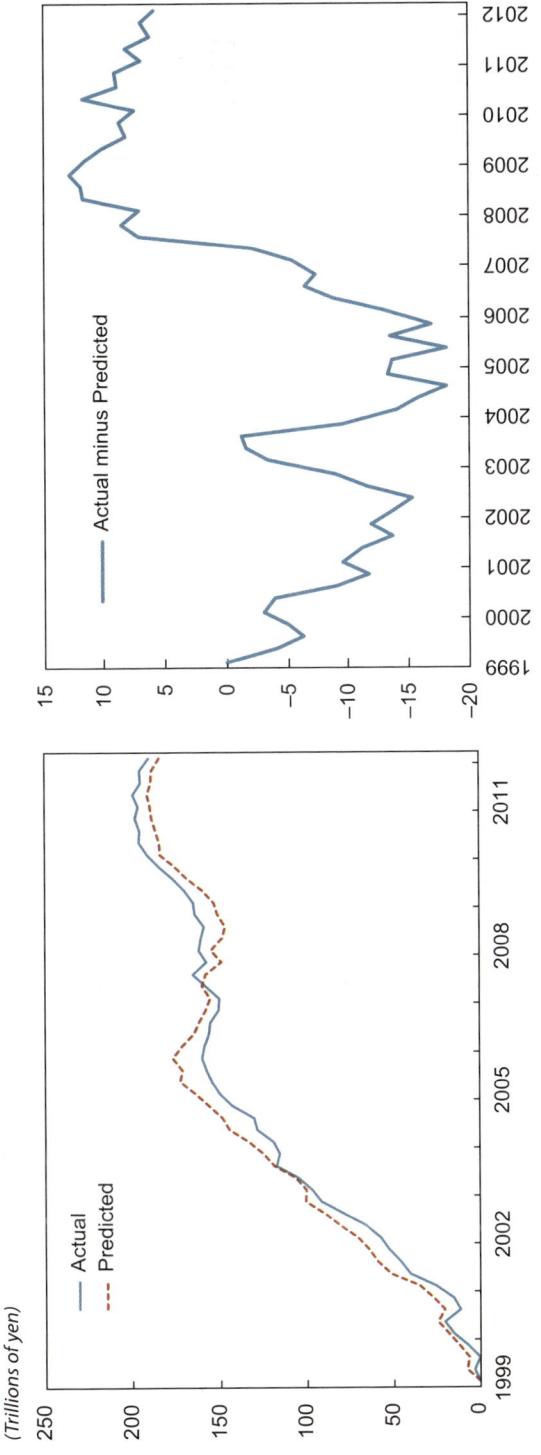

Sources: Bank of Japan, Flow of Funds statistics; Japan Post Bank; and IMF staff estimates.
Note: JGB = Japanese government bonds.
[1] Depository corporations include the Japan Post Bank, with the figures after 2007 estimated from company reports. Insurance funds include Japan Post Insurance. Social security funds include the Government Pension Investment Fund. Other domestic includes households and corporations. Domestically licensed banks include major and regional banks.
[2] Predicted purchases of JGBs by depository corporations are based on total net issuance, social security fund purchases, Bank of Japan purchases, and foreign purchases.

TABLE 8.2

Projected Net Purchases of Japanese Government Bonds, 2013–17
(Annual average; trillions of yen)

	Pre-Abenomics	Abenomics: complete package	Abenomics: incomplete package
Net JGB Issuance	25.9	25.3	28.7
Bank of Japan	14.7	20.0	20.0
Depository Corporations	5.0	−5.5	6.9
Insurance and Pension Funds	9.0	9.0	9.0
Social Security Funds	−4.0	−4.0	−4.0
Other Domestic	0.0	0.0	0.0
Foreigners	1.2	5.8	−3.3

Source: IMF staff projections.
Note: The Bank of Japan net purchases of Japanese government bonds (JGBs) are 50 trillion yen both in 2013 and 2014. Net purchases by insurance and pension funds are based on historical trends. Net purchases by social security funds are based on trends in the last four years.

Based on these historical relationships and hypothetical scenarios discussed earlier, Japanese banks' JGB holdings are projected for 2014–17 as follows (as explained further in Arslanalp and Lam 2013) and as summarized in Table 8.2.

- *Net JGB issuance.* Cumulative net issuance of JGBs over the medium term is based on IMF general government gross debt projections under the three scenarios provided in IMF (2013). In all these scenarios, general government debt is assumed to be issued as follows: 75 percent in JGBs, 20 percent in Treasury bills, and 5 percent in local government bonds, in line with the broad pattern of debt issuance in recent years.

- *Central bank purchases.* The BoJ's net JGB purchases over 2013–14 are projected based on the April 2013 policy announcement (¥50 trillion each in 2013 and 2014), and its holdings are assumed to be constant thereafter (that is, we assume the BoJ will roll over any JGBs maturing in its portfolio over the following three years). Under the pre-Abenomics scenario, the BoJ's JGB purchases are projected based on the Open-Ended Asset Purchasing Method introduced in January 2013.

- *Social Security Fund purchases.* Social security funds are assumed to remain net sellers of JGBs under current demographic trends by ¥4 trillion per year.

- *Insurance and pension fund purchases.* Insurance and pension funds are expected to broadly maintain their liability-driven investment strategy, and to continue buying about ¥9 trillion of JGBs per year on a net basis.

- *Foreign purchases.* The foreign share of JGBs is projected to increase from 4½ percent at the end of 2012 to 7 percent by the end of 2017 under complete policies, but fall to 2 percent under incomplete policies, as the rise in the risk premium does not assuage foreign investors' concerns about fiscal sustainability. The figures of 7 percent and 2 percent represent the highest and lowest foreign share registered in the JGB market since 2000.

A final simplifying assumption is that net purchases of JGBs and other domestic bonds by major and regional banks take place proportional to their current holdings. That essentially means that, under the scenarios, major and regional banks maintain their relative shares in the JGB, local government, and corporate bond markets (some cases in which this may not hold will be discussed below).

Based on these assumptions, Japanese banks' interest rate risk is calculated as mark-to-market losses to Tier 1 capital from a hypothetical 100-basis-point parallel rise in the domestic yield curve, in line with the methodology of the BoJ in the Financial System Report and as shown in the equation.

$$\text{Interest rate risk exposure} = \frac{\text{Domestic bond holdings} * \text{Duration}}{\text{Tier 1 capital}}$$

For the duration of banks' JGB holdings, we assume a gradual reduction given that the BoJ is expected to expand the duration of its JGB holdings under the QQE.[1] For Tier 1 capital, we assume that bank capital grows in line with nominal GDP (that is, mainly through retained earnings and not through capital raising, in line with the current market guidelines of large financial institutions).[2]

Based on this framework, the scenarios highlight that the interest rate risk exposures of Japanese banks could decline substantially over the next two years as the BoJ becomes a large buyer of JGBs (Figure 8.8). In particular in the near term, both complete and incomplete Abenomics scenarios show a substantial decline in

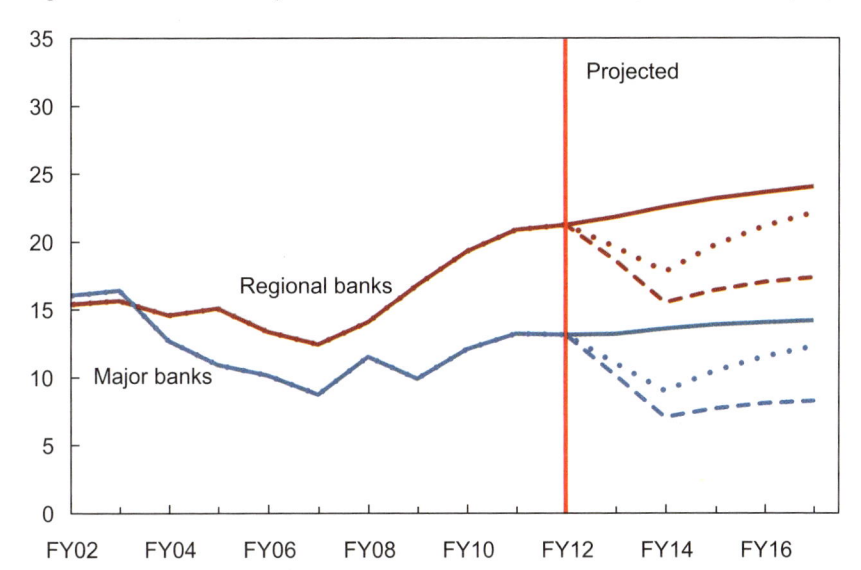

Figure 8.8 Banks' Sensitivity to a 100-Basis-Point Interest Rate Shock *(Percent of Tier 1 capital)*

Sources: Bank of Japan; and IMF staff estimates and projections.
Note: Solid lines (—) represent the pre-Abenomics scenario; dashed lines (- -) the Abenomics: complete package scenario; and dotted lines (⋯) the Abenomics: incomplete package scenario.

---

[1] In particular, we assume the average remaining maturity of domestic bond holdings will decline from 2.5 to 2 years for major banks and from 4 to 3.5 years for regional banks over 2013–14.
[2] Alternatively, we can assume that Tier 1 capital will grow at a constant rate of 4.2 percent. This would take into account the average return on equity of Japanese banks (about 6 percent) and the average dividend payout ratio of Tokyo Stock Exchange listed companies (about 30 percent). The results are broadly the same.

the interest rate risk exposures of major and regional banks on account of large BoJ purchases, as well as fiscal consolidation, higher profitability, and Tier 1 capital growth due to structural reforms under the complete scenario. In contrast, under the pre-Abenomics baseline, the interest rate risk exposures of major and regional banks would have risen steadily over the medium term, highlighting growing financial stability risks. As such, financial sector stability would benefit greatly from successful Abenomics, with risks expected to shift from interest to market risk as portfolio rebalancing commences.

At the same time, the scenarios suggest that interest rate risk may rise again if structural and fiscal reforms disappoint over the medium term. Under such an incomplete policy package, banks' JGB holdings and interest rate risk exposure may rise quickly again, as banks may, once again, have to absorb large government financing needs and their profitability and Tier 1 capital growth may decline because of lower growth. Consistent with the analysis in Chapter 3, where we showed that a complete policy package was critical to overcome the structural headwinds from population aging and to achieve the two-percent inflation target in a stable manner, these results indicate that a complete policy package is also vital for reducing interest rate risk in the banking sector and, ultimately, reducing tail risks from the fiscal–financial nexus.

JAPANESE FINANCIAL INSTITUTIONS EXPANDING ABROAD

An important component of portfolio rebalancing is greater cross-border lending activity. Cross-border activities of Japanese financial institutions have risen over the past few years, particularly to Asia. As a result, major Japanese banks have attained an important global and regional footprint, with their cross-border consolidated claims abroad increasing since 2005, reaching nearly $3 trillion (about 15 percent of total banking and trust assets) as of March 2013, according to data from the Bank for International Settlements. Claims on Asia have more than doubled since the global financial crisis, and now account for about 10 percent of total foreign consolidated claims. The expansion abroad has made Japanese banks key players in regional and global syndicated loans and project finance. Overseas gross profits now account for about 30 percent of total gross profits (about half of which arise from net interest income, with higher net interest margins on foreign loans than domestically). At the same time, major brokerage firms and life insurers have sought acquisitions or strategic partnerships overseas.

The current trend is often compared to previous episodes of overseas expansion by Japanese financial institutions. Those can be broadly classified into three waves: (1) the rapid expansion in the 1980s until the bursting of the asset-price bubble in 1990; (2) the expansion during the mid-1990s; and (3) the expansion abroad beginning from 2006, which temporarily slowed during the global financial crisis (Figure 8.9). A question to explore would be how the current trend of overseas expansion compared to these earlier episodes and whether the growing cross-border activity will continue under Abenomics.

Figure 8.9 Japanese Financial Institutions: Global Ranking and Expansion Overseas

1. Major Global Banks, by Asset Size

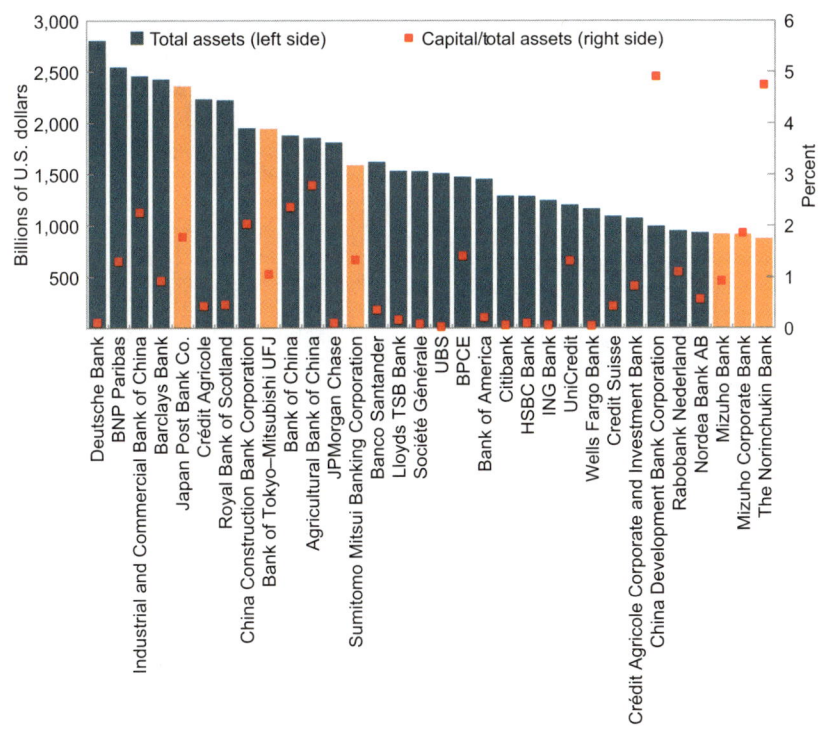

Source: BankersAccuity.

2. Foreign Direct Investment Abroad, by Industry

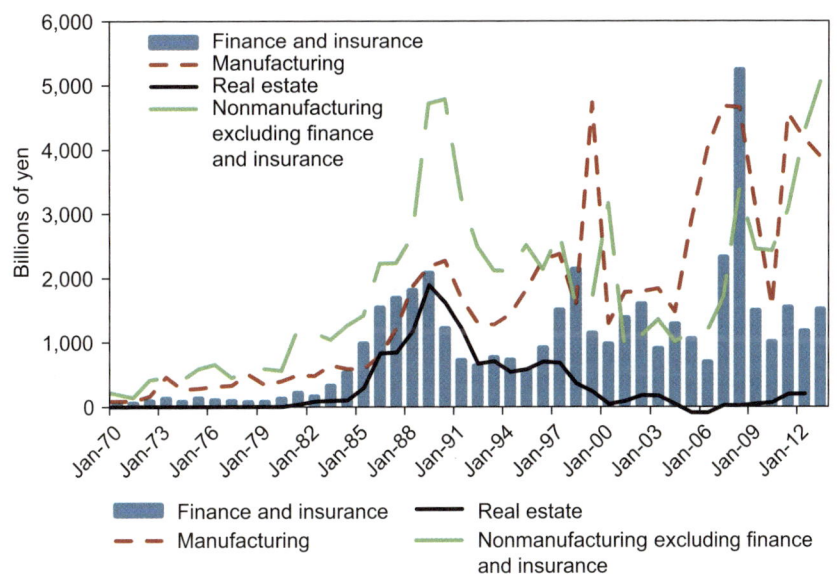

Sources: Haver Analytics; and Japan Ministry of Finance.

Figure 8.9 (Continued)

3. External Bank Assets and Liabilities

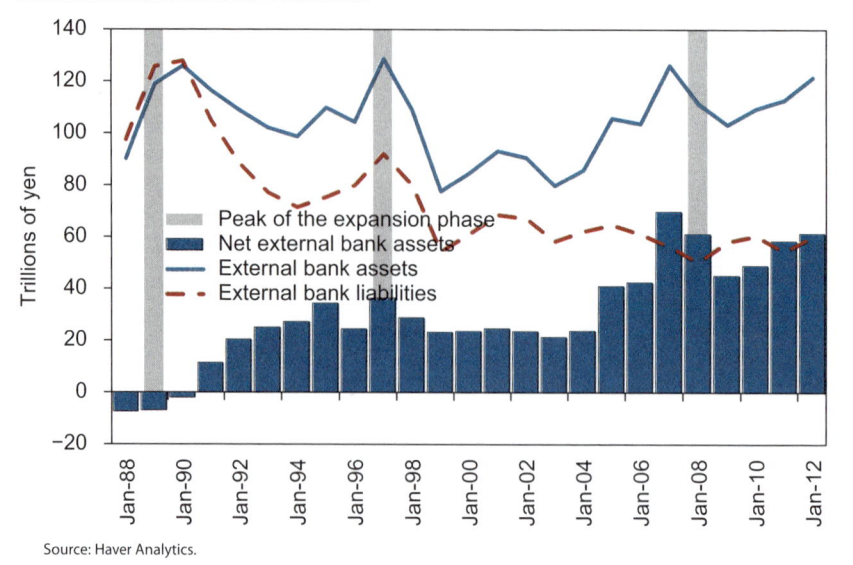

4. Consolidated Foreign Claims for Japanese Banks

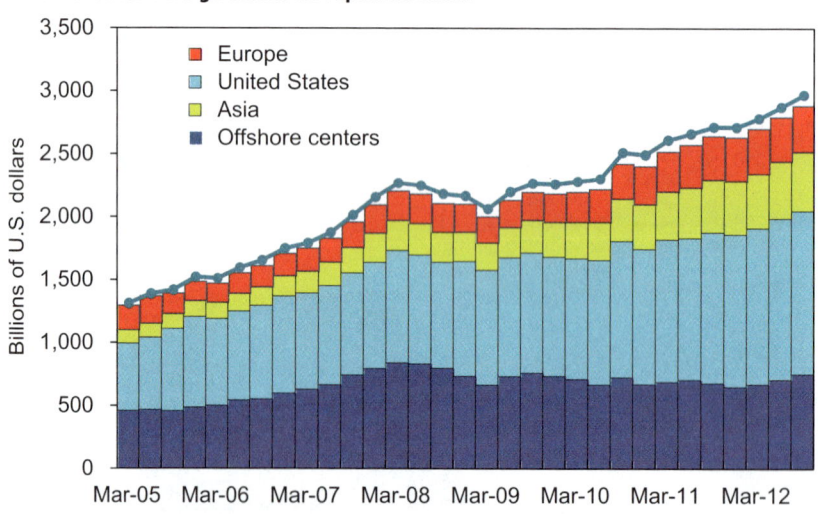

5. Banks' Net Foreign Currency-Denominated External Assets

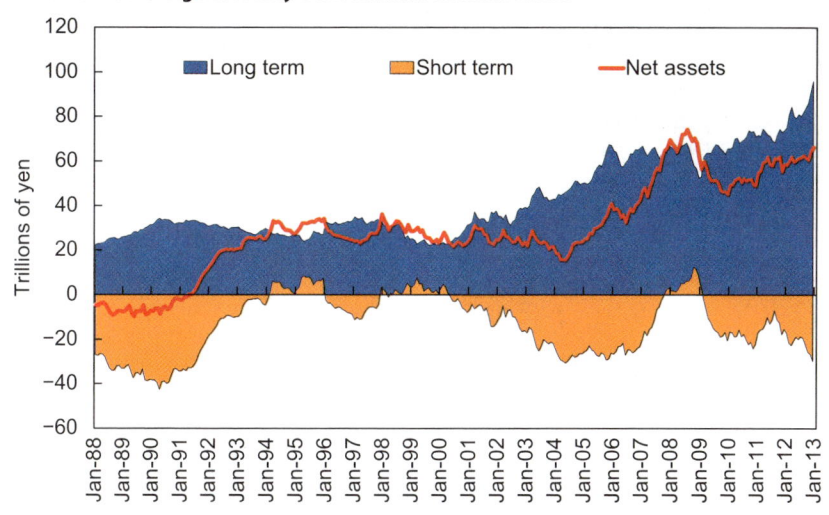

Source: Japan Ministry of Finance.

6. Banks' Yen-Denominated Net External Assets

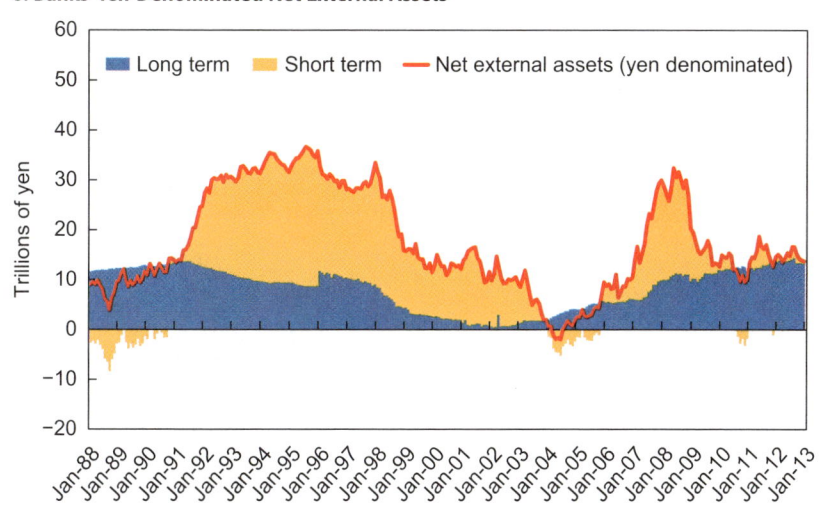

Source: Japan Ministry of Finance.

Several domestic and regional factors contribute to the increasing trend of overseas activity among Japanese financial institutions.

- *Limited domestic opportunities have generated a need for major Japanese banks to expand abroad.* As noted, domestic credit demand was sluggish in the past few years because of stagnant growth, though it has picked up recently. Large corporations have limited funding needs as they accumulated sizable surpluses (rising to about 6 percent of GDP). Structural factors—such as high leverage among SMEs, population aging, and sluggish growth in Japan's regions—have limited domestic opportunities. At the same time, lingering deflation has limited the decline of the real interest rate to sufficiently stimulate credit demand. The shrinking net interest margin on loans (about 0.6–1.2 percent now relative to about 1.2–2.1 percent in the early 2000s) tends to limit banks' core profitability as interest income accounts for more than two-thirds of their total income.

- *Major banks weathered the global financial crisis well and have capacity to take on more foreign exposures.* They have abundant yen liquidity supported by a stable deposit base, and, as noted, further strengthened their capital adequacy after the global financial crisis, in part to meet the Basel III requirements. The resilience of Japanese banks' balance sheets has placed them in a good position to further expand overseas, despite lingering global and regional uncertainty.

- *Regional and global factors, such as large financing needs in emerging Asia, have offered new business opportunities for Japanese banks.* Major banks have benefited from the increasing outward foreign direct investment and trade linkages of Japanese firms. Financing needs for infrastructure in emerging Asia are large (about $8 trillion), according to data from the Asian Development Bank. These generate demand for cross-border financial activity between Japan and various foreign direct investment destinations.

- *Deleveraging of European banks since 2010 has accelerated the pace of overseas expansion.* Japanese banks, among other local Asian banks, have stepped up financing to gain market share against the scale-back of European banks in the region.

To analyze the role of these factors more formally for their contribution to the rise in cross-border bank lending, Lam (2013) conducted an empirical analysis to assess the determinants of banks' overseas expansion. The analysis also assesses whether and how the current expansion is different from previous episodes. Several other studies also looked into the factors contributing to cross-border banking through factor analyses and institutional features (Shirota 2013, Focarelli and Pozzolo 2005).

The empirical results suggest that global and regional factors explain a large part of the rise of foreign claims. Regarding domestic factors, the resilience of the major Japanese banks, particularly the strengthening of capital adequacy and low nonperforming loans, even during the global financial crisis, was found to contribute around one-third of foreign claims growth. As such, cross-border expansion is likely to continue under Abenomics. The empirical estimates suggest that the substitution effect between domestic and overseas lending contributed about 5 percent to the growth of foreign claims in Japan, indicating that recovering domestic opportunities may moderately slow, rather than reverse, overseas expansion.

Although Japanese financial institutions and the economy as a whole would benefit from a more diversified income base through banks' expanding abroad, a gradual and cautious approach in overseas strategies is warranted. Expanding overseas will nevertheless help financial institutions improve their profitability by better allocating their liquidity and developing local markets in Asia. But banks may also favor a gradual expansion to maintain their balance sheets under the global regulatory reform agenda (for example, Basel III requirements). A rapid expansion could lead to buying foreign assets at high prices or entering unfamiliar local markets that could eventually result in heavy losses, as happened in the late 1980s and 1990s.

POTENTIAL RISKS

Although the analysis in this chapter suggests that, if successful, Abenomics has the potential to reduce banks' interest rate risk exposures, weaken bank–sovereign linkages, and encourage more cross-border activities, new risks to the financial system may emerge. In particular:

- *Foreign exchange funding risks.* Quantitative and qualitative monetary easing could lead Japanese financial institutions (major banks and insurance companies) to go overseas more aggressively as they reallocate their portfolios. Higher overseas exposures may add to funding risks as securing stable and long-term dollar funding has remained a challenge for Japanese financial institutions. Supervisors should encourage banks to further improve their resilience against shocks by strengthening their funding sources and risk management, such as by closely monitoring the overseas maturity mismatch and foreign currency-denominated loan-to-deposit ratios. Cross-border collateral arrangements—in place with Singapore and Thailand and agreed to be established with Indonesia—could also help reduce local currency funding risks in overseas markets.[3] Cross-border risk monitoring arrangements with foreign supervisory authorities can also help monitor risks from these activities, including foreign exchange funding risks. In that regard, the supervisory agencies in Japan have signed the Financial Stability Board's Multilateral Framework for sharing the information of global, systemically important banks through the data gap initiatives in early 2013 based on discussions at the board.

- *Japanese regional banks.* A key risk factor for regional banks is low profitability stemming from weak loan demand in their core business areas. As a result, an important source of income for these banks is interest generated from long-term domestic bonds. In that context, if credit demand in regional economies is slow to pick up, and given limited opportunities for cross-border expansion, regional banks may decide to maintain their JGB holdings or even extend their maturity further, making them more susceptible to interest rate risk. This could happen especially if structural reforms disappoint, yielding an incomplete policy package. Though regional banks

---

[3] Under these arrangements, Japanese banks can draw funding from the host overseas central bank by posting JGBs as collateral with the BoJ. Haircuts are determined by the host central bank and the BoJ acts as custodian.

individually are small, as a group they are systemically important (with about 40 percent of banking system assets excluding the Japan Post Bank and agricultural cooperatives).
- *Rising risk premium.* A lack of medium-term fiscal adjustment may lead to a rising risk premium in JGB yields, as discussed in Arslanalp and Lam (2013). This could lead to substantial losses in the financial system, despite the current decline in JGB holdings, and undermine financial stability.

POLICY OPTIONS

The authorities have taken a number of steps to strengthen the financial sector's ability to provide risk capital to the economy and facilitate more portfolio rebalancing abroad. In January 2014, the Japan Exchange Group, the Tokyo Stock Exchange, and Nikkei launched a new index, JPX Nikkei 400, a return-on-equity-focused index to encourage companies and investors to pay more attention to corporate governance and profitability. In early 2014, the Government Pension Investment Fund decided to shift part of its domestic equity allocation from the Tokyo Stock Price Index (TOPIX) to the new index, which could prompt other institutions to follow. In January 2014, the government launched tax-free investment accounts designed to encourage Japanese households—with more than $16 trillion in financial assets—to put more of their saving into stocks, bonds, and investment trusts instead of parking them in bank accounts. In February 2014, the BoJ decided to extend its facilities to stimulate bank lending and support economic growth by one year, while doubling their size and extending their repayment period to four years.

While BoJ asset purchases could take up a significant amount of interest rate risk from Japanese banks in the next two years, their JGB holdings and related interest rate risk exposures could rise again in the absence of accompanying fiscal and structural reforms. Strengthening capital requirements for domestically active banks and private sector-led consolidation in the regional banking sector could help mitigate downside risks of incomplete policies on the more vulnerable parts of the banking sector. By strengthening their capital base, such policies could also allow these banks to take better advantage of the potential reduction in their interest rate risk exposure and increase lending to SMEs and other corporations. And that could, in turn, support the authorities' growth objectives by enhancing the provision of risk capital.

But further provision of risk capital will require actions that go beyond banks. Specifically:
- *Securitization.* There is room for boosting securitization activity backed by small business loans, possibly by encouraging more information sharing across multiple credit registries on the repayment and default history of individual firms. There may also be scope for greater coordination between the Ministry of Finance and the BoJ to facilitate greater use of the central bank's existing growth-supporting facilities for asset-backed lending (by further easing terms on BoJ facilities, including by lowering funding costs

and extending the maturity of the loans). Risks and abuses associated with the originate-to-distribute framework underlying securitization could be contained by requiring originators to hold an equity position/loss absorption buffer on the underlying loans.
- *Venture capital.* The Government Pension Investment Fund reforms first proposed in November 2013 and adopted in October 2014, along with the shift in the portfolio targets, are an encouraging development in this regard. A further shift in targets toward riskier assets such as venture capital could spur faster growth in funding for new businesses. As was seen in the United States, the 1979 reform of the Employment Retirement Income Security Act allowed pension funds to invest in high-risk assets leading to an increase in venture capital funding, a rising share of corporate research and development financed by venture capital firms, and better quality patenting (measured by citation accounts) associated with this.
- *Restructuring and exit of nonviable SMEs.* As noted, the persistence of nonviable firms, kept afloat in part by restructured loans and progressively easier terms of financing, impedes credit intermediation and risk taking in several ways, such as by deterring the entry of new firms and the expansion of healthy firms, and by eroding the risk assessment capabilities at banks. Achieving turnover rates that reflect underlying fundamentals will involve phasing out credit guarantees, overhauling bankruptcy procedures, and, where needed, consolidating regional banks whose capital buffers are weakened by calling in nonperforming loans. At the same time, small business entry could be facilitated by reducing the time and cost of starting businesses, including through streamlining business registration procedures and upgrading credit registries and personal credit information.

CONCLUSION

In this chapter we explored how the domestic and cross-border balance sheets of Japanese institutions may change under the government's new policies. Indeed, portfolio rebalancing is a key element of the transmission of the BoJ's monetary easing program. It would also facilitate higher economic growth through greater provision of risk capital and weaken bank–sovereign linkages. On the latter, a key vulnerability of Japan's financial system is its high exposure to interest rate risk as a result of large JGB holdings, and the results presented in this chapter suggest that this risk will persistently decline if Abenomics is successful. In contrast, incomplete Abenomics that fails to raise potential growth and restore fiscal sustainability implies that interest rate risk exposure could quickly rise again. This is because banks may once again have to absorb large government financing needs and their profitability, and Tier 1 capital growth could decline in the absence of sufficiently ambitious structural reforms.

The present analysis finds that Japanese banks are well positioned to scale up foreign exposures, thanks to their relatively resilient balance sheets and continued growth in Asia. Stronger domestic growth in Japan under successful Abenomics could mitigate the pace, but is unlikely to reverse the expansion as global and regional pull-factors play a more prominent role in the growth of cross-border claims. At the same time, increasing cross-border activity could pose funding risks and supervisory challenges, and require continued close monitoring.

We discussed a number of policy options to expand the provision of risk capital. The analysis presented in this chapter suggests that additional policy efforts should focus on intermediation (securitization and venture capital) and on take up on the demand side (exit and entry of firms, corporate restructuring).

REFERENCES

Arslanalp, S., and R. Lam. 2013. "Outlook for Interest Rates and Japanese Banks' Risk Exposures under Abenomics." IMF Working Paper No. 13/213. International Monetary Fund, Washington, DC.

Bank of Japan. 2013. Financial System Reports, October 2013. http://www.boj.or.jp/en/research/brp/fsr/index.htm/.

Caballero, R.J., T. Hoshi, and A.K. Kashyap. 2008. "Zombie Lending and Depressed Restructuring in Japan." *American Economic Review* 98 (5): 1943–77.

Focarelli, D., and A. F. Pozzolo. 2005. "Where Do Banks Expand Abroad? An Empirical Analysis." *The Journal of Business* 78 (6): 2435–64.

International Monetary Fund. 2012. "Japan: Financial System Stability Assessment Update." IMF Country Report No. 12/210, Washington. www.imf.org/external/pubs/ft/scr/2012/cr12210.pdf.

———. 2013. "Japan: Article IV Consultation Report," IMF Country Report No. 13/253. Washington. www.imf.org/external/pubs/ft/scr/2013/cr13253.pdf.

Lam, R. 2013. "Cross-Border Activity of Japanese Banks." IMF Working Paper No. 13/235. International Monetary Fund, Washington, DC.

Lam, R., and J. Shin. 2012. "What Role Can Financial Policies Play in Revitalizing SMEs in Japan?" IMF Working Paper No. 12/291. International Monetary Fund, Washington, DC.

Nabar, M., and M. Syed. 2011. "The Great Rebalancing Act: Can Investment Be a Lever?" IMF Working Paper No. 11/35. International Monetary Fund, Washington, DC.

Shirota, T. 2013. "What Is the Major Determinant of Credit Flows through Cross-Border Banking?" Bank of Japan Working Paper Series, No. 13-E-5, Tokyo: Bank of Japan.

CHAPTER 9

Stimulating Private Investment and Innovation

Joong Shik Kang

With Abenomics now nearly two years underway, the economy now needs to transition from a stimulus-driven to a self-sustained recovery. With the fiscal stance expected to turn contractionary and headwinds from Japans' shrinking labor force because of population aging, capital accumulation and productivity gains need to become the main drivers of potential growth. Fortunately, the current business conditions (Figure 9.1) provide a favorable backdrop for higher corporate investment (see Chapter 3).

In this chapter we discuss past corporate investment trends and the key drivers of private investment, and formulate policy options to stimulate innovation. Specifically, we try to answer the following questions:

- How has Japan performed in terms of private investment over the last several decades?
- What has been driving the decline in corporate investment, especially by small and medium-sized enterprises (SMEs)?
- What kinds of policies could help boost investment?

During Japan's boom years in the 1980s, when growth averaged 4½ percent per year, private investment was an important driver for this expansion, accounting for more than a third of growth (Figure 9.2). However, since the asset-price collapse of the early 1990s, the investment-to-GDP ratio has declined steadily and was 16½ percent in 2013, down from its peak of 25 percent in 1990.[1] Accordingly the contribution to growth from private investment has also declined sharply and has been negative since the global financial crisis. As discussed in Chapter 6, productivity growth has remained solid in Japan, with weak investment and the shrinking labor force the main contributors to the sharp slowdown in potential growth during the Lost Decade.

This chapter finds that the main common factors driving investment depend on firm characteristics such as size, sector, overseas exposure, and capital intensity. We find that expectations of future profitability and the deterioration of the demand outlook, as well as trend appreciation of the yen prior to the onset of

---

[1] Strong private investment in the 1980s was partly driven by the asset bubble and, as such, it was not sustainable.

148 Stimulating Private Investment and Innovation

Figure 9.1 Tankan Survey: Overall Enterprise Business Conditions *(Percent)*

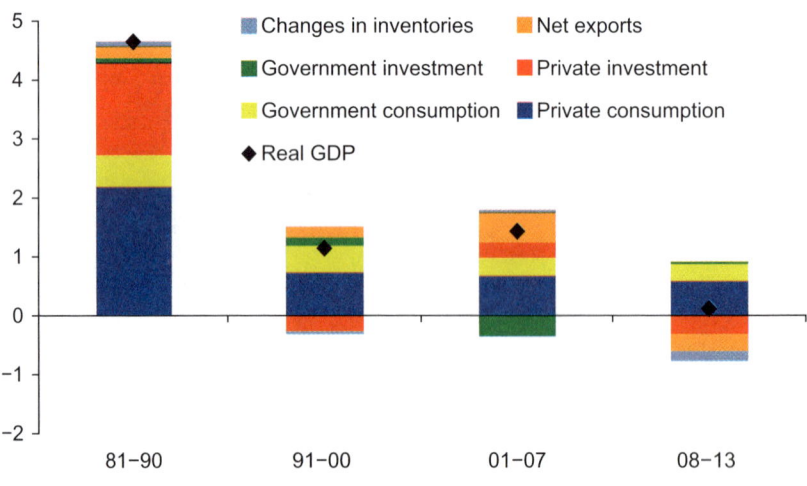

Source: Bank of Japan.

Figure 9.2 Contributions to Growth *(Percent, annualized)*

Sources: Cabinet Office; and IMF staff estimates.

Abenomics, seem to be common factors behind the steady investment decline. By sectoral composition, private investment shifted markedly toward manufacturing in the 2000s, particularly in the main exporting sectors, as weak growth prospects caused by slowing consumer demand and stagnant land prices shrank business opportunities for SMEs at home and hence deterred their capital investments.

RECENT INVESTMENT TRENDS

Behind the decline in total investment since the asset bubble burst in the 1990s is a sharp adjustment of nonresidential investment, which fell from about 20 percent of GDP in 1991 to 13½ percent as of 2013, lower than the post-bubble period average of about 14 percent (Figure 9.3). The moderation of nonresidential investment growth has increased the age of the existing capital stock, estimated to have reached 16 years, about three to four years older than that the United States. Although investment has begun to improve following the large decline during the global financial crisis, its pace remained moderate during the first two years of Abenomics. Japanese firms have expanded abroad, in particular to emerging Asia, over the last decade to tap into rising demand, utilize cheaper labor costs in emerging market economies, and to counter the effects of the yen's trend appreciation. Nonetheless, firms' investment abroad does not appear to substitute for domestic investment (Figure 9.4), with both generally rising in tandem, albeit with greater divergence lately. Tanaka (2012) also finds that the empirical evidence does not support that foreign direct investment hollows out domestic manufacturing or employment.

As noted in Syed and Lee (2010), the composition of investment also shifted in the 2000s. During the recovery of 2003–07, large manufacturing firms drove fixed investment to a great extent, particularly in the main exporting sectors: automobiles, machinery, electronics, and steel (Figure 9.5). As a result, domestic investment and trading partner demand have become increasingly correlated, and both exports and investment contracted sharply during the global financial crisis. On the other hand, investment by SMEs and firms operating in the services sector has been relatively stagnant in real terms: the share of the nonmanufacturing sector in overall investment fell from 70 percent in 2000 to just over 50 percent

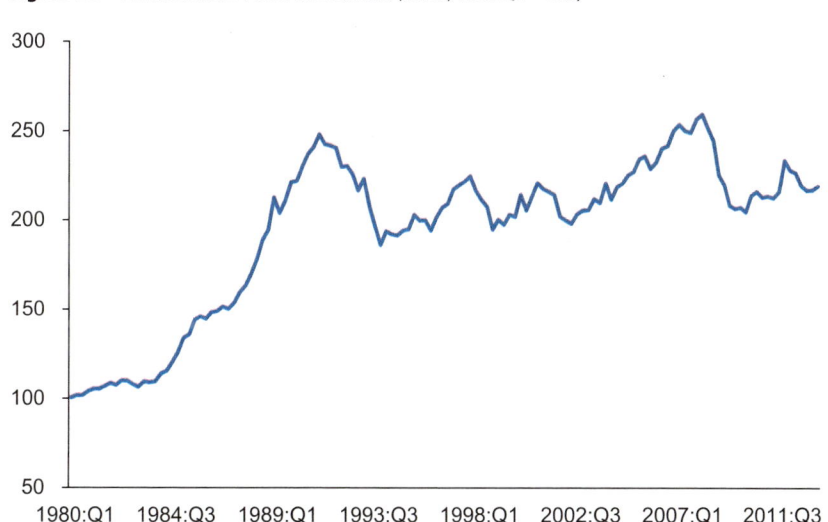

Figure 9.3 Real Business Fixed Investment *(Index, 1980:Q1 = 100)*

Sources: Cabinet Office; and IMF staff estimates.

Figure 9.4 Corporate Investment and Foreign Direct Investment *(Percent of GDP)*

Sources: Bank of Japan; Cabinet Office; and IMF staff estimates.

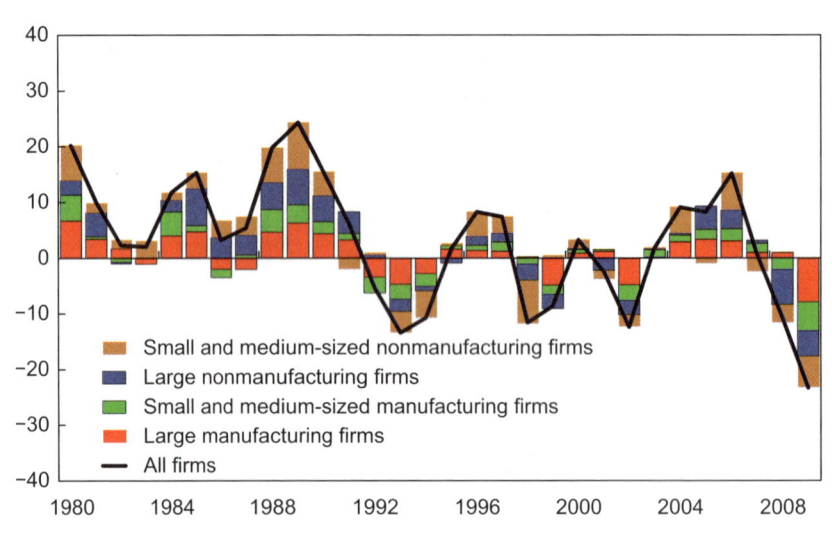

Figure 9.5 Business Fixed Investment *(Year-over-year percent change)*

Sources: Japan Ministry of Finance; and IMF staff estimates.

in 2007. This decline contrasts sharply with developments in comparator economies with similar initial conditions, where the share of nonmanufacturing investment rose to about 80 percent during the same period (Figure 9.6).

SMEs have been a major source of employment and growth, but their weak performance has hindered their role in the Japanese economy. As Lam and Shin (2012) note, the sector accounts for nearly 70 percent of total employment and over 50 percent of manufacturing value-added (Figure 9.7). SME businesses span

Figure 9.6 Composition of Investment by Sector *(Percent of total at constant 1995 prices)*

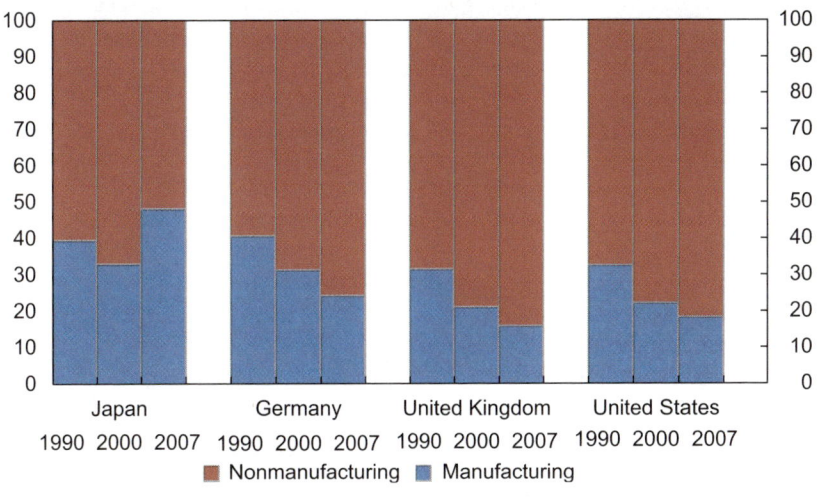

Source: EU KLEMS Database.
Note: Excludes finance, insurance, real estate, and public utilities.

Figure 9.7 Employment Share of Small and Medium Enterprises across Advanced Economies *(Percent)*

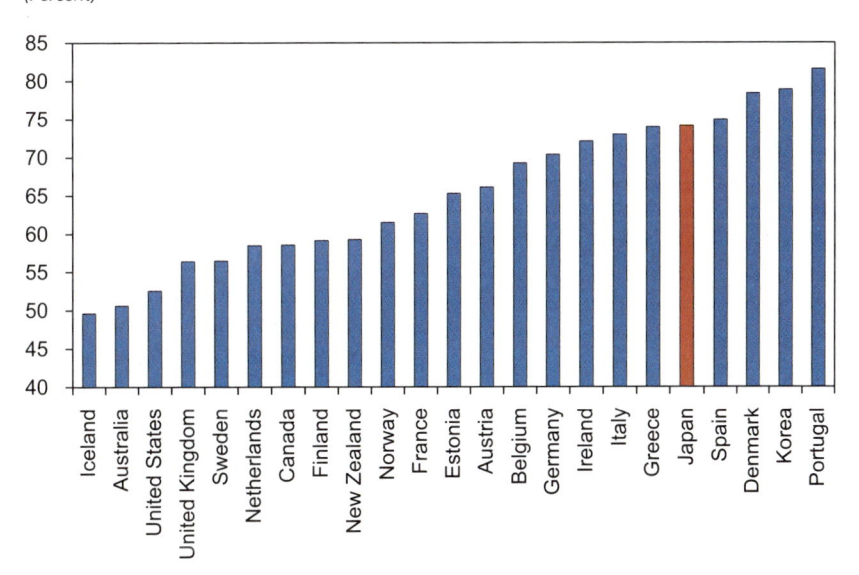

Source: Ayyagari, Beck, and Demirgüç-Kunt (2005).

many industries, have historically served as key suppliers to large manufacturing firms, and are the backbone of the services sector. Over the last decade, however, SMEs have no longer been a thriving source of growth. The profitability and investment of these firms have declined significantly and business registration in net terms has been stagnant since the global financial crisis, despite very accommodative financing conditions.

Amid this trend, Syed and Lee (2010) noted that the capital efficiency of Japanese firms is relatively low, pointing to the need for more innovation. For example, although the capital intensity (measured by the net capital stock per person) of the Japanese economy has been rising since the 1970s and is high compared with advanced economy peers (Figure 9.8), capital productivity (measured by output per net capital stock) has declined and is now appreciably lower than that in the

Figure 9.8 Net Capital Stock per Person Employed *(Thousands of U.S. dollars, constant 2000 prices)*

Source: European Union, Annual Macro-Economic (AMECO) Database.

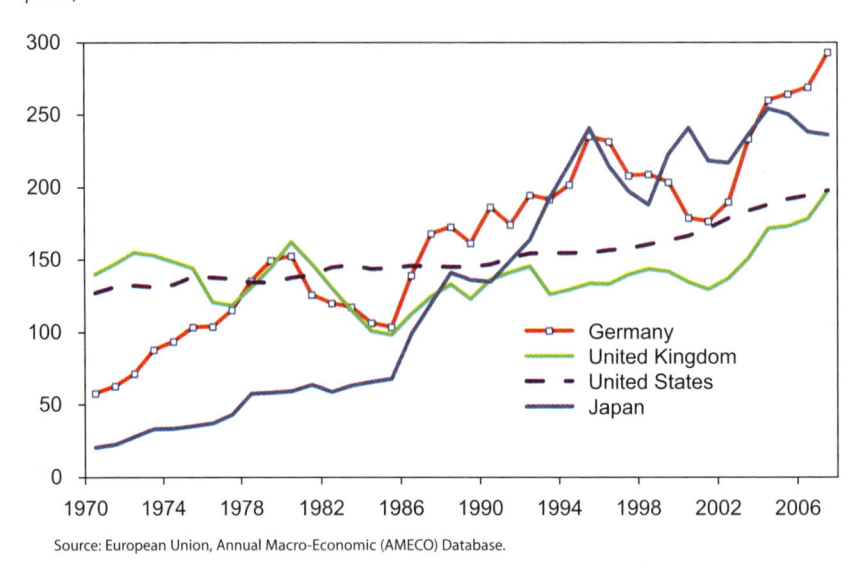

Figure 9.9 Capital Productivity *(GDP divided by net capital stock)*

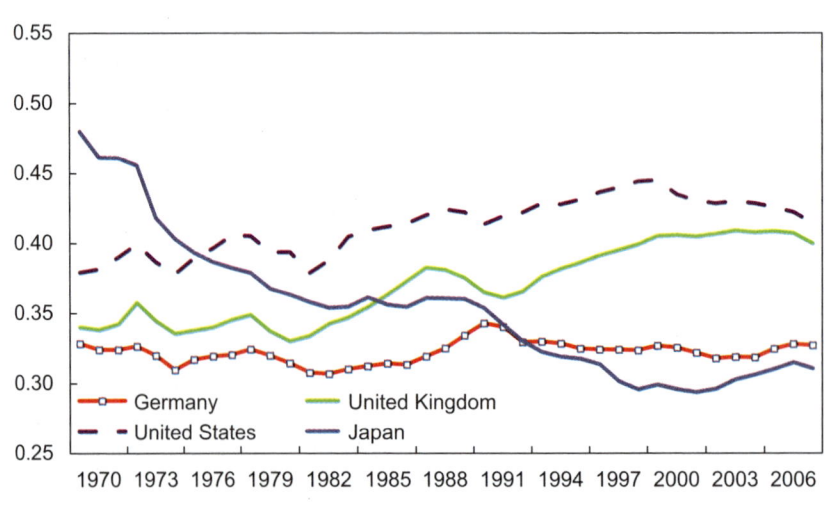

Sources: European Union, Annual Macro-Economic (AMECO) Database; and IMF staff estimates.

United Kingdom and the United States (Figure 9.9).[2] This suggests the need for more innovation and intangible investment to boost the efficiency of Japan's capital stock, including through increased spending on research and development.

Japanese firms' research and development spending as share of GDP is the third-highest in the Organization for Economic Cooperation and Development (OECD), but its benefit in raising productivity growth has lagged over the last two decades (OECD 2005, Brandstetter and Nakamura 2003). Several contributing factors have been identified in the literature:

- The waning importance of process and incremental product innovation in which Japan has traditionally excelled, and the lack of "radical product innovation" (Sakakibara and Tsujimoto 2003);
- Vertically integrated structures and weaknesses in areas in which collaboration with a broad range of organizations is critical, such as services and software (Takeishi and Fujimoto 2003);
- Weak links between research and development sectors (universities, businesses, and the public sector);
- A relatively low degree of openness to foreign investment, and the underdeveloped venture capital industry (see also Chapter 8).

Syed and Lee (2010) noted that the low share of services in business research and development also stands out and may be contributing to low productivity in the sector, which, at 12 percent, contrasts sharply with the 43 percent in the United States and an OECD average of 25 percent. By type of investment, capital spending related to information and communication technology is low. A large proportion of the acceleration in labor productivity in the United States since the mid-1990s originated in services that use information and communication technology intensively, including retail, wholesale, finance, and telecommunications. But the contribution to labor productivity of services using such technology is low in Japan and has declined significantly since 1995 (OECD 2008).

WHAT EXPLAINS THESE TRENDS?

What has led to the trend decline in private nonresidential investment over the last two decades? Among the explanations, one would expect that, with the burst of the asset-price bubble and stock market collapse in 1990s, weak domestic demand and lower profitability initially impaired investment, while higher-than-warranted real interest rates owing to deflation could have played a role later on. The exchange rate may have contributed positively during the carry-trade period and negatively afterward.

The estimation of aggregate private nonresidential investment based on several traditional models generally confirms this pattern (Kang 2014). In line with the investment literature (Lee and Rabanal 2010, among others), investment in Japan

---

[2]The fact that the capital stock is older in Japan than in the United States likely contributes to lower capital productivity as well.

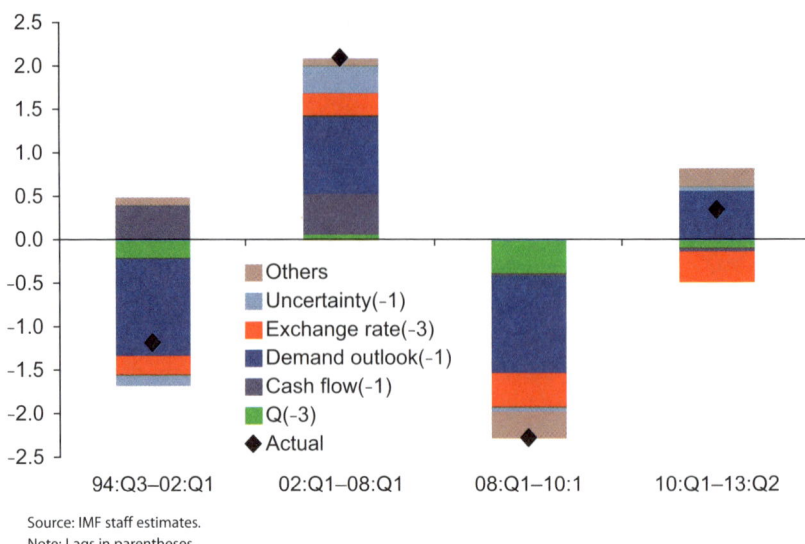

Figure 9.10 Contribution to the Change in the Investment-to-Capital Ratio *(Percent)*

Source: IMF staff estimates.
Note: Lags in parentheses.

is positively associated with expectations of future profitability, summarized by Tobin's Q,[3] and better liquidity conditions, which are captured by cash flows. Elevated uncertainty, proxied by the standard deviation of consensus growth forecasts, and exchange rate appreciation have also hindered private investment. But in terms of economic significance, business expectations of medium-term demand growth (domestic and external) have been the key factor driving private nonresidential investment during the slump and recovery periods. Together with the finding that high real interest rates have hurt corporate investment, this suggests that deflation has been detrimental for investment, both directly through higher financing costs and indirectly through diminished expectations of future demand and by lowering the opportunity cost of cash holdings.

Model estimates highlight the following factors during four key time periods (Figure 9.10):

- After the bubble burst in the 1990s, the domestic demand outlook deteriorated sharply, together with yen appreciation, leading to a large decline in private investment.
- Investment recovered in the 2000s on the back of an improved demand outlook, partly as a result of a booming global economic environment, and improved liquidity conditions. The reversal of yen appreciation and less growth uncertainty also contributed to higher investment over this period.
- During the 2008–09 global financial crisis, in addition to the sharp deterioration in both domestic and foreign demand, the sustained large appreciation of the yen on the back of safe-haven flows contributed to the large decline in private investment.

---

[3]The ratio of the market value of a firm's assets to the replacement cost of the firm's assets.

Figure 9.11 Elasticity of Fixed Investment to Fundamentals

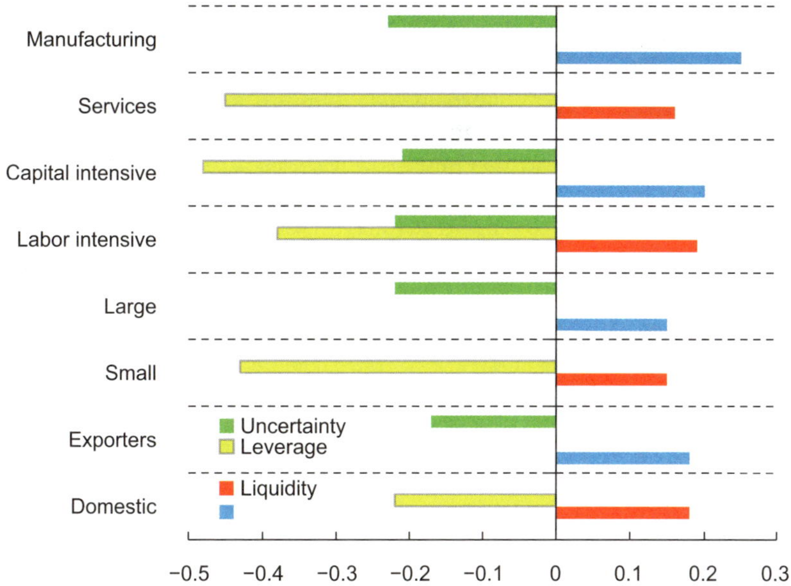

[Bar chart showing Uncertainty, Leverage, Liquidity, and (Tobin's Q) elasticities across categories: Manufacturing, Services, Capital intensive, Labor intensive, Large, Small, Exporters, Domestic]

Sources: Worldscope; and IMF staff estimates.
Note: As summarized by Tobin's Q.

- Since 2010 despite the gradual recovery in the global economy and improvement in the demand outlook, continued yen appreciation has slowed the investment recovery.

Throughout these episodes, what stands out is the importance of the demand outlook, including external conditions. Model estimates using firm-level data confirm the importance of economic fundamentals for fixed investment (Syed and Lee 2010).[4] Although investment is positively related to expectations of future profitability, as summarized by Tobin's Q, it is negatively associated with leverage and uncertainty (Figure 9.11). The coefficient on cash flow is positive but not statistically significant, suggesting that the average listed firm in Japan is not financially constrained. This is consistent with the view that liquidity is abundant in Japan and that large firms typically hold excess cash.

Confirming the results from the aggregate analysis, the determinants of investment have changed over time. Declining investment rates in the 1990s seem to mainly reflect diminished profit expectations, consistent with the hypothesis that low demand for investment because of declining profitability was the key factor during the 1990s. By contrast, the stronger relationship observed between investment, leverage, and uncertainty in the full sample (1990–2008) seems to reflect the behavior of Japanese firms during the 2000s.

Syed and Lee (2010) also found that factors driving investment also differ significantly based on firm characteristics, including size, sector, overseas exposure,

---

[4]Intangible investments are also driven by economic fundamentals, although to a smaller extent.

and capital intensity. For larger firms, manufacturers, exporters, and those using capital-intensive technology, profit expectations and uncertainty have powerful effects on investment. This may reflect their greater exposure to international competition, as well as to fluctuations in domestic and overseas macroeconomic conditions. By contrast, investment is more sensitive to cash flow for smaller firms, service providers, non-exporters, and those using labor-intensive technology. This cross-sectional variation in the coefficient on cash flow supports its interpretation as an indicator of financing constraints. For the smaller group of firms, despite progress with corporate restructuring, a legacy of excess leverage and dependence on debt financing continues to hold back investment. This effect is concentrated in those firms that have high debt and low profitability, suggesting threshold effects.

For SMEs, weak growth prospects with slowing consumer demand and stagnant land prices have shrunk business opportunities and deterred capital investments (Lam and Shin 2012). SMEs' anemic credit growth is attributable in part to their structural weaknesses, with nonviable firms kept afloat through the provision of low interest rates and the help of public credit support measures (such as full-value credit guarantees) (Figure 9.12). Firm-level data and sectoral corporate balance sheets show that many SMEs have high leverage and low profitability. The global financial crisis further weakened the financial position across SMEs, particularly those with low credit worthiness. Finally, regulatory barriers and the lack of market development have also played a role by adding to the costs of starting a business and limiting the types of credit available, among other things.

The preference of Japanese firms for large cash holdings (see Chapter 6) may also have hindered investment growth, aside from constraining wage and dividend growth (Figure 9.13). The accumulation of cash and deposits has occurred

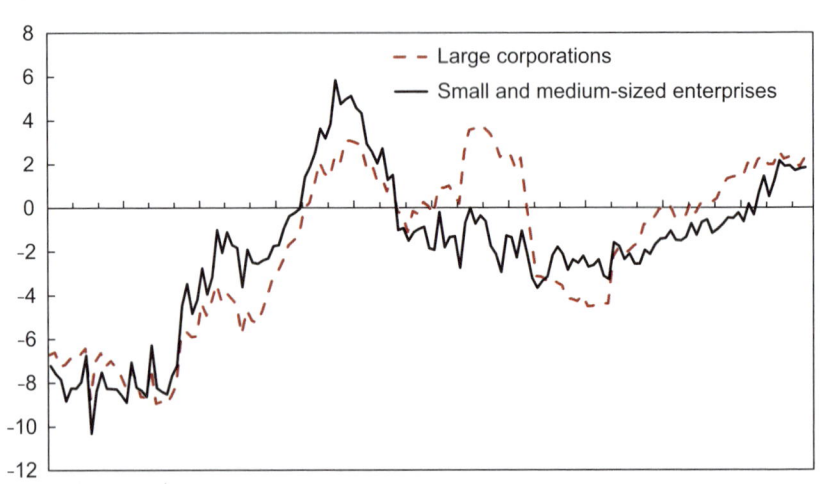

Figure 9.12 Bank Lending to the Corporate Sector *(Percent; year-over-year)*

Source: CEIC.

Figure 9.13 Listed Companies' Cash and Cash Equivalents Holdings *(Percent of market capitalization; average, 2004–12)*

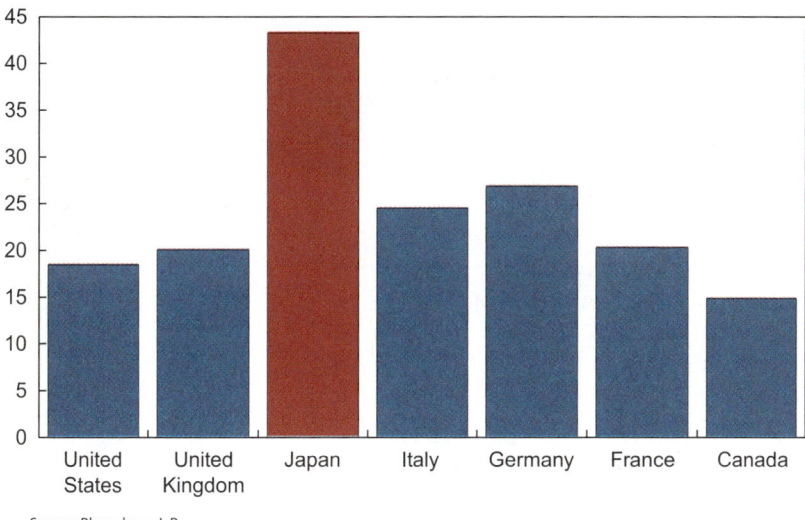

Source: Bloomberg, L.P.

Figure 9.14 Cash and Overseas Investment *(Percent of GDP)*

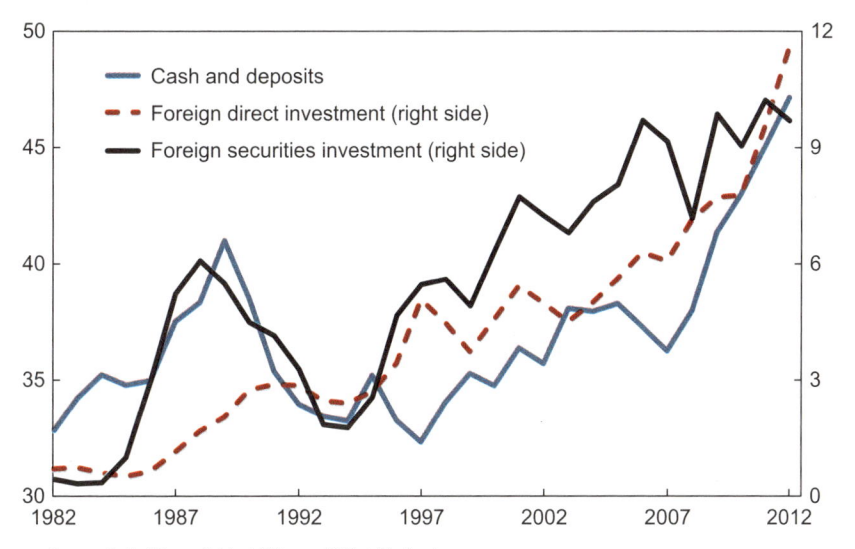

Sources: Bank of Japan; Cabinet Office; and IMF staff estimates.

against the backdrop of greater overseas investment (Figure 9.14) and reduction in debt (Figure 9.15), implying that, in principle, firms' balance sheets are now strong enough to accommodate higher investment, wages, and dividends. Kinoshita (2013) notes that the Japanese legal framework contributes to large cash holdings as bankruptcy procedures may increase managers' preference for

Figure 9.15 Corporate Sector Gross Debt *(Percent of GDP)*

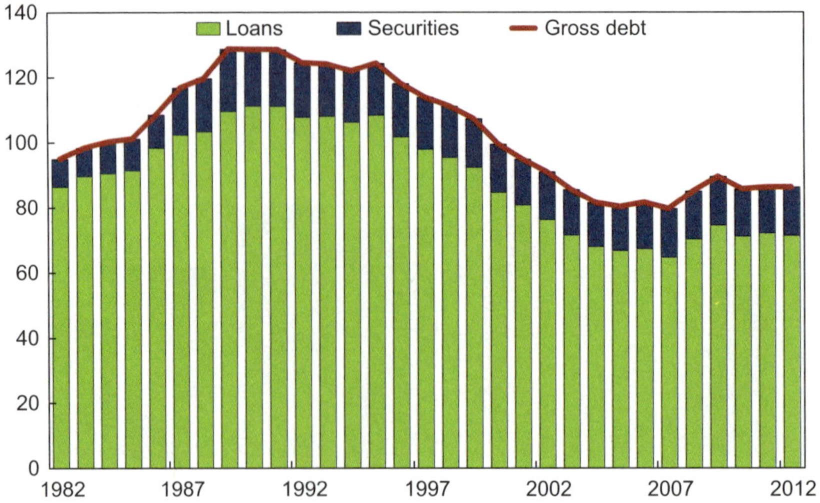

Sources: Bank of Japan; and IMF staff estimates.

precautionary cash holdings. Takeover regulations, enforcement of enterprise law, and the share ownership structure also do not pressure managers enough to act in the interests of shareholders. Entrenched deflation expectations are another important determinant of large cash holdings in Japan, because a deflationary environment lowers the opportunity cost of holding cash for both managers and shareholders.

However, weaker corporate governance than in other advanced economies may also contribute to large cash holdings and lower investment. Specifically, some internationally comparable indicators, including an index of corporate governance outcomes (de facto corporate governance) and a firm-level governance index (Aggarwal and others 2010), suggest that corporate governance might be weaker in Japan than in other advanced economies. As a consequence, managers in Japan might have more leeway to pursue "individual benefits" rather than maximize shareholder value, thus choosing to hold more cash and investing less. Aoyagi and Ganelli (2014) found that better corporate governance reduces cash holdings.

Furthermore, as discussed in Chapter 5, the high statutory and effective corporate income tax rate in Japan impedes investment and creates debt bias and incentives for income shifting. Using estimates for the elasticity of corporate taxable income, de Mooij and Saito (2014) note that investment could be boosted by around 0.4 percent for each percentage point reduction in the corporate income tax rate. They also add that, based on international and Japan-specific empirical estimates of corporate tax elasticities, between 10 and 30 percent of the static revenue loss could be recovered in the long run through dynamic scoring, although Japan's offset may be closer to the lower bound of this range.

POLICY IMPLICATIONS

Both aggregate and firm-level analyses suggest that policies should focus on the following areas to increase investment: (1) improving the demand outlook; (2) increasing the return on investment; (3) reducing uncertainty; and (4) improving access to external financing to reduce the cost of capital, especially for smaller and domestically oriented firms.

1. The successful implementation of structural reforms, the third arrow of Abenomics, is crucial to increase private investment and raise potential growth. Even though such measures typically take some time to roll out, they could have a positive impact on private investment even in the near term by improving confidence in the domestic demand outlook. The estimation results on aggregate investment imply that improving the outlook to 2006–07 levels would raise private nonresidential investment about 5 percent (or about 0.5 percent in terms of the investment-to-GDP ratio).

2. Although corporate income tax reform could stimulate incentives to invest (Cummins, Hassett, and Hubbard 1995), a cut to the rate is not self-financing and the government faces tight fiscal constraints, as noted in Chapter 5 and in de Mooij and Saito (2014). Any rate reduction must therefore be part of a more comprehensive fiscal reform plan. If revenue losses from a rate reduction are offset by base broadening measures within the corporate income tax, the scope for a cut is limited and reform runs the risk of undoing positive investment effects. However, eliminating some special tax incentives, abolishing the special treatment of SMEs, and bringing about a modest rate reduction could simplify the corporate income tax and yield benefits in the form of lower income shifting and lower debt bias. One promising additional reform option is to introduce an allowance for corporate equity, applied to incremental investment, which could significantly reduce marginal effective tax rates while eliminating debt bias, with fiscal costs incurring only gradually.

3. Reducing uncertainty would help lower the risks associated with long-term investment decisions. These can be affected by uncertainty about many, potentially exogenous, aspects of the operating environment—such as demand, prices, costs, and exchange rates—as well as risks related to policies. Potential options include promoting the use of financial instruments to manage risks, further strengthening the business climate, and credible and concrete medium-term fiscal consolidation that would remove concerns about tail risks and reduce the debt overhang.

4. Improving access to external financing would lower the cost of capital for smaller firms and those in the services sector. Incomplete financial products, regulatory rigidities, gaps in the legal framework, or information asymmetries between financiers and firms are especially acute for start-ups. These typically represent an important source of innovation and will become even more essential as production processes are revamped in response

to a changed postcrisis global landscape. Potential options include widening the pool of venture capital funding available for start-ups in new emerging sectors, broadening eligible collateral to allow for a wider range of securitization beyond real estate and other fixed assets, and greater risk-based lending.[5]

In addition, several financial policy measures could help foster a more dynamic SME sector and lift productivity through reducing leverage and improving incentives for corporate restructuring. To this end, policies could focus on the following areas: (1) gradually phasing out credit support measures, (2) encouraging consolidation of regional and *shinkin* banks with low profitability by raising their capital requirements, (3) accelerating SME restructuring, (4) promoting risk-based financing by encouraging use of asset-based lending and deepening capital markets, and (5) streamlining regulatory measures to reduce the time and cost of starting businesses.[6]

1. Special credit guarantees with full coverage of the loan value need to be phased out as the recovery takes hold. Over time, reducing the normal guarantee coverage ratio from 80 to 60 percent in line with international averages (IMF 2006) and scrutinizing the rollover of guarantees would ensure market discipline in monitoring credit risk by banks.

2. Increasing the capital requirement for domestically oriented banks from the current 4 percent would facilitate consolidation. For instance, about 5 percent of smaller banks would have a capital shortfall if the capital requirement for those banks was raised to 6 percent of risk-weighted assets (still below the minimum requirement of internationally active banks at 8 percent).[7]

3. The public asset management company could be refocused to advance SME restructuring. This would encourage the restructuring and exit of nonviable SMEs by using debt-equity swaps to incentivize banks and SMEs for out-of-court voluntary workouts (Laryea 2010).

4. The authorities (government and municipalities) could take the lead in originating and trading electronically registered claims for firms and households, which could avoid the risks of double assignment of claims. Capital markets for securitized loans could be developed further by revising the investment restrictions for institutional investors (for example, pension

---

[5]See Chapter 8 for a full discussion of the provision of risk capital.
[6]Addressing structural weaknesses and accelerating SME restructuring could have a noticeable impact on the economy's growth potential. Based on simulations with the IMF's Global Integrated Monetary and Fiscal model, addressing SME structural weaknesses could raise aggregate productivity by about ¼ percentage point, which in turn would lift long-term growth 0.1–0.2 percentage points from the baseline.
[7]This may risk a contraction in credit in the near term as regional banks deleverage to meet the capital requirement, but the contraction could largely be mitigated by bringing in new capital through equity issuance, lower dividend payouts, or a temporary public capital injection. Over the medium term, higher capital would put these institutions in a stronger financial position to take on risk.

funds) to encourage alternative investments such as securitized loans and venture capital (see Chapter 8).
5. The coverage of credit registries could be broadened through a more centralized database and by including a consumer data bureau for personal credit information. This could be facilitated by linking the proposed taxpayer identification system to the collection of credit information of firms and individuals.

As noted, corporate governance reforms would also help by removing some of the bottlenecks that encourage high corporate cash holdings and prevent a more pro-growth use of resources. Among the various options considered by the government, the introduction of a stewardship code, aimed at increasing fiduciary responsibilities of institutional shareholders, would encourage managers to maximize shareholders' value. The recent launch of the JPX-Nikkei Index 400, which includes only profitable companies with good corporate governance, is also expected to have a positive impact.

More ambitious measures could be considered to improve corporate governance to discourage excessive corporate savings such as expanding the use of outside directors and complementing a stewardship code with a corporate governance code for firms.

CONCLUSION

This chapter investigated the causes of the steady decline in investment after the asset-price bubble burst. In sectoral composition, private investment shifted markedly toward the manufacturing sector in the 2000s, particularly in the main exporting sectors, as weak growth prospects with slowing consumer demand and stagnant land prices shrank business opportunities for SMEs at home and hence deterred their capital investments. Over this period, the capital efficiency of Japanese firms was relatively low, pointing to the need for more innovation. Indeed, higher investment will be essential to move Abenomics to the next phase in which growth is increasingly self-sustained rather than stimulus driven.

This chapter finds that the main common factors driving investment depend on firm characteristics such as size, sector, overseas exposure, and capital intensity. It also finds that expectations of future profitability and the deterioration of the demand outlook, as well as the trend appreciation of the yen prior to the onset of Abenomics, seem to be common factors behind the steady investment decline. Model estimates using firm-level data confirm the importance of economic fundamentals for fixed investment.

The key policy implications include improving the level and certainty of the demand outlook, enhancing the provision of risk capital, and reforming corporate income tax and corporate governance. As such, the goal of increasing investment will, to a large extent, depend on how ambitious the structural reforms will be under Abenomics' third arrow. As noted in previous chapters, if successful, there will be important synergies with the other objectives of exiting deflation and achieving fiscal sustainability.

REFERENCES

Aggarwal, R., I. Erel, M. Ferreira, and P. Matos. 2010. "Does Governance Travel Around the World? Evidence from Institutional Investors," Fisher College of Business Working Paper No. 2009-008. Ohio: Ohio State University.

Aoyagi, C., and G. Ganelli. 2014. "Un-Stash" the Cash! Corporate Governance Reform in Japan." IMF Working Paper No. 14/140. International Monetary Fund, Washington, DC.

Ayyagari, M., T. Beck, and A. Demirgüç-Kunt. 2005. "Small and Medium Enterprises across the Globe." www.tilburguniversity.edu/webwijs/files/center/beck/.../globe.pdf.

Brandstetter, L., and Y. Nakamura. 2003. "Is Japan's Innovative Capacity in Decline?" NBER Working Paper No. 9438. Cambridge, Massachusetts: National Bureau of Economic Research.

Cummins, J.G., K.A. Hassett, and R.G. Hubbard. 1995. "Tax Reforms and Investment: A Cross-Country Comparison." *Journal of Public Economics* 62 (1–2): 237–73.

de Mooij, R., and I. Saito. 2014. "Japan's Corporate Income Tax: Facts, Issues, and Reform Options," IMF Working Paper No. 14/138. International Monetary Fund, Washington, DC.

International Monetary Fund. 2006. "Republic of Korea: Selected Issues." IMF Country Report No. 06/381, Washington, DC.

Kang, J.S. 2014. "Balance Sheet Repair and Corporate Investment in Japan." IMF Working Paper No. 14/141. International Monetary Fund, Washington, DC.

Kinoshita, N. 2013. "Legal Background to the Low Profitability of Japanese Enterprises." Center on Japanese Economy and Business Working Papers No. 316. New York: Columbia University.

Lam, R.W., and J. Shin. 2012. "What Role Can Financial Policies Play in Revitalizing SMEs in Japan?" IMF Working Paper No. 12/291. International Monetary Fund, Washington, DC.

Laryea T. 2010. "Approaches to Corporate Debt Restructuring in the Wake of Financial Crises." IMF Staff Position Note No. 10/02. International Monetary Fund, Washington, DC.

Lee, J., and P. Rabanal. 2010. "Forecasting U.S. Investment." IMF Working Paper No. 10/246. International Monetary Fund, Washington, DC.

Organization for Economic Cooperation and Development (OECD). 2005. *OECD Economic Survey of Japan*. Paris: OECD.

———. 2008. *OECD Science, Technology, and Industry Scoreboard*. Paris: OECD.

Sakakibara, K., and M. Tsujimoto. 2003. "Why Did R&D Productivity of Japanese Firms Decline?" ESRI Discussion Paper Series No. 47. Tokyo: Economic and Social Research Institute, Cabinet Office.

Syed, M., and J. Lee. 2010. "Japan's Quest for Growth: Exploring the Role of Capital and Innovation." IMF Working Paper No. 10/294. International Monetary Fund, Washington, DC.

Takeishi, A., and T. Fujimoto. 2003. "Modularization in the Car Industry: Interlinked Multiple Hierarchies of Product, Production and Supplier Systems," in *The Business of Systems Integration*, edited by A. Prencipe, A. Davies, and M. Hobday. Oxford: Oxford University Press.

Tanaka, A. 2012. "The Effects of FDI on Domestic Employment and Workforce Composition." RIETI Discussion Paper Series, No. 12-E-069. Tokyo: Research Institute of Economy, Trade, and Industry.

CHAPTER 10

Japan's Role in the Global Economy and Spillover Effects of Abenomics

DENNIS BOTMAN AND JOONG SHIK KANG

The previous chapters have shown that successful Abenomics could help Japan achieve higher growth, lower government debt, and stronger financial sector stability. But what would be the implications of this for key trading partners and the rest of the world? Abenomics can affect other countries through higher import demand if growth increases, through competitiveness changes following exchange rate moves, through capital flows amid portfolio rebalancing in light of the quantitative and qualitative monetary easing framework, and by affecting global risk sentiment in case the policy package is incomplete.

Concerns at the start of Abenomics, especially in Asia, focused on potential spillovers on trade and capital flows. Specifically, trading partners worried that the depreciation of the yen would lower their price competitiveness, while capital inflows from Japan could create additional exchange rate pressure. These did not materialize in the first two years of Abenomics, showing that the domestic private sector response was not fully forthcoming.

In this chapter, we summarize special features of Japan's integration with the global economy and discuss how these will affect the potential spillover effects of Abenomics, including:

- *Outsourcing production.* Japan's overseas production increased steadily since the asset bubble burst. Labor cost differentials (vertical integration) and the host country's market size (to tap into local demand) have been important determinants of Japan's outward foreign direct investment (FDI). As a result, sales by overseas subsidiaries now exceed exports by firms in Japan. This phenomenon matters for possible spillover effects as the response of exports to changes in the yen may be more tempered than used to be the case in the past.

- *High-tech inputs in the global supply chain.* Although firms based in Japan have lost some of their global market share, partly owing to the rising role of emerging market economies and increased overseas production, Japan still remains an important player in global trade by providing high-tech inputs to the Asian and global supply chain. These supply-chain linkages matter for potential spillover effects from Abenomics as they tend to mute the effects of exchange rate changes on competitiveness.

- *Rising cross-border credit exposures.* Japan's households are prolific savers, funding not only most of the government's very large financing requirements (see Chapters 5 and 8), but also a stream of capital to the rest of the world, as evidenced by the country being the largest international creditor. Banks and major life insurers have actively started to expand abroad again after the global financial crisis. The factors that have driven these cross-border activities include limited domestic opportunities, a capacity to take on more foreign exposures, large financing needs in emerging Asia, and the deleveraging of European banks. Despite greater opportunities at home, as noted in Chapter 8, this trend is likely to continue under Abenomics, creating a source of benign spillover effects (Lam 2013).

- *Safe-haven effects.* Japan is a major safe haven. When risk-off episodes occur, policymakers in safe-haven countries may have to deal with sharp real appreciations or surges in capital flows.[1] Transitory real appreciation may create hefty adjustment costs to the economy and, subsequently, economic dislocation when exchange rates eventually revert back. These safe-haven effects arise in Japan without noticeable changes in capital flows. Instead they transpire through complex financial transactions such as derivatives positions. Persistently low interest rates and historically low volatility made the yen a favored funding currency for carry trades and rendered it a significant driver of cross-currency positioning. These considerations matter for evaluating the depreciation of the yen that has occurred so far during Abenomics, and the inward spillovers to Japan from global economic conditions and the resulting spillbacks to other countries.

Next, we discuss how these factors have contributed to relatively mild spillover effects in the first two years of Abenomics notwithstanding the sharp depreciation of the yen. Japan's exports have been subdued, imports have been relatively strong, and portfolio rebalancing by financial institutions toward foreign assets has been more than offset by greater inflows by foreign investors into Japan. However, several factors behind these slow responses are expected to wane, suggesting the possibility of greater spillover effects going forward. At the same time, the global context has also changed. With the beginning of the Federal Reserve's tapering, neighboring countries have experienced tightening financing conditions, leading them to be less concerned about possible capital inflows from Japan.

We then assess the future potential spillover effects from Abenomics. First, we discuss potential effects based on the IMF's G20MOD model.[2] The simulations suggest that, if all three arrows of Abenomics are successfully deployed

---

[1] Risk-off episodes in this chapter refer to large swings in global risk aversion as proxied by the VIX (a volatility index). During such periods, investors reallocate resources toward lower yielding investments which are perceived to have lower risk.

[2] G20MOD is the IMF's global macroeconomic model developed to support the G20's Mutual Assessment Process. The model has 23 blocks, comprising all G20 countries and three aggregate country groups (other non-euro-area European Union countries, other industrial countries, and the rest of the world), and treats each G20 member separately to allow policies to be considered and tailored to every member's individual circumstances.

and succeed in raising growth and inflation and bringing down public debt, spillover effects to the Group of Twenty economies are positive, albeit small (about 0–0.1 percent of GDP) in the short term, before rising over the medium term once the effects of structural reforms translate into higher growth in Japan. Second, we argue that, in practice, overall spillover effects as well as the impact on individual countries would be more complex because of the unique features already mentioned that are not fully captured in general equilibrium models. Finally, we discuss how Abenomics may affect the probability of a medium-term tail risk. Specifically, the combination of high government debt and large net foreign assets implies that the materialization of fiscal risks and tail events could have important spillovers on other countries if heightened risk aversion in Japan spreads progressively to bond and stock markets in other economies. Insofar as Abenomics succeeds in putting the debt path on a downward trajectory over the medium term (Chapter 5) and thus enhances financial sector stability (Chapter 8), these potential adverse spillover effects might be prevented.

UNIQUE FEATURES OF JAPAN'S GLOBAL ROLE

Firms' Overseas Production

Intraregional trade has expanded rapidly since 1990, largely owing to dynamic economies such as China. Nonetheless, Japan's intraregional exports as a share of global GDP have remained remarkably stable—even during the global financial crisis—and account for more than two-thirds of industrial countries' intraregional trade. Japan's deepening regional integration has largely been driven by the outsourcing of production by Japanese firms to neighboring countries, especially China, Hong Kong SAR, and Singapore. This integration affects the interpretation of changes in Japan's export structure. Its increased outsourcing and upstream position has facilitated the shift in technology content to other Asian countries, adding to the apparent convergence in export structures. Rising similarity could thus reflect increased complementarities, as well as competition.

Japan's stock of outward FDI is concentrated mainly in the United States, followed closely by Asia, reflecting the increased presence of Japanese corporations in the region. The euro area has continued to attract around one-fourth of Japan's outward FDI. IMF (2011) models its outward FDI flows by employing a gravity-model framework. The analysis suggests that labor cost differentials—vertical integration—have been a main driver of FDI. Host-country market size has recently become another important determinant of outward FDI. This is also consistent with the expansion of the country's multinational operations, especially in Asia, to tap into local demand. Originally, Japan's outward FDI complemented its trade pattern (for example, exporting parts and capital goods to factories and subsidiaries financed by FDI). But since 2000 it has become increasingly aimed at servicing local markets, substituting for its exports (Figure 10.1).

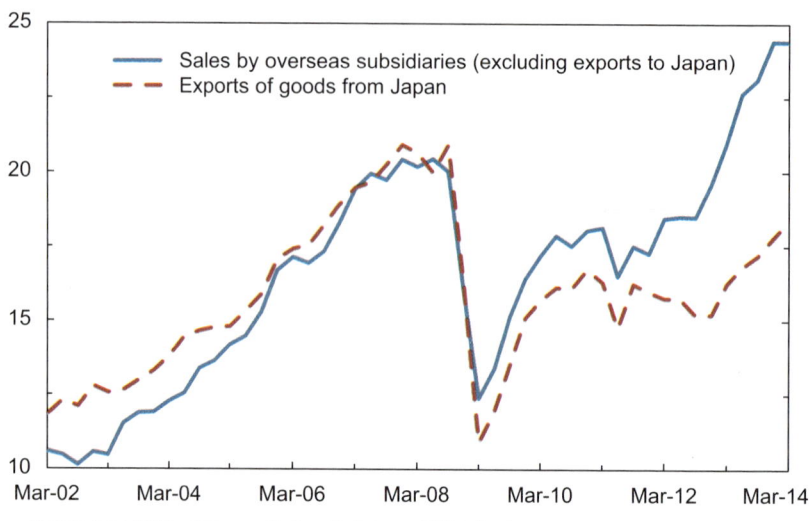

Figure 10.1 Exports versus Sales of Overseas Subsidiaries *(Trillion Yen)*

[Figure: Line chart showing "Sales by overseas subsidiaries (excluding exports to Japan)" and "Exports of goods from Japan" from Mar-02 to Mar-14, ranging from about 10 to 25 trillion yen.]

Sources: Japan Ministry of Economy, Trade and Industry; and IMF staff estimates.

Supply Chain

The importance of supply-chain linkages, both domestically and in relation to other countries, came to the fore during the March 11, 2011 earthquake, which struck a wide area in the northeast, including Tokyo.[3]

Assessing the economic ramifications was highly difficult, partly because of uncertainty about the duration of widespread electricity shortages and increasing uncertainty about global economic conditions in light of the escalating euro area crisis. Supply-chain factors also complicated this assessment. Just-in-time production, in combination with more extensive supply chains, created additional uncertainty about supply disruptions and their transmission to other sectors and regions in Japan as well as internationally. Japan is a key source of demand for final goods and an important producer of intermediate components and capital goods in the regional supply chain, especially in electronics. The earthquake highlighted the fragility of tightly integrated global production networks.

The country's contribution to "foreign value added" is especially high in economies engaged in assembly or processing activities, such as Taiwan Province of China, Thailand, and China, particularly for high-tech exports, such as electronic equipment and motor vehicles. Nonetheless, Japanese exports have the lowest share of foreign value added in the region, underscoring the country's upstream position in the regional production chain (IMF 2011). For example, it accounts for one-fifth of the world's semiconductor production and in the machinery and reactors

---

[3] Japan's strongest earthquake on record unleashed a vast tsunami and subsequent nuclear accidents and a radiation crisis. The Cabinet Office estimated the direct economic cost of the disaster at 16.9 trillion yen ($210 billion or 3.6 percent of 2011 GDP).

Figure 10.2 Import Content from Japan for Gross Exports *(Percent)*

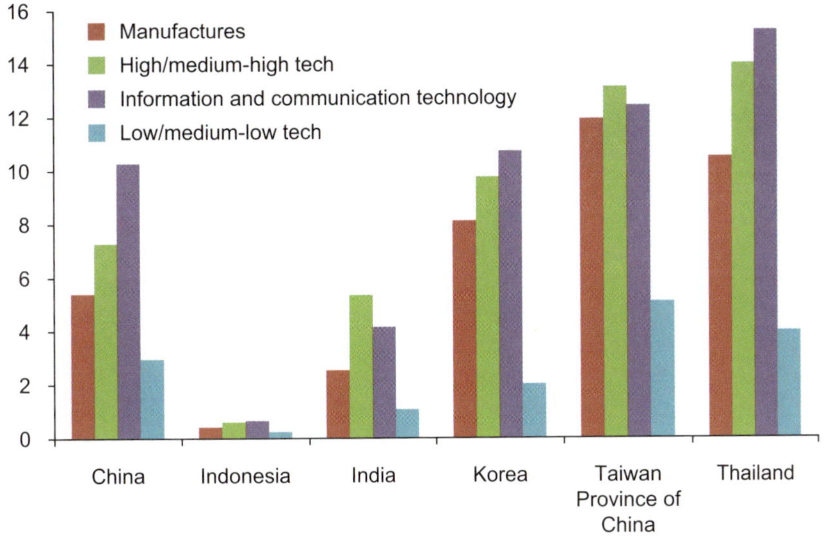

Source: IMF staff estimates.

sector it accounts for more than a third of global exports of machinery and wafers, providing more than 50 and 35 percent of U.S. and Chinese imports, respectively. As Japan has increased the sophistication of its export basket, it maintains a lead in specialized core components. This has enabled it to maintain a bilateral trade surplus with most countries in Asia and capture a significant share of value added in other Asian countries' exports. For example, Japanese companies account for about 10 percent of value added in Chinese exports of electrical equipment.

With the vertical integration of global production processing, a significant amount of imported intermediate inputs are embodied in final exports, mitigating the impact of currency movements on export prices and limiting the deterioration of price competitiveness of neighboring countries in response to yen depreciation (Figure 10.2). This also affects price competitiveness in third markets compared to competitors who rely less on Japan for intermediate inputs. The substitution of intermediate inputs for Japanese inputs in trading partners would further mitigate the negative effects from currency appreciation, but at the cost of lower domestic production (IMF 2013).

Global Financial Role

Because of its large external surpluses, Japan has accumulated one of the world's largest net foreign asset positions. The approximately $3.3 trillion net international investment position at the end of 2013 reflects both official reserves (mostly held in the form of U.S. Treasury securities) and a large net private position in bonds. The private position (more than 80 percent of the net international investment position) primarily consists of the outward investments of banks, life insurers, and corporate pension funds in U.S. Treasuries and both U.S. dollar and yen-denominated corporate bonds.

In terms of financial linkages, the expansion of Japanese financial institutions abroad in the 1980s and 1990s was partly successful (Lam 2013). During the mid to late 1980s, these institutions rapidly raised overseas exposures in tandem with the outward FDI of real estate and construction companies, though that ended abruptly with losses incurred after the domestic asset bubble burst. Subsequently, in the years leading up to the Asian financial crisis (1997–98), banks funded overseas loans to developing Asia mostly through foreign exchange financing. Banks incurred sizable valuation losses and higher nonperforming loans after the Asian financial crisis, forcing them to recede from overseas lending. Losses abroad added to financial vulnerabilities at home (for example, credit risks in small and medium-sized enterprises and declining interest rates), and contributed to Japan's subsequent banking crises in the early 2000s.

As noted in Lam (2013), the cross-border activities of Japanese financial institutions have risen again over the past few years, particularly to Asia. Overseas loans by major banks are growing and major Japanese banks have attained an important global and regional presence, particularly in the areas of syndicated lending and project finance. Foreign claims on Asia have recouped the decline at the height of the global financial crisis. As noted in Chapter 8, several regional and domestic factors have contributed to overseas expansions since the crisis. Stagnant growth and limited domestic credit demand have added incentives for financial institutions to seek opportunities abroad. Modest global uncertainty, large growth differentials, and the resilience of domestic banking systems are key drivers for cross-border claims. Outside Japan, growth in Asia and deleveraging of European banks in the region contributed to a rise of cross-border lending. The yen's appreciation in the past years might have added incentives for expanding abroad.

The trend of expanding abroad is not limited to banks. Major life insurers have begun to strengthen their overseas business, especially in Asia, by acquiring or affiliating with local insurers for long-term profitability. They usually expand via incremental capital and building alliances typically involve minority stakes rather than aggressive acquisitions.

Japan's debt and equity markets are among the top five international markets in size, but are primarily geared toward domestic investors. Foreign investors hold less than 5 percent of Japanese government bonds (JGBs), of which about one-fifth are in Asia. By comparison, more than 30 percent of U.S. Treasuries and about 55 percent of German bunds are held abroad. However, foreign investors account for about 15 percent of the cash turnover in JGBs and 65 percent of futures markets transactions. Participation in the equity market is larger, with one-fourth of market capitalization held abroad, but less than one-half of a percent accounted for by investors in Asia.

Given its domestic focus, Tokyo as a financial marketplace is not a major intermediary of global capital flows. Foreign issuance of equity and debt in Japan has been negligible in recent years, and bonds placed by Japanese issuers abroad amount to only 1½ percent of global outstanding cross-border debt securities. At 14 percent of GDP, the sum of gross capital inflows and outflows in Japan's balance of payments—a crude measure of financial market turnover—is considerably smaller than in other systemic economies.

Safe-Haven and Carry-Trade Effects

The yen remains an important global currency, although its share in global reserve holdings has declined in the past decade. Yen holdings currently account for 2 percent of reported foreign exchange reserves as measured by turnover. The foreign exchange market in Tokyo remains the third largest in the world, albeit well behind London and New York. In recent years, the yen has not only been a funding currency for foreign-exchange carry trades but a preferred investment currency during global turmoil. This has contributed at times to relatively abrupt currency movements in response to shifts in sentiment.

As such, the yen is widely considered a safe-haven currency, which appreciates when global investors' behavior becomes more risk-averse or economic fundamentals are more uncertain. Since 2008, the yen appreciated steadily against the U.S. dollar in effective terms in the aftermath of various shocks. First, the global financial crisis was associated with a large real exchange rate appreciation by over 20 percent. Second, in May 2010, higher market distress about peripheral European sovereigns led to a large jump in the VIX (a volatility index), followed by a 10 percent yen appreciation against the euro within a matter of weeks. Third, following the March 2011 earthquake, the yen appreciated further on expectations of sizable repatriation of foreign assets by insurance companies, which in fact did not occur. Fourth, on February 25, 2013, uncertainty surrounding the outcome of the Italian elections led to a whopping intraday appreciation of the yen against the euro of 5¼ percent and about 4 percent against the U.S. dollar. These examples illustrate that appreciation of the yen during episodes of increased global risk aversion is recurrent. Indeed, since the mid-1990s, there have been 12 episodes during which the yen has appreciated in nominal effective terms by 6 percent or more within one quarter and these often coincided with events outside Japan.[4]

Safe-haven currencies tend to have low interest rates, a strong net foreign asset position, and deep and liquid financial markets. Japan meets all these criteria. After controlling for the carry trade, Habib and Stracca (2012) find that safe-haven status is robustly associated with stronger net foreign asset positions (an indicator of external vulnerability) and, to a lesser extent, with the absolute size of the stock market (an indicator of market size and financial development). For advanced economies, in addition to the net financial asset position, the public debt-to-GDP ratio and some measures of financial development and the liquidity of foreign exchange markets (measured by the bid-ask spread) are associated with safe-haven status.

Although being a safe-haven country may appear enviable when risk-off episodes recur, policymakers in safe-haven countries face the challenge of dealing with sharp real appreciations or surges in capital flows. Transitory real appreciation may create hefty adjustment costs to the economy, and subsequently,

---

[4]These include the Asian financial crisis, the 2008 Lehman shock, the 2010–11 escalation of the euro area crisis, and uncertainty surrounding the debt ceiling debate in the United States.

economic dislocation when exchange rates eventually revert back (for example, Bussière, Lopez, and Tille 2013). The longer lasting the real appreciation and surge in capital flows, the greater the potential for vulnerabilities to build up in either private or public sector balance sheets.[5] Moreover, in economies with already low inflation and interest rates close to the zero bound, real appreciations driven by risk-off episodes could feed deflation risks and place downward pressures on aggregate demand (IMF 2012a, de Carvalho Filho 2013).

Although the yen's safe-haven status has been well documented (for example, Ranaldo and Söderlind 2010, de Bock and de Carvalho Filho 2013), the mechanisms through which risk-off appreciations occur have received considerably less attention. In this regard, a casual glance at the data reveals a curious feature: large movements in the yen during risk-off episodes occur without any detectable movements in net capital in- or outflows. A similar observation holds for the large depreciation that has occurred since late 2012, which coincided with the emergence of Abenomics as well as waning safe-haven effects and widening trade deficits. As such, a forensic investigation of what drives large movements in the yen fills a void in the literature, with potential important implications for spillover analysis and the role of macroeconomic policies to address excessive exchange rate volatility.

Botman, de Carvalho Filho, and Lam (2013) use the risk-off indicator proposed by de Bock and de Carvalho Filho (2013), which identifies the onset of risk-off episodes with large increases in the VIX relative to its 60-day historical moving average.[6] Botman, de Carvalho Filho, and Lam (2013) find that safe-haven effects in Japan work differently than in other countries. Specifically and in contrast to the experience of the Swiss franc, there is little evidence that yen risk-off appreciations are driven by capital inflows. Neither do expectations about the relative stance of monetary policies appear to be an important factor. Instead, the authors present supporting evidence that portfolio rebalancing through offshore derivative transactions appears to be a key factor behind risk-off appreciations (Figure 10.3). This could possibly reflect self-fulfilling expectations of currency appreciation. In addition, risk-off appreciations could be driven by transactions between residents or among nonresidents. Alternatively, portfolio rebalancing could be achieved with little or no transaction as prices adjust to changes in beliefs that are common to market participants.

Prior to the global financial crisis, persistently low interest rates and historically low volatility made the yen a favored funding currency for carry trades. Moreover, the strong appetite for risk that characterized 2003–07 led to a steady buildup in these positions, and rendered the carry trade a significant driver of cross-currency positioning.[7]

---

[5]Sorsa and others (2007) identified expectations of appreciation spurred in part by capital inflows as a driver of liability dollarization in Southeastern European countries. A similar phenomenon appears to have occurred in Turkey during the buildup to the crisis of 2000–01 (IMF 2004) and in Iceland before the global financial crisis (IMF 2012b).

[6]Bekaert, Hoerova, and Duca (2010) show the VIX can be decomposed into risk aversion and uncertainty. However that decomposition is not very informative because risk aversion and uncertainty are highly correlated.

[7]The discussion on carry trade is based on IMF (2011), Chapter IX.

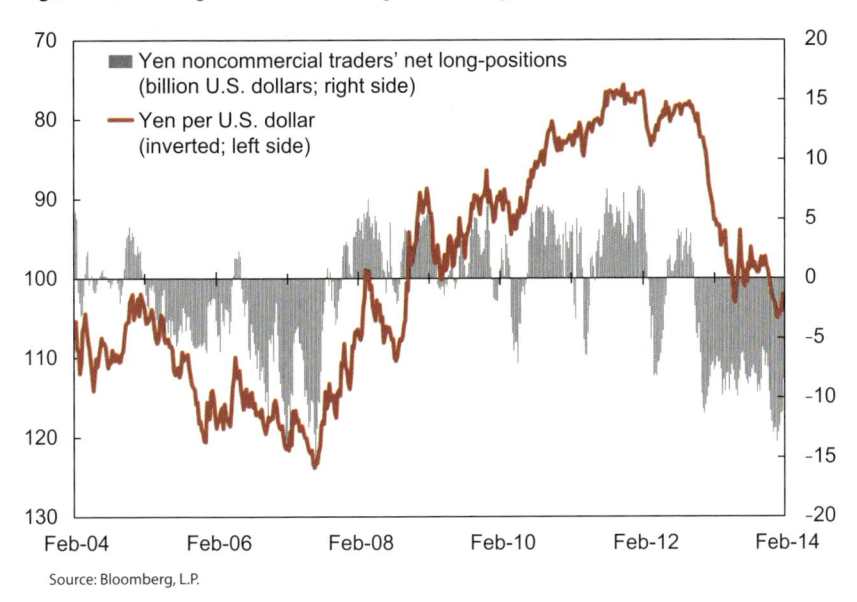

Figure 10.3 Chicago Mercantile Exchange Yen Trading Position

Source: Bloomberg, L.P.

Quantifying the size and destination of these positions is challenging as the range of instruments has grown over the years, including complex off balance sheet transactions that are less easily detected in balance of payments and capital-flow statistics. The trade has also come to encompass a range of different investor classes, from Japanese retail investors (so-called Mrs. Watanabe) to more sophisticated global brokerage houses and hedge funds. In 2007, near the peak, estimates of the yen-funded carry trade ranged from $100 billion to $2 trillion. IMF (2011) estimates the sensitivity of the carry trade to fundamentals following the methodology of Hattori and Shin (2009), using the net interoffice assets of foreign banks operating in Japan as an indicator of the scale of the yen-funded carry trade. These net interoffice assets are then modeled as a function of international policy-rate differentials (yen versus average of the Australian dollar, U.S. dollar, and euro) and the VIX. The results suggest that an average widening of the interest differential by about 220 basis points would prompt an increase in the carry trade of about ¥4.3 trillion.

SPILLOVER EFFECTS FROM ABENOMICS

Trade and Financial Spillovers during Abenomics' First Year

Contrary to initial concerns, spillover effects through trade from the sharp depreciation of the yen were not substantial during Abenomics' first year. Real export growth has been subdued, while that of trading partners has remained robust, including to Japan. These features of Japan's role in the global economy have an important bearing on spillover effects seen so far.

Specifically, during previous episodes of depreciations by more than 20 percent, it took about six to eight quarters for the trade balance to improve, with both exports recovering and imports moderating (Figure 10.4). These J-curve effects appeared to have been more drawn out this time considering the faster pace of yen depreciation, which could reflect capacity constraints caused by rush demand ahead of the consumption tax hike as well as the need for exporters to replenish profit buffers following years of yen strength during the postcrisis period. Furthermore, as noted, firms have increasingly relied on overseas production as a substitute for exports and supply chain interactions have muted the effect of yen depreciation on competitiveness. Elevated import demand for mineral fuels has also contributed to the weaker trade balance after all nuclear power plants were closed after the earthquake in March 2011.

Likewise, despite the sharp yen depreciation and creation of liquidity, capital outflows from Japan have so far been limited. Weekly portfolio flows show that foreign investors continued to pour into Japanese equity markets (cumulative about ¥18 trillion from November 2012 to the end of 2013), more than offsetting net sales of domestic bonds and notes (cumulative about ¥4.4 trillion) during the same period. Domestic investors scaled down foreign bond holdings significantly during the first half of 2013 (cumulative about ¥11.2 trillion) before net purchases rose again in the second half (cumulative about ¥8.7 trillion). They sold foreign equities steadily from November 2012 throughout 2013 (cumulative about ¥6.8 trillion). Net assets held in the retail investment trusts (*toshin* funds)—particularly on equity funds—increased in early 2013 after net declines in 2012. The increase, however, was mostly driven by valuation effects rather than increasing outflows.

Figure 10.4 Sharp Yen Depreciations and the Trade Balance *(Percentage points of GDP)*

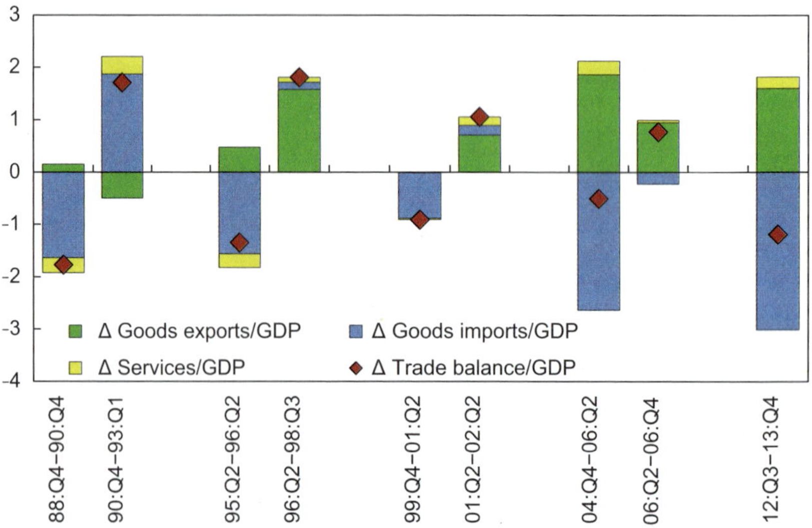

Source: IMF staff estimates.

Potential Spillover Effects over the Medium Term: A Model-Based Evaluation

Spillovers from Abenomics are complex and conditional on the new macroeconomic policies being fully completed (the three arrows). Spillover channels of a successful effort to revitalize the Japanese economy are likely to operate through the exchange rate, higher growth in Japan, and financial interlinkages. IMF (2013) use the IMF's G20MOD for illustrative simulations and considers each arrow of Abenomics in separate scenarios to quantify their contribution to key macroeconomic indicators and spillover effects. As such, it is similar in spirit to the analysis in Chapter 3 on the domestic effects of Abenomics and in Chapter 8 on the financial stability implications of complete and incomplete reforms.

Simulation results show that, while varying across countries and regions, the net spillover effects are generally positive, though small. Successful reflation in Japan would affect other countries through (1) yen depreciation and a corresponding appreciation of trading partner currencies, (2) higher growth in Japan as well as the global economy, and (3) lower interest rates in trading partners owing to capital inflows and higher global savings from falling debt in Japan. In sum, the negative spillovers arising from yen depreciation would be offset by positive spillovers through the other two channels. Japan's rising current account surplus implies capital inflows into trading partners, reducing interest rates and stimulating investment and growth. Higher growth in Japan increases import demand. From the simulations, structural reforms in Japan appear to exert particularly important positive spillover effects.

To understand the impact of a sharper depreciation of the yen (relative to the more gradual depreciation in these simulations), IMF (2013) also considers a case in which the yen real effective exchange rate depreciates by an additional 10 percent in the near term and is sustained at this level. This broadly corresponds to the estimated contribution of quantitative and qualitative monetary easing to the depreciation of the yen, with the rest accounted for by the widening of the trade deficit, the larger interest rate differential with the United States, and waning safe-haven effects. The simulation shows smaller net growth spillovers in this case, with some economies including China, Germany, and Korea slowing in the near to medium term before benefiting in the long term. As such, credible structural and fiscal policies are essential in Japan to generate positive spillovers, while in their absence monetary policy would become overburdened and the exchange rate would be the main transmission channel with adverse effects on trading partners.

Beyond Model Simulations

However, in the near term, overall spillover effects, as well as the impact on individual countries, will likely be more complex because of the unique features of the Japanese economy that are not fully captured in the model simulation just described.

- *Portfolio rebalancing.* Regarding the financial channel, the Bank of Japan's JGB purchases could cause a substantial rebalancing of financial institutions' portfolios, potentially leading to large financial spillovers to other countries. The effects of capital inflows on recipient countries would not be uniform, but would depend on their cyclical conditions. While easier financing conditions can support growth in economies with slack and little inflation, they could raise overheating risks for those with already rapid credit growth and rising asset prices, although this concern may have been reduced since the U.S. tapering started.

- *Foreign direct investment.* Financial spillover effects could also occur through FDI. It has been observed that a rise of 1 percent of GDP in Japanese FDI boosts growth by 0.5–0.7 percentage point in recipient countries. Empirical analysis also suggests that overseas production and outward FDI are sensitive to real effective exchange rate movements. For instance, a 10 percentage point depreciation in the real effective exchange rate would slow the overseas production ratio by 1.3 percentage points. Nonetheless, outward FDI is a long-term trend since firms aim to locate where the demand is growing and take advantage of cost differentials. It is unlikely that increasing overseas production or FDI abroad would be reversed given the relatively high rate of return on these investments.

- *Supply chain.* For the trade channel, increased vertical integration of the production network implies that a significant amount of imported intermediate inputs from Japan would somewhat offset the effect of yen depreciation on trading partners' export prices while higher growth and exports would benefit other countries through the supply-chain structure.

- *Interest rate differential.* A sustained different stance in monetary policies between the Bank of Japan and other major central banks, in particular the Federal Reserve, would increase the incentive for Japanese investors to rebalance their portfolios toward foreign assets. An illustrative scenario analysis (IMF 2014) that takes into account increasing pressure on bank profits from large excess reserves, higher domestic credit growth, governance reforms at the Government Pension Investment Fund, and rising interest rate differentials with the United States, estimates that potential capital outflows could rise significantly as Abenomics proceeds. While the vast majority of these funds are expected to flow to advanced economies, emerging market economies would also benefit, not only from direct regional flows that could moderate the expected tightening of financing conditions but also indirectly as outflows from Japan to advanced economies would lessen the tightening of financial conditions there.

- *Overseas expansion.* In terms of banks' expanding abroad, as noted in Chapter 8, Lam (2013) argues that the trend of expanding overseas is likely to continue, but its pace will depend on a supportive domestic economy and careful risk supervision. Although stronger domestic growth might slow the expansion pace, it is not expected to reverse the trend unless incomplete policies under Abenomics elevate domestic financial stability risks. Increasing cross-border activity could add to funding risks while exacerbating supervisory challenges that require continued close monitoring.

Spillovers from Tail Risks[8]

Financial stress in Japan has measureable spillovers on global financial markets, including those in Asia. Specifically, given Japan's role as a global lender and its large domestic needs for funding as a result of the government's high financial requirement, a key risk for Japan and the rest of the world stems from a spike in JGB yields. IMF (2011) simulated a range of fiscal crisis scenarios originating in Japan featuring different assumptions regarding the impact of the crisis on worldwide market confidence.[9]

The first scenario features a fiscal crisis contained within Japan. A sudden loss of confidence in fiscal sustainability raises long-term nominal interest rates, while heightened risk aversion also hits the stock market and reduced confidence leads households and firms to postpone their consumption and investment. Combined with fiscal consolidation and yen depreciation, such a scenario would have major implications for Japan, but the spillover effects would be relatively modest on other countries: a weighted-average peak output loss of 4.4 percent in Japan, 0.1 percent in euro area periphery countries, 0.2 percent in other advanced economies, and 0.4 percent in emerging market economies.

As such, spillovers will only be material if heightened risk aversion in Japan spreads progressively to bond and stock markets in other economies, including emerging markets. Although Japanese financial markets are relatively isolated, during periods of uncertainty global financial markets face elevated risks of falling market confidence and herd behavior. Depending on the extent of spillovers to market confidence, the costs to other countries can reach as high as 3 percent of GDP.

In addition, spillovers could be amplified as most JGBs are held by Japanese financial institutions. This suggests that a shock to JGB yields might have a direct spillover to other markets, by impacting Japan's financial sector balance sheets and prompting a withdrawal by financial firms from foreign markets. However, even under the most severe scenario, the regional impact of a reduction in foreign loans is limited. Assuming that banks reduce their foreign loans in proportion to their share of loans to each jurisdiction, the impact on local banking systems is relatively minor, ranging from 0 to 2 percent expressed as a fraction of total domestic credit. The key exceptions are the offshore financial centers, Hong Kong SAR and Singapore, where the impact ranges from 3 to 6 percent. As these centers are effectively cross-border intermediaries, the effect on the local economy will quite likely be limited.[10]

In essence, successful Abenomics that put debt on a downward path will prevent such a medium-term tail risk from emerging and therefore avoid the possibility of sharp negative spillovers through financial stress in the future.

---

[8]This section is based on Chapter VII, Chapter IX, and Chapter X of IMF (2011).
[9]These results are derived from a refined version of the structural macroeconometric model of the world economy documented in Vitek (2010), which features extensive linkages between the real and financial sectors, both within and across Group of Twenty economies.
[10]Interbank network analysis confirms that a withdrawal of Japanese funding would not be severe enough to trigger systemic distress in other countries.

CONCLUSION

Japan's share in global growth started to wane as firms and the financial sector grappled with the Lost Decade. However, during that period, secular shifts took place that simultaneously strengthened Japan's footprint in the world economy in general and Asia in particular. For example, firms' FDI increased markedly, particularly to countries with strong domestic demand, and Japan became a key upstream player in the global and regional supply chain. Banks, too, have actively expanded abroad in recent years. With low interest rates in Japan, financial linkages also manifested themselves as a result of the yen carry-trade, while the country remained among the largest providers of global liquidity each year owing to its stable current account surplus, which also continued to cement its status as a safe-haven country.

These factors are not only spillover channels themselves, they also tend to mitigate the transmission of Abenomics to other countries. Overall, model-based simulations suggest that a complete package of reforms that achieves the Bank of Japan's inflation target puts the debt-to-GDP ratio on a declining trajectory, and raising potential growth through structural reforms would create positive, albeit modest, spillovers to other countries, even though direct competitors may be affected adversely in the short run as a result of the weaker yen. The trend of banks and firms expanding overseas may slow in this case as demand for credit, competitiveness, and consumer confidence increase in Japan, but it is unlikely to change in a material way. Capital outflows could be more substantial in the period ahead compared to Abenomics' first two years, which would contribute to keeping financial conditions in recipient countries accommodative amid tapering in the United States. Finally, a complete package of reforms would help to avoid negative spillovers from a potential tail risk in light of Japan's rapidly rising debt under the pre-Abenomics baseline.

REFERENCES

Bekaert, G., M. Hoerova, and M.L. Duca. 2010. "Risk, Uncertainty, and Monetary Policy." NBER Working Paper No. 16397. Cambridge, Massachusetts: National Bureau of Economic Research.

Botman, D., I.E. de Carvalho Filho, and R.W. Lam. 2013. "The Curious Case of the Yen as a Safe Haven Currency: A Forensic Analysis." IMF Working Paper No. 13/228. International Monetary Fund, Washington, DC.

Bussière, M., C. Lopez, and C. Tille. 2013. "Currency Crises in Reverse: Do Large Real Exchange Rate Appreciations Matter for Growth?" MPRA Paper No. 44096. Munich: Munich Personal RePEc Archive.

de Bock, R., and I. de Carvalho Filho. 2013. "The Behavior of Currencies during Risk-off Episodes." IMF Working Paper No. 13/08. International Monetary Fund, Washington, DC.

de Carvalho Filho, I. 2013. "Risk-off Episodes and Swiss Franc Appreciation: the Role of Capital Flows." Unpublished. International Monetary Fund, Washington, DC.

Habib, M.M., and L. Stracca. 2012. "Getting Beyond Carry Trade: What Makes a Safe Haven Currency?" *Journal of International Economics* 87 (1): 50–64.

Hattori, M., and H.S. Shin, 2009, "Yen Carry Trade and the Subprime Crisis." *IMF Staff Papers* 56 (2): 384-409.

International Monetary Fund. 2004. "Debt-Related Vulnerabilities and Financial Crises—An Application of the Balance Sheet Approach to Emerging Market Countries." http://www.imf.org/external/np/pdr/bal/2004/eng/070104.htm.

———. 2011. "Japan: Spillover Report." IMF Country Report No. 11/183, Washington.

———. 2012a. "Switzerland: Selected Issues Paper." IMF Country Report No. 12/107, Washington.

———. 2012b. "Iceland: Ex Post Evaluation of Exceptional Access under the 2008 Stand-by Arrangement. IMF Country Report No. 12/91, Washington.

———. 2013. "IMF Multilateral Policy Issues Report." 2013 Spillover Report—Analytical Underpinnings and other Background Papers, Washington.

Lam, R.W. 2013. "Cross-Border Activity of Japanese Banks." IMF Working Paper No. 13/235. International Monetary Fund, Washington, DC.

Ranaldo, A., and P. Söderlind. 2010. "Safe Haven Currencies." *Review of Finance* 14 (3): 385–407.

Sorsa, P., B.B. Bakker, C. Duenwald, A.M. Maechler, and A. Tiffin. 2007. "Vulnerabilities in Emerging Southeastern Europe—How Much Cause for Concern?" IMF Working Paper No. 07/236. International Monetary Fund, Washington, DC.

Vitek, F. 2010. "Policy Analysis and Forecasting in the World Economy: A Panel Unobserved Components Approach." IMF Working Paper No. 12/149. International Monetary Fund, Washington, DC.

Contributors

Chie Aoyagi, a Japanese national, is currently an Economist in the IMF's Regional Office for Asia and the Pacific in Tokyo. Her research focuses on structural reforms in Japan. She joined the IMF in 2012. Prior to that, she was an assistant equity analyst and economist at Nomura Asset Management. She graduated in 2008 from the University of California, Los Angeles with a bachelor's degree in International Development.

Serkan Arslanalp is a senior economist in the Monetary and Capital Markets Department of the IMF, contributing to the *Global Financial Stability Report* on issues related to sovereign risk, financial stability, and capital markets. He has participated in the recent Financial Sector Assessment Program (FSAP) Update for Japan. Mr. Arslanalp joined the IMF in 2004 and worked in the Fiscal Affairs Department on a range of surveillance and program countries, including the Stand-By Arrangement program on Ukraine in 2008. He holds an undergraduate degree in Economics from the Massachusetts Institute of Technology and a PhD in Economics from Stanford University.

Dennis Botman is a Deputy Division Chief in the IMF's Asia and Pacific Department. He joined the IMF in 2002 and has worked on various assignments, including the Economic Modeling Division in the Research Department and in the Fiscal Affairs Department. Prior to his current assignment he was the IMF's Resident Representative in the Philippines. His research covers a variety of topics, including general equilibrium modeling, financial crises and speculative attacks, aging and social security reform, and public finance. He holds a PhD from the University of Amsterdam, the Netherlands.

Stephan Danninger is a Division Chief in the IMF's Asia and Pacific Department. He joined the IMF in 2000 and has worked on various assignments, including the IMF's World Economic Studies Division responsible for the publication of the *World Economic Outlook* (WEO). His research covers a variety of topics, including determinants of countries' export competitiveness, fiscal reforms, cross-country spillovers of financial stress, and growth enhancing structural reforms. He holds a PhD from Columbia University, New York.

Giovanni Ganelli, an Italian national, joined the IMF in 2003. Before being assigned to the Regional Office for Asia and the Pacific in Tokyo in August 2012, he was based at the IMF's headquarters in Washington, D.C., where he worked in the Fiscal Affairs and European Departments, and the IMF's Institute for Capacity Development. During his IMF career he has participated in work on various countries in Europe, Asia, and Africa. He is currently a member of the IMF team that carries out the annual Article IV consultation with Japan. He holds a PhD in Economics from the University of Warwick (UK). His research focuses on fiscal policy issues.

Joong Shik Kang is an Economist in the IMF's Asia and Pacific Department. Prior to this, he worked in the Research Department, on several multilateral surveillance issues, including the *World Economic Outlook*, G20 surveillance, and commodities. His research covers a variety of topics, including international risk sharing, internal devaluation, global rebalancing, and exchange rates. Mr. Kang is a national of the Republic of Korea and received his BA at Seoul National University and MS and PhD degrees at the University of Wisconsin-Madison.

Raphael Lam is currently the IMF's Deputy Resident Representative to China. In previous positions at the IMF, he has covered a range of Asian economies, including China, Japan, and Hong Kong SAR. He has participated in the Japan Financial Sector Assessment Program and was involved in regional surveillance in Asia. During his tenure in the European Department, he participated in the IMF's lending program to Iceland during the global financial crisis and worked on Sweden and Israel. His research interests include finance, trade and investment, and regional development and spillovers. He has a PhD in Economics from the University of California and was a lecturer at the University of California, Los Angeles. He has worked in the research department of the Hong Kong Monetary Authority and has also served as research visiting scholar at the Hong Kong Institute of Monetary Research.

Malhar Nabar is a Senior Economist in the IMF's Asia and Pacific Department, covering Japan. Prior to this, he worked on China and Hong Kong SAR and in the Regional Studies Division for the Asia-Pacific region. Before Mr. Nabar joined the IMF in 2009, he was on the faculty at Wellesley College. His research interests are in financial development, investment, and productivity growth. Mr. Nabar holds a PhD in economics from Brown University.

Ikuo Saito is an Economist in the IMF's Asia and Pacific Department. He works on Japan, the Federated States of Micronesia, and the Republic of the Marshall Islands. Before joining the IMF, he worked for the Japanese Ministry of Finance, where he was deputy director in charge of tax and international finance issues. He received a BA in law from the University of Tokyo, an MA in international policy studies from Stanford University, and an MPA from Syracuse University.

Jerald Schiff is Deputy Director of the IMF's Asia and Pacific Department (APD) and Mission Chief for Japan. He previously served as a Senior Advisor in the Office of the Managing Director of the IMF, as well as Assistant Director of APD and Divison Chief in the European Department. Mr. Schiff received his AB at Cornell University and MS and PhD degrees at the University of Wisconsin. He has also taught at Tulane University and the American University School of International Service and worked in the U.S. Department of Treasury.

Chad Steinberg is a Senior Economist at the IMF and works currently in the Emerging Markets Division of the Strategy, Policy, and Review Department. He spent four years as Regional Representative in Tokyo and Desk Economist on Japan. He has published extensively on growth and labor reform issues in Japan, including on female labor force participation. Mr. Steinberg holds a BA from the University of Pennsylvania and a PhD and NPP from Harvard University.

Index

Page numbers followed by italic *f* or *t* refer to figures or tables, respectively.

A

Abe, Shinzō, 3
Abenomics
   conceptual basis of, 3, 51
   corporate investment and, 61–62
   debt projections, 54, 63, 69, 70*f*
   effects on the financial sector, 125
   financial sector policies, 6–7
   fiscal policies, 4–5, 30, 46, 70
   growth strategy of, 5–6, 30, 94, 96
   implications for cross-border lending, 138–143
   implications of population aging for, 29, 43–47, 49
   interest rate projections under, 60–61, 61*f*, 63
   labor market reforms to support implementation of, 108
   medium-term projections, 29, 46
   monetary easing strategies, 25–26, 27, 30, 36
   monetary policy of, 12–13, 24–26, 30, 33–34, 46
   outcomes to date, 7–8, 29, 30–36, 31*f*, 47
   perceptions and expectations regarding, 3
   policy coordination in, 26
   portfolio rebalancing toward risk capital under, 125–132, 144–146
   projected economic outcomes of, 45*f*, 63
   risks of, 30, 44–47, 49, 132–138, 143–144
   stimulus measures, 4–5
   structural reforms to promote growth, 96–97
   three arrows of, 3, 97*f*
   See also Global spillover effects of Abenomics
Aging, population
   causes of, 36–37, 39
   challenges for Japan, v
   as contributing factor in recent economic declines, 2
   dissaving behaviors, 43, 47–48
   effects on inflation and growth, 40–43, 41*f*, 55, 93
   global risks from, 48–49
   health care spending and, 83
   implications for Abenomics policies, 29, 43–47, 48–49
   implications for fiscal consolidation, 87
   implications for fiscal-monetary policy coordination, 24
   implications for the labor market, 37, 39–42, 47, 48, 108
   interest rates and, 60
   international comparison of, 36*f*
   labor participation of older workers, 114–115
   linkages to national economic performance, 37–40, 47–48
   pension eligibility, 82
   political economy and, 38, 39
   public debt and, 51, 65–66
   public spending trends and, 71
   trends and projections, 36*f*, 93
Agricultural sector, 6, 101–102

Allowance for corporate equity, 80
Antimonopoly Act, 101
Asian financial crisis (1997), 1, 42, 55–56, 67
Asset-price collapse of 1990s
 bubble development and, 13
 corporate investment since, 147, 149, 153, 161
 course of recovery from, 14
 effects on demand, 1
 growth declines related to, 92–93
 Japan's debt levels and, 54, 67
 monetary policy responses, 13–14
Australia, 104
Austria, 100

B

Bank of Japan
 Abenomics implementation, 3–4
 asset purchase program of 2000s, 17, 20, 24–25, 26–27
 communication and transparency of monetary policy, 21
 exit from monetary easing policies, 46–47
 forward guidance role of, 21–23, 27
 government bond purchases, 4, 6, 17, 26, 136, 144
 monetary easing policy in Abenomics, v, 25–26
 shortcomings of policy responses to deflation, 2
Birth rate, 2, 39, 72
Business environment
 barriers to exit and entry, 130–132, 145
 corporate tax rate, 6, 71, 77–80, 78f, 79f, 87, 96, 103, 103f
 firm-level governance, 103, 158, 161
 growth-promoting reforms in, 96
 immigration–entrepreneurship linkage, 99
 policy reforms to promote competitiveness, 101–102
 strategies to promote foreign direct investment, 104

C

Carry-trades, 169, 170–171
Child care, 113–114, 123
China, 104, 165, 166
Competitiveness
 global spillover effects of, 163
 growth strategies based on increasing, 96, 101–102
 trends, 8, 78–79
Comprehensive Monetary Easing policy, 17, 23
Consumer confidence, 3, 4–5, 8, 36, 63, 175. *See also* Inflation and growth expectations
Consumption tax
 debt levels and, 55–56, 69
 debt-to-GDP ratio projections and, 57–58
 implementation of Abenomics reforms, 5, 8, 30, 36, 43–44, 57, 77
 international comparison, 74, 75f
 lessons from 2014 increase, vi
 rationale for increasing, for fiscal consolidation, 71, 74–77, 75f
 recommendations for fiscal consolidation, 87–88
 regressivity and equity concerns, 76–77, 86
 revenue, 73
Corporate investment
 Abenomics implementation and, 31f
 cash holdings *versus*, 156–158, 157f, 161
 contributions to growth, 147, 148f
 current conditions favoring higher, 147, 148f
 determinants of, 7, 147–148, 153–158, 154f, 161
 firm size and, 149–151, 150f
 foreign investment by Japanese corporations, 149, 157f
 international comparison, 151f, 157f
 in Lost Decade, 1
 policy reforms to promote, as growth strategy, 96–97, 102–103, 159–161

recent patterns and trends, 147, 148*f*, 149–153, 149*f*, 150*f*, 161
research and development spending, 153
sectoral distribution of, 148, 149–150, 151*f*
Credit system
bank lending to corporate sector, 156*f*
cross-border lending by Japanese banks, 138–143, 139*f*, 140*f*, 141*f*, 164, 167–169
data collection and dissemination, 161
deflation effects on, 11
demand, 7, 8, 20, 39, 130–131
effects of monetary easing on, 20
future challenges and opportunities for policymakers, 7
policies to expand provision of risk capital, 144–145, 146
policies to promote corporate investment, 159–161
population aging effects in, 39
risks of Abenomics in, 143–144
securitization product issuance, 126, 129*f*, 144–145
small business loans, 126–129
zombie borrowers, 93, 102, 132

D

Debt-to-GDP ratio
causes of rise in, 51, 54–57, 67
corporate sector, 158*f*
current, v, 51
future challenges and opportunities for policymakers, v, 67, 69–71
interest rate growth differential and, 59–65
Japan's commitment to lower, 53, 56–57
population aging and, 41*f*, 51, 54, 55
projections, 45*f*, 53, 54, 57–58, 58*f*, 70*f*
recent patterns and trends, v, 54, 56
risks from, 51, 53–54
See also Fiscal consolidation; Public debt

Deficit spending, 24
Deflation
causes of, 1, 15
in course of 1990s asset bubble, 14
declines in growth and, v, 1, 93
effectiveness of quantitative easing policies on, 17–20, 18*f*
effects on compensation, 11
future challenges for Japan, v
mechanisms for transmission of population aging effects on, 37–40
policies to counter effects of population aging on, 44
policy coordination to address, 23–24
population aging as obstacle to recovery from, 40, 43, 48
price-level targeting to address, 16
recent patterns and trends, 12*f*
shortcomings of policy responses to, 2
Demand and consumption
business expectations of, investment behavior and, 153–154, 155, 159
in credit market, 7, 8, 20, 39, 130–131
effects of global financial crisis on, 93–94
goals of monetary easing, 25
for health services, 84, 87, 100
in Lost Decade, 1
outcomes of Abenomics policies, 8, 30–32, 31*f*
policy responses contributing to recent economic problems, 2
population aging and, 37, 37*f*, 39–40, 41*f*, 42, 43, 48
projected effects of Abenomics on, 4, 45*f*
stimulus spending effects on, 55
Dot-com bubble, 15

E

Earthquake, Great East Japan (2011), 1, 2, 53, 54, 56, 67, 166, 169
Energy sector, 102
Entrepreneurship, 99
Equity markets

Abenomics effects on, 31*f*, 35, 35*f*
  effects of monetary easing policies on, 18, 20
  foreign investment in, 168, 172
Excess cost growth, 66
Exchange rate
  in Abenomics reforms, 4, 25, 45*f*
  corporate investment patterns and, 153, 154
  in course of 1990s asset bubble, 14
  effects of monetary easing policies on, 19, 20
  global implications of policy outcomes, 8–9, 173
  patterns and trends, 169, 171*f*
  population aging and, 38, 41*f*, 42, 43, 48
  trade balance and, 172, 172*f*
  yen as funding currency for carry-trades, 169, 170–171
  yen's safe-haven status, 169–170
Exports
  Abenomics impact on, 30–32, 31*f*
  exchange rate fluctuations and, 172, 172*f*
  foreign direct investment and, 165, 166*f*
  foreign value added of, 166–167
  future prospects, 8, 29
  global spillover of Abenomics effects on, 163, 165
  outcomes of Abenomics to date, 8
  patterns and trends, 103–104, 165, 166*f*, 172, 172*f*
  prospects for growth and, 94
  regional, import content from Japan for, 167, 167*f*
  regional competitiveness, 167
  trade agreements to promote growth, 104

F

Financial crisis. *See* Asian financial crisis (1997); Global financial crisis (2008)

Financial intermediation, 7, 102, 128*f*
Financial sector
  Abenomics strategies for reform in, 6–7
  asset allocations, 127*f*
  capital flows after Abenomics implementation, 35, 35*f*
  challenges for Japan, v
  cross-border lending activities of, 138–143, 139*f*, 140*f*, 141*f*, 164, 167–169
  effects of Abenomics policies on, 125
  effects of asset bubble collapse, 93
  effects of quantitative easing policies on, 17–20, 18*f*, 19*f*
  growth-promoting reforms for, 96, 102–103
  international comparison of asset size of major banks, 139*f*
  policies to expand provision of risk capital, 144–145, 146
  policies to prevent bubbles, 13
  recommendations for reforms in, vi
  risks for banks holding government bonds, 132–138
  risks of Abenomics for, 143–144
  small business loans, 126–129
  stresses of 1990s economic shocks, 14
  transition to higher risk environment, 6, 7
Financial Stability Board, 143
Finland, 94, 100
Fiscal consolidation
  challenges, 87
  consumption tax increase for, 74–77
  corporate income tax reform for, 77–80
  goals of Abenomics, 30, 56, 63
  government bond yields and, 53, 60
  health care reform for, 83–84
  institutional setting for, 71
  intergenerational equity considerations, 69, 77, 84–87
  pace of, 69–70, 86, 88
  pension reform for, 80–83
  population aging and, 24, 38, 43, 44, 47–48, 87

recommended policies to promote, 71, 87–88
risks of exit from deflation in, 69
spending cuts *versus* tax increases for, 70–71
Fiscal Investment and Loan Program, 59
Fiscal policy
  Abenomics strategies, 3, 4–5, 46
  the Lost Decade and, 11
  effectiveness of, since 1980s, 55–56
  monetary policy coordination with, 12, 23–24, 26
  population aging considerations in, 43–44, 48
  recommendations for reforms in, vi
  See also Fiscal consolidation
Fiscal Structure Reform Act, 56
Flexicurity, 118–120
Foreign investment
  corporate income tax rate and, 78–79
  cross-border lending by Japanese banks, 138–143, 139f, 140f, 141f, 164
  export patterns and, 165, 166f
  foreign yen holdings, 169
  by Japanese corporate sector, 149
  in Japanese equity markets, 168, 172
  in Japan's government bond market, 53–54, 62, 136, 168
  outward, 130, 131f
  population aging and, 43
  projected effects of Abenomics on, 45f
  promoting, to promote growth, 104
  spillover effects of Japan's overseas production, 163, 165, 174
  yen as funding currency for carry-trades, 169, 170–171
Forward guidance from central bank, 12, 21–23, 26, 27
France, 91

G

G20, 53, 56
Germany, 62, 91, 93, 100, 111, 168
Global economy
  challenges for Japan, v, 9
  generalizability of Abenomics to, vi
  Japan's linkage in, 176
  See also Global spillover effects of Abenomics
Global financial crisis (2008)
  current health of bank balance sheets, 126, 129f
  effects on growth, 93–94
  exchange rate fluctuations in, 169
  Japan's debt levels and, 54
  labor market outcomes of, 107
  outcomes in Japan, 1, 56
Global Integrated Monetary and Fiscal model, 29, 40
Global spillover effects of Abenomics
  channels for transmission of, 8–9, 163–164, 173, 176
  experience to date, 164, 171–172
  foreign direct investment as source of, 174
  interest rate differentials and, 174
  Japan's safe-haven status as source of, 164, 169–171
  model simulations, 173–174
  portfolio rebalancing as source of, 173–174
  risk of, 164–165, 173–176
  supply-chain linkages as source of, 163, 166–167, 174
  from tail risks, 175
  through cross-border credit exposures, 164, 167–169
  through Japan's overseas production and investment, 163, 165
Government bonds
  Abenomics goals and outcomes for, 3, 4, 26, 30
  Abenomics policy effects on, 132–138
  central bank purchase of, 4, 6, 17, 26, 136, 144
  composition of investor base, 52–53, 52f, 60, 61f, 62, 134f
  current demand for, 6–7
  effects of monetary easing on, 18, 18f

financial sector holdings of, 126, 132
foreign ownership of, 53, 62, 168
funding structure risks, 53
global market, 62
global spillover risks from spike in, 175
impact of Lost Decade policies in, 12
international comparison of domestic ownership of, 52, 52*f*
population aging and, 38
potential risks of Abenomics, 46
projected purchases, 136, 136*t*
projected yields, v, 53–54, 62
public debt projections and, 59, 67
purchases by depository corporations, 135*f*
risk implications of interest rate rise for bank holders of, 132–138, 137*f*, 144
source of low yields, v, 59
Government Pension Investment Fund, 81, 144, 145
Growth
Abenomics outcomes to date, 8, 30–32, 31*f*
Abenomics strategies to promote, 4–6
Abenomics targets for, 94
causes of recent lags in, v, 1, 91, 92–94
contributions to, 147, 148*f*
course of recovery from 1990s asset bubble, 14
economic agreements to promote, 103–104
effects of global financial crisis on, 93–94
effects of population aging on, 40–43, 41*f*, 47–48, 55
examples of sustained increases in, 94–96, 95*f*, 95*t*, 96*f*
female labor force participation and, 112
financial sector reforms to promote, 102–103
foreign labor force participation and, 97–100
future challenges for, v, 94, 147
international comparison, 92*f*
Japan's potential rate, 92*f*, 94, 94*t*

labor participation and, 62–63
policies to counter effects of population aging on, 44
projected effects of Abenomics on, 45*f*, 46
recent patterns and trends, v, 1, 91–94, 92*f*
recent signs of recovery, 2
structural reforms to promote, 91, 96–97, 97*f*, 104–105
See also Inflation and growth expectations; Lost Decade

H

Health and long-term care system
copayment rates, 84
demand for long-term care workers in, 99–100, 100*f*
patterns and trends, 55, 65–66, 72*f*, 73, 83
population aging implications for, 38, 51, 54, 66, 83
projected spending, 38, 51, 54, 66, 66*f*, 71, 83
reform options, 83–84
Honebuto no Hoshin, 56
Hong Kong, 165, 175
Household investment
asset allocations, 127*f*
in Lost Decade, 1
recent reforms to increase, 144
Household savings
patterns and trends, 42, 43*t*
population aging and, 42–43, 42*t*

I

Immigration policy, 6, 86–87, 97–100, 98*f*, 108, 114, 123
Imports
Abenomics implementation and, 31*f*, 32
exchange rate and, 42, 172
services, 104

Indonesia, 143
Inflation
  Abenomics outcomes for, 4, 8, 32–33, 33f, 36, 45f
  Abenomics policy targets, 24, 26
  in course of 1990s asset bubble, 13, 14
  effects of monetary easing policies on, 19
  effects of population aging on, 40–43, 41f, 47–48
  interest rate linkage, 15–16, 60
  mechanisms for transmission of population aging effects on, 37–40
  recent patterns and trends, 12f
  targets in policy responses to 1990s economic shocks, 15–16
  wage rates and, 120
  See also Deflation; Inflation and growth expectations
Inflation and growth expectations
  Abenomics implementation and, 3, 4, 32, 33f, 125
  central bank transparency and, 21–22, 23, 26–27
  government bond yields and, 60
  interest rates and, 15–16, 60
  monetary easing and, 17, 19, 20, 25, 26, 32, 46
  population aging and, 40, 44
  private investment and, 154, 155, 158
  wages and, 120–121
Initial public offerings, 130, 131f
Insurance industry
  asset allocations, 128f, 136
  cross-border activities, 168
Interest rates
  corporate investment patterns and, 154
  forward guidance from central bank on, 21–23
  future challenges and opportunities for policymakers, v
  global spillover effects of Abenomics and, 174
  inflation linkage, 15–16, 60
  policy responses to 1990s economic shocks, 14, 15–16
  population aging and, 39, 40, 43, 60
  projected effects of Abenomics on, 4, 45f, 60–61, 61f
  public debt projections and, 59–65
  recent patterns and trends, 14, 15f
  risks for banks holding government bonds, 132–138, 137f, 144
Intergenerational equity issues, 69, 77, 84–87
Investment. *See* Corporate investment

J

JPX Nikkei 400 index, 144, 161

K

Koizumi administration, 56, 73

L

Labor market
  Abenomics effects to date, 32, 32f
  Abenomics growth strategies, 6
  employment in small- and medium-sized enterprises, 150–151, 151f
  employment patterns and trends, 108–109, 109f
  employment protection policies, 116–117, 119f
  female participation in, 97, 98f, 108, 112–114, 112f, 113f, 115, 115f, 117, 118f, 123
  foreign worker participation in, 6, 86–87, 97–100, 98f, 108, 114, 123
  future challenges and opportunities for policymakers, v–vi, 6, 107–108
  global financial crisis effects in, 107
  in health and long-term care sector, 99–100, 100f
  income share, 110, 110f
  increasing older worker participation in, 114–115, 123

international comparison of workforce participation, 98f
lifetime employment system, 107
nonregular workers in, 1, 6, 107, 111, 111f, 115–118, 115f, 123
population aging and, 37, 39–42, 47, 48, 108
potential growth gains from reform of, 94–96, 96f
potential inflationary outcomes of reforms in, 108
projections, 62–63, 108
protections for part-time workers, 118–120
recent growth lags and, 93, 94
recommendations for reforms in, 123–124
reforms to promote growth, 96, 97–100
reforms to support Abenomics implementation, 108, 123, 124
sectoral variation in nonregular employment, 116, 116f
sectoral variation in unemployment, 109
sensitivity to output fluctuations, 109
severance pay system, 117
See also Wages and compensation
Land markets
in development of 1990s asset bubble, 13
population aging and, 37, 41f
projected effects of Abenomics on, 45f
Life expectancy, 36, 39, 72
Lost Decade
conditions leading to, 1, 11
growth outcomes of reform responses, 5, 51
lessons from monetary policy during, 14–16, 26–27
signs of recovery from, 2

M

Manufacturing sector, 39–40, 93, 101f, 116f, 122f, 139f, 148, 149, 151f

Minimum wage, 121–123
Monetary policy
Abenomics strategies, 3–4, 8, 12–13, 24–26, 46
central bank communication and transparency of, 21
in development of 1990s asset bubble, 13
fiscal policy coordination with, 12, 23–24, 26
forward guidance in, 12, 21–23
lessons from Lost Decade experience, 14–16, 26–27
population aging considerations in, 48
recommendations for reforms in, vi
responses to 1990s asset bubble shock, 13–14
shortcomings of, in response to deflation, 2, 11–12, 26
transmission channels, 4, 12

N

Netherlands, 95–96
New Zealand, 94, 95
Nonregular workers, 1, 6, 107, 111, 111f, 115–118, 115f, 123
Nuclear power, 2

O

Organisation for Economic Co-Operation and Development, 73, 74f, 107

P

Parental leave policies, 113–114
Pension system
asset allocations, 127f, 128f
contribution rate, 82, 86
contributions from dependent spouses, 82–83
effects of 2004 reforms, 65, 71
eligibility age, 81–82, 85–86
intergenerational equity issues, 85–86

macroeconomic indexing of benefits, 81
population aging and, 55, 65
recommendations for fiscal
  consolidation, 87–88
replacement ratio, 82, 85–86
share of social security spending, 72*f*,
  73
spending, 55, 65, 80–81
tax treatment of benefits, 83, 86
transition to higher-risk investing, 145
Political economy, population aging and,
  38, 39
Portfolio rebalancing
  Abenomics outcomes in, 33–34, 34*f*
  allocation to safe assets in recent past, 1,
    127–128*f*
  cross-border lending in, 138–143
  global spillover effects of, 163, 173–174
  goals of Abenomics, 7, 9, 51
  monetary easing and, 25, 125
  population aging and, 38, 47
  risks of Abenomics, 143, 145–146
  shift toward risk capital under
    Abenomics, 51, 125–132, 144–146
Productivity
  capital, 152–153, 152*f*
  growth prospects and, 94
  growth rate and, 92–93
  patterns and trends, 101, 101*f*
  population aging and, 39–40
  recent signs of recovery, 2
  reducing labor market duality to
    increase, 115–116
  research and development spending
    and, 153
  sectoral differences, 101
  strategies for promoting, 101–102
  wage growth and, 109–110, 110*f*
Public debt
  future prospects, 53, 67
  gross and net, 57
  population aging and, 38, 43–44, 51,
    65–66
  projected effects of Abenomics on, 45*f*,
    69, 70*f*

recent patterns and trends, 4, 56, 58*f*,
  67
reform strategy of Abenomics, 4, 5
spending patterns, 51
sustainability analysis, 53, 57–59,
  63–65, 64*f*, 67
See also Debt-to-GDP ratio
Public spending
  In Abenomics plan, 30, 31*f*
  for earthquake reconstruction, 53, 54,
    56
  fiscal–monetary policy coordination
    and, 24
  growth rate and, 93
  in health care system, 38, 51, 54, 65,
    66, 66*f*, 71, 83
  interest payments, 73
  international comparison, 73, 74*f*
  on pension system, 55, 65, 80–81
  population aging and, 38, 51, 55,
    65–66
  projections, 71
  recent patterns and trends, 72
  tax increase *versus*, as fiscal
    consolidation strategy, 70–71
  See also Public debt; Stimulus spending
Public works spending, 51, 55, 73

Q

Quantitative and qualitative easing
  Abenomics implementation, v, 3–4,
    12–13, 24–26, 27, 29, 30, 36
  composition of asset purchase programs,
    20, 24–25, 25*f*, 26–27
  effectiveness of policies in 2000s,
    17–20, 18*f*, 21*f*
  exit risks, 46–47, 49
  forward guidance in, 21–23
  global spillover effects of, 163
  impact of Lost Decade policies, 12
  implications of population aging for, 44
  lessons from Lost Decade policies,
    26–27
  transmission channel components, 25

R

Real estate investment trusts, 19
Regulatory regime
  Abenomics growth strategies, 6
  barriers to firm exit and entry, 130–132, 145
  cross-border risk monitoring, 143
  employment protection policies, 116–117, 118–120
  growth-promoting reforms of, 96, 97
  transition to higher risk environment in financial sector and, 6, 7
Research and development, 153
Retirement age, 114, 115
Risk environment
  of Abenomics, 30, 143–144
  cross-border lending by Japanese banks, 143
  effects of monetary easing on, 20
  exit from monetary easing policies and, 47
  financial sector policies to ameliorate, 144–145
  financial sector transition to higher, 6, 7, 102
  global spillover effects from government bond shocks, 175
  global spillover effects of Abenomics, 164–165
  implications of interest rate rise for banks holding government bonds, 132–138, 137f
  portfolio allocation toward higher, under Abenomics, 125–132
  yen as safe-haven currency, 169–170

S

Savings rate
  consumption tax increase and, 76
  population aging and, 42–43, 42t
  projections, 53
  recent reforms to increase, 144
  trends, 120

Services sector, 6, 39–40, 101, 102, 104, 116f, 121, 122f, 149–150, 153
Singapore, 143, 165, 175
Small- and medium-sized enterprises, 111
  bank lending to, 156f
  credit access, 7, 130–131, 145, 156f
  economic significance, 150–151
  employment in, 150–151, 151f
  financial policy reforms to support, 1, 02, 6, 159, 160
  income and debt shifting by, 79–80
  investment patterns, 149, 150f, 156
  sluggish wage growth in, 111
Social security spending, 51, 55, 65, 71, 72, 72f, 73, 87, 136
Special economic zones, 101, 123
Stimulus spending, 4–5, 23–24, 29, 30, 54–55, 56, 67
Structural policies
  Abenomics reform strategy for, 3, 5–6, 8
  future challenges and opportunities, v–vi
  population aging considerations in, 44, 48
  to promote corporate investment, 159–161
  to promote growth, 91, 96–97, 97f, 104–105
Supply-chain linkages, Japan's, 163, 166–167, 174
Sustainability
  of Abenomics outcomes to date, 8
  challenges for Japan, v, 9
  debt analysis, 53, 57–59, 63–65, 64f, 67
  goals of Abenomics, 51
Sweden, 94, 95–96

T

Tax policy
  Abenomics strategies for, 5, 30
  corporate rate, 6, 71, 77–80, 78f, 79f, 87, 96, 103, 103f, 158, 159
  on dividend income, 103, 103f
  female labor force participation and, 114

for fiscal consolidation, 70–71
international comparison of corporate rate, 77–78, 78*f*
outcomes of Abenomics reforms of, 8
reforms of 1990s, 55
revenue generation in Lost Decade, 54
revenue patterns and trends, 72–73, 73*f*
treatment of pension income, 83, 86
See also Consumption tax
Technological innovation, 153
Thailand, 143, 166
Trade. *See* Exports; Imports
Trade agreements, 6, 96, 103–104
Trans-Pacific Partnership, 6, 30, 104

U

Unemployment insurance, 119, 119*f*
United Kingdom, 109, 111
United States, 91, 93, 109
 foreign ownership of government bonds of, 168
 forward guidance from central bank in, 21–22
 Japan's foreign direct investment in, 165
 monetary easing policies, 19
 policy effects on Japanese government bonds, 62
 recovery from Great Depression in, 23

V

Venture capital, 7, 130, 145, 159–160

W

Wages and compensation
 deflation effects on, 11, 120–121
 educational attainment and, 123*f*
 effects on inflation, 120
 foreign labor force participation and, 99
 international comparison, 122*f*
 minimum rates, 121–123
 nonregular workforce and, 111*f*
 overtime payment, 119–120
 patterns and trends, 109–110, 110*f*, 120
 population aging effects on, 29, 38, 42, 48
 recent signs of improvement in, 8
 recommendations for reforms in, 124
 reforms to support Abenomics implementation, 29, 108, 124
 sectoral variation in, 122*f*
 sources of slow growth in, 110–111, 120–121
 unemployment insurance, 119, 119*f*
Women in workforce, 97, 98*f*, 108, 112–114, 112*f*, 113*f*, 115, 115*f*, 117, 118*f*, 123

Z

Zero interest rate policy, 2, 14, 15, 17, 22–23
Zombie borrowers, 93, 102, 132